Future of World Forests : Their Use and Conservation

Future of World Forests : Their Use and Conservation

Praveen Taank

CYBER TECH PUBLICATIONS
4264/3, Ansari Road, Daryaganj, New Delhi-110002 (India)
Ph.: 011-23244078, 011-43559448 Fax: 011-23280028
E-Mail: cyberpublicationsdelhi@yahoo.com
Website: www.cybertechpublications.com

FUTURE OF WORLD FORESTS : THEIR USE AND CONSERVATION

Praveen Taank

First Edition 2011

Published by :

G.S. Rawat for **Cyber Tech Publications**
4264/3, Ansari Road, Daryaganj, New Delhi-110002 (India)
Ph.: 011-23244078, 011-43559448 Fax: 011-23280028
E-Mail: cyberpublicationsdelhi@yahoo.com
Website: www.cybertechpublications.com

CONTENTS

Preface

The processes of exchange between forests and the atmosphere and with the consequences of these exchanges for the growth and production of forests and for the composition of the atmosphere. For this purpose, we may think of forests in a number of different ways. Forests function as the major terrestrial interface between the atmosphere and the earth: they interact with the atmosphere to condition life on the earth. On the one hand, the atmosphere provides driving variables for processes in forests; on the other, forests feed back to modify the atmosphere, very efficiently removing gases and particles from the atmosphere. For example, we can divide them on a phytogeographical basis into boreal, temperate and tropical forests (Malhi *et al.* 1999), on a phenological basis into deciduous and evergreen forests, or on a morphological basis into broadleaved and needle-leaved (largely coniferous) forests.

However, at the present time, we have scarcely sufficient data to classify them on the basis of exchange processes into a range of functional types. A succession of recent international programmes has very substantially increased the extent of quantitative information available about forest processes, particularly in the boreal and temperate regions, compared with the situation 25 years ago (Jarvis *et al.* 1976) but our knowledge base is still to a large extent anecdotal. In this chapter, we attempt to pull together the strands of new information relating to exchange processes resulting from the development of new technology and the explosion of measurement programmes over the last 10 years and to derive some generalizations, based on functional attributes.

—*Author*

1

Introduction

INTRODUCTION

Forests function as the major terrestrial interface between the atmosphere and the earth: they interact with the atmosphere to condition life on the earth. On the one hand, the atmosphere provides driving variables for processes in forests; on the other, forests feed back to modify the atmosphere, very efficiently removing gases and particles from the atmosphere. This chapter is concerned with the processes of exchange between forests and the atmosphere and with the consequences of these exchanges for the growth and production of forests and for the composition of the atmosphere. For this purpose, we may think of forests in a number of different ways.

For example, we can divide them on a phytogeographical basis into boreal, temperate and tropical forests (Malhi *et al.* 1999), on a phenological basis into deciduous and evergreen forests, or on a morphological basis into broadleaved and needle-leaved (largely coniferous) forests.

However, at the present time, we have scarcely sufficient data to classify them on the basis of exchange processes into a range of functional types. A succession of recent international programmes has very substantially increased the extent of quantitative information available about forest processes, particularly in the boreal and temperate regions, compared with the situation 25 years ago (Jarvis *et al.* 1976) but our knowledge base is still to a large extent anecdotal. In this chapter, we attempt to pull together the strands of new information relating to exchange processes resulting from the development of new technology and the explosion of measurement programmes over the last 10 years and to derive some generalizations, based on functional attributes.

Spatial and temporal scales

Spatial scales

On a large spatial scale, say 100 km, a natural forest is a haphazard mosaic of individual trees and patches of different species and ages, occasioned by microenvironment, topography and disturbance, such as windthrow and fire events. At the other extreme, intensively managed forest generally comprises uniform compartments (woodlots or coupes) each of a single species of tree of similar age and size, comprising a range of species and ages, on a spatial scale of up to 1 km. A sustainably managed forest, whether maintained by natural regeneration or planting, should comprise compartments covering a range of ages from regeneration through to harvest.

The unit for intensive study of exchange processes may be several compartments or part of a compartment, commonly referred to as a stand, the size of which depends on the processes investigated and the methodology used.

For measurements of net ecosystem exchange (NEE) of scalars* such as CO_2, water vapour, CH_4 and other trace gases by eddy covariance, the scale of the stand is necessarily similar to that of the compartment (< 100 ha), whereas for measurements of net primary productivity (NPP) the sample plot may be as small as 0.1 ha. While from an economic perspective a stand is generally defined in terms of the keystone species, i.e. the trees, from a functional ecosystem perspective the understorey, ground vegetation and, particularly, the soil components can be just as important.

While the stand is an appropriate scale at which to assess forest-atmosphere interactions, it is necessary to move to the smaller scales of tree, branch and leaf, coarse and fine roots and soil microorganisms to explain the magnitude and to understand the constraints on NEE. Conversely, to appreciate interactions between the atmosphere and a forest comprising compartments of different species and ages on an overall scale of about 10-100 km, it is necessary to adopt different strategies to scale up or to obtain spatially integrated measurements.

Temporal scales

Exchanges between the atmosphere and a young forest stand regenerating or regrowing after disturbance such as harvesting or fire is critically dependent on the phase of the successional cycle. During the first 5 or 10 years after disturbance in temperate forests, the trees are small, the understorey vegetation damaged and the soil may be churned up and exposed. Because of the changing height, structure and inherent physiological activity of trees and stands with age and development, processes within the stand and coupling of the stand to the atmosphere change during the course of a rotation. For example, a recently disturbed area is likely to be losing carbon to the atmosphere as CO_2; subsequently, as the trees come to occupy the site fully, the area will accumulate carbon strongly during a phase of rapid growth that may last for decades, depending on the species of trees and site conditions, before old-growth forest may become a net source of carbon to the atmosphere in some circumstances.

However our capability to measure exchanges of H_2O, CO_2, CH_4, N_2O and other trace gases is sufficiently new that only specimen, usually mature, stands during a rotation have so far been studied, over periods as short as a few months up to 5 years. Stages during the natural or managerial succession have not so far been systematically studied. We now recognize that investigations of chronosequences are needed to obtain temporally integrated estimates of the exchanges of water vapour and trace gases for a range of forest types to be able fully to understand the interactions and to construct lifetime budgets. Furthermore, management operations (e.g. planting, thinning and harvesting) and natural disturbances (e.g. wind-throw and fire) occur at irregular intervals with major consequences for pools and fluxes, particularly at the larger spatial scales, and thus also impose a requirement for long sequences of data or, at the least, for campaigns to sample different stages in a chronosequence, for example substituting spatial variability for temporal variability.

Interannual variability

In addition, at any time during growth of a new plantation or natural forest succession, there may be appreciable variability from year to year in the exchanges of trace gases as a result of variability in the weather. For example, dry tropical forests may become a source of CO_2 in years of relatively low solar radiation inputs and high temperature, such as were caused by the eruption of Mt Pinatubo (Grace *et al.* 1995a,b), and may occur particularly during El Niño years (Tian *et al.* 1998). Water vapour and CO_2 exchanges of temperate deciduous forest are particularly sensitive to the length of the growing season as defined by the times of budburst and leaf senescence, which may vary by 2-3 weeks from year to year (Goulden *et al.* 1996); temperate coniferous forests are similarly affected by the length of the photosynthetic period, particularly in northern maritime latitudes (Valentini *et al.* 2000).

In the boreal forest, exchanges are even more sensitive to the timing of the onset of the spring thaw, which can vary from year to year by 2-3 weeks and may result in a change in the annual sequestration of carbon of 1 Mg ha^{-1} so that a stand may be a sink for CO_2 one year and a source the next (Goulden *et al.* 1998; Lindroth *et al.* 1998; Bergh & Linder 1999). Thus, measurements made in a single year at some arbitrary time in the succession, or even over a few years such as the initial 5-year 'commitment period' of the Kyoto Protocol, may give a misleading picture of the long-term exchange capacity of the forest. For this reason, measurements should extend over periods of at least 5 years, in order to define the major drivers and constraints on the fluxes. However, such lengthy periods of observation have so far been made on only a handful of stands.

Historical development

Although the basic concept of measurement of vegetation-atmosphere exchanges by eddy covari-ance was enunciated in the 1930s (see Sutton 1953), the technique was essentially confined to the measurement of sensible heat flux because of the difficulty in obtaining sufficiently fast sensors for water vapour, CO_2 and other trace gases (Swinbank 1951). In the 1960s, water vapour fluxes were successfully measured continuously over short periods using fine-wire thermojunctions wetted with single strands of cotton (the Evapotron and Fluxatron: Dyer & Maher 1965; Dyer & Hicks 1967) but generally flux measurements were made by the Bowen ratio or flux-gradient method, sometimes automated into an energy balance system.

This approach, while practical over crops and grassland (e.g. Biscoe *et al.* 1975), was particularly difficult (and expensive) to apply over forest because of the extremely small size of the gradients as a result of canopy height and surface roughness (Thom *et al.* 1975; Jarvis *et al.* 1976). Consequently between the mid 1970s and the early 1990s there was a major gap in measurement of trace gas fluxes while researchers awaited improvements in the eddy covariance and eddy accumulation approaches. Developments in sensor technology since 1990 (Baldocchi *et al.* 1996; Moncrieff *et al.* 1996, 1997; Aubinet *et al.* 2000) have led to near-continuous measurements by eddy covariance of canopy-atmosphere exchanges of momentum water vapour, CO_2 and other trace gases, first in campaigns lasting months, then over a year and now over periods of up to 5 years.

Exchanges of radiation, momentum, sensible heat and water vapour by forests have been relatively well understood for some time (e.g. Stewart & Thom 1973; Biscoe *et al.* 1975; Rutter 1975; Thom 1975; McNaughton & Jarvis 1983; Raupach 1988; Shuttleworth 1989) and stand-scale fluxes have been progressively documented over the past 30 years (e.g. Jarvis *et al.* 1976; Ruimy *et al.* 1995; Baldocchi & Meyers 1998). Consequently, these exchanges are treated relatively briefly, with the emphasis on new concepts and data. A broader, more comprehensive treatment is given to fluxes of the several trace gases of importance as pollutants and to CO_2, of particular importance in relation to 'global warming' and the reduction of net CO_2 emissions of anthropogenic origin. Understanding fluxes of trace gases has increased substantially in recent years in direct relation to the development and application of the new measurement technologies. Considerable impetus has been provided by major national and international experiments on land-atmosphere interactions that have included forests as a major land surface cover (e.g. HAPEX-MOBILHY, Andre *et al.* 1986; HAPEX-SAHEL, Moncrieff *et al.* 1997; ABRACOS, Gash *et al.* 1996; EUROFLUX, Valentini *et al.* 1999; MEDEFLU, FLUXNET, Running *et al.* 1999; BOREAS, Sellers *et al.* 1995, 1997; LBA, Kabat *et al.* 1999) as well as by more restricted and local campaigns (e.g. Hollinger *et al.* 1994; Greco & Baldocchi 1996; Baldocchi 1997; Kelliher *et al.* 1997; Schulze *et al.* 1999).

The stand system

For simplicity we consider forest stands as being extensive and relatively uniform in the horizontal and treat exchanges with the atmosphere as largely one-dimensional processes in the vertical, acknowledging none the less that advection may at times exercise a major influence. We define the upper boundary as a horizontal plane at the height of the eddy covariance flux station, approximately twice the height of the trees, and the lower boundary as a horizontal plane either at the soil surface or at some depth below the rooting zone.

At the outset, we consider the environmental variables driving exchange processes as independent variables at the scale of the stand, subsequently recognizing the increasing importance of feedbacks with increase in the spatial scale, so that the driving variables become progressively dependent variables (McNaughton & Jarvis 1991).

STAND ENERGY BALANCE

Conservation of energy requires that the influxes and effluxes of energy should equate, i.e.

$$R_n = H + XE + G + 1 + S + (jF_c \qquad [1.1]$$

where R_n is the net absorbed all-wave ıadiation flux, H the sensible heat flux, XE the latent heat flux (i.e. the energy equivalent of the evaporation and transpiration of water), G the flux of sensible heat into storage in the soil, / the flux of sensible and latent heat into storage in the air column, 5 the flux of sensible heat into storage in the trees and other vegetation, and $\backslash iF_c$ the energy equivalent of CO_2 exchange. Each of the quantities in Eqn 10.1 can be both an influx and an efflux. Conventionally, effluxes are treated as positive and influxes as negative, with the exception of R_n for which a net influx is treated as positive and a net efflux as negative.

Conceptually this is a one-dimensional model and supposes an area of forest sufficiently extensive and uniform for horizontal gradients and fluxes to be negligible. However, with a few exceptions in the tropical and boreal regions, most forests, and more particularly stands within forests, are too small to meet this requirement. Advection terms can be added to this equation but the practical difficulties in evaluating small horizontal gradients are such that this is rarely done and horizontal transport is neglected. None the less, 'footprint analysis' of flux source areas around a flux measurement tower in a stand (Schuepp *et al.* 1990) indicates that about 90% of the measured flux originates within a radius of about 50-700 m from the tower for flux-measuring instrumentation placed about

10 m above the canopy surface; various empirical estimates suggest that horizontal gradients become negligible within 200-300 m of a stand edge, so that any horizontal flux component neglected is likely to be very small.

The first two terms on the right-hand side of Eqn 10.1 $(H+kE)$ are together generally much larger than the storage and photosynthetic terms, accounting for around 90% of the energy exchange, except in very open, sparse forest when the exchange with the soil may at times be large (~ 100 Wm^{-2}) (Jarvis *et al.* 1976).

The ratio of sensible heat transfer to latent heat transfer, the Bowen ratio $(P = H/A,E)$, is a functional descriptor of energy use by forest stands. Originally conceived to represent partitioning of absorbed net radiation, the Bowen ratio is particularly useful now that we are able to measure the sensible and latent heat fluxes independently and routinely by eddy covariance and to appreciate that advection and entrainment of warm or dry air are the norm rather than the exception where forests are concerned.

Similar stands in different climates partition the available energy in different ways, as do dissimilar stands in the same environment. In a maritime environment on the Atlantic fringe of Europe, for example, high humidities suppress evaporation so that transpiration rates of spruce are low, with midday summer values of p of 2 or more; in the more continental climate of central Europe, with higher temperatures and larger water vapour saturation deficits, values of p for spruce are 1 or less. Similarly, stands of different species on different soils in the same climatic region have very different ranges of p.

Because forest areas are on the whole small or fragmented, the variables driving fluxes in a stand have very largely been determined elsewhere, frequently outwith the forested area. Air both advected and entrained into the forested area is likely to be very different in temperature, humidity and trace gas composition to the air in the surface layer, particularly in the early morning, so that these variables can be regarded initially as independent driving variables.

Energy balance closure provides a useful test of the competence of the measurement techniques. Rearranging Eqn 10.1, net radiation, less all the storage terms, should equate to the sum of the sensible and latent heat fluxes for complete closure, i.e. larger the zenith angle, the higher the reflectance, so that on sunny days as the day progresses, albedos decline to a minimum at midday rising again in the afternoon, the minimum becoming progressively lower as the season advances to midsummer. The lower albedos for coniferous canopies result from the spire-like form of the tree crowns, with multiple reflections and scattering among them, so that when seen from above, the spaces between the tree crowns appear as black holes.

The more planar surfaces of broadleaved canopies result in higher albedos that depend more strongly on larger leaf area densities in the upper canopy and leaf inclination angles closer to horizontal than in coniferous canopies. In the tropics albedos of evergreen species tend to be lower than in the boreal region on sunny days because of the smaller zenith angles (Pinker *et al.* 1980; Pinker 1982); in the boreal region they are up to 5% higher in winter when there is some snow retained on the canopy (Betts & Ball 1997; Baldocchi *et al.* 2000). The albedos of deciduous broadleaved trees are up to 5% lower in the winter when they are leafless.

Midday or mean daily canopy reflectances for photosynthetically active radiation (PAR) or photosynthetic photon flux density (PPFD) from closed forest canopies are no more than 3-5% because of strong absorption in the waveband 350-700 nm but may reach 7% in winter, and in open stands vary depending on canopy leaf area density and the type of understorey (e.g. Hassika & Berbigier 1998). Above canopies the relation between incident PPFD and solar radiation is relatively conservative (2.0 + 0.1 l imolJ^{-1}), although within canopies selective absorption of PPFD, particularly in the red waveband, reduces this ratio substantially (Sattin *et al.* 1997). The red:far-red ratio, important for phytochrome photoequilibrium and for neighbour detection in canopies (Gilbert *et al.* 1995), also changes with depth into a canopy as a result of preferential absorption of red radiation by chlorophyll. From a typical value of 1.3 in sunlight, this ratio falls to an order of magnitude less below canopies of leaf area index larger than about 4.

Long-wave radiation exchange

There have been few regular or continuous measurements of incident, reflected or emitted thermal radiation above forest canopies until very recently because of the lack of appropriate network-standard instruments. Thus estimates in the past have been based on the relationship between measured solar radiation exchange and net radiation balance (e.g. Monteith & Szeicz 1961) or on calculation based on simple assumptions regarding canopy and sky temperatures. Forest canopies are in general well coupled to the atmosphere (see section 10.5) so that leaf temperatures, particularly of small narrow leaves in unstable conditions, are close to air temperature, and the emissivity of leaves in the waveband range 10-14 l im is 0.97 + 0.02 (Gates 1980), i.e. very close to that of a black body. Energy balance models of forest canopies have also been solved iteratively to yield leaf temperatures to provide more accurate estimates of thermal radiation emission (e.g. Baldocchi 1997). Both the incoming and outgoing long-wave fluxes are large, although the difference between the net long-wave flux is small relative to the net solar radiation in daytime but is crucial to canopy temperature at night.

Net all-wave radiation balance

The net all-wave radiation absorbed by a canopy (i.e. the measured sum of net short-wave and net long-wave radiation, R_n) defines the energy available to drive energy-requiring processes, in the absence of advected and entrained convective energy. As such, it is particularly important for driving transpiration from the understorey and the ground vegetation but less so for driving transpiration from the overstorey, which is usually more strongly driven by the atmospheric water vapour saturation deficit, because of the strong coupling of forest canopies to the atmosphere for much of the time (see section 10.6). Because the net long-wave exchange is comparatively small there is a close relation between net all-wave radiation and net solar radiation. The net all-wave radiation measured over a broadleaved canopy is about 0.7*Q* to 0.75*Q*, whereas over conifers it may exceed 0.85*Q* because of the small albedo. This is one reason why coniferous canopies are particularly effective in warming the atmosphere.

MOMENTUM EXCHANGE

The aerodynamically rough surfaces of forests enhance rates of exchange of momentum and scalars between forests and the atmosphere relative to surfaces of other shorter, terrestrial vegetation. The frictional and form drag of forests on the boundary layer airflow very effectively captures the momentum from the airflow. Expressed in energy terms, the flux of momentum over typical forest surfaces exceeds that over shorter vegetation by a factor of five or more for the same wind speed. The exchange of momentum between forests and the atmosphere provides the primary driving energy for the local exchange of scalars entrained in the atmospheric surface layer. A detailed mathematical description of the turbulent structure within the vegetation boundary layer is given by Thom (1975) and lies beyond the scope of this chapter, though see also Chapter 12. More recent descriptions of the subject are provided by Garratt (1992), Kaimal and Finnigan (1994) and Raupach *et al.* (1996).

In considering a simple, dimensional Fickian approach to mass and momentum transfer across the boundary layer of the forest canopy, the turbulence generated by the frictional drag of terrestrial surfaces is the primary regulator of scalar transport. The enhanced momentum exchange is reflected in the potential for a greatly enhanced exchange of scalar quantities, such as water vapour, trace gases, CO_2 and particles, and is manifest in large values of the leaf boundary layer and canopy aerodynamic conductances and small values of the corresponding transfer resistances (see section 10.5).

None the less, the degree to which the potential rates of exchange are realized is also determined by processes at the leaf, branch and stem surfaces which regulate the source or sink strength. Examples of the rates of exchange of a range of trace gases to illustrate typical upper limits for rates of exchange of these gases.

EXCHANGE OF SCALARS

Exchanges of scalars (water vapour, trace gases, particles) between forests and the atmosphere can be expressed as a flux (*F*) driven by a difference in 'concentration' (*AX*) and constrained by a conductance (*g*) or resistance (*r*), i.e.

$$F = g\text{-}AX = AX/r \qquad [1.3]$$

Depending on the scalar and whether the net flux is towards or away from the canopy, the flux is constrained by a catena of conductances or resistances along the pathway between sources or sinks on the surfaces of leaves, twigs and branches, or within leaves, and the source or sink in the atmosphere, notably the conductances of the stomata and stomatal antechambers, the conductance of the leaf cuticle and other tree surfaces, the conductances across the leaf boundary layers, and the aerodynamic conductances through the canopy and across the canopy boundary layer to a reference location above.

While the application of conductance and resistance approaches are the norm for current applications, it is necessary in important cases to recognize that fluxes are bidirectional and that multiple sources and sinks within forest canopies increasingly require more complex treatments to describe the interaction of biological production, uptake and chemical processing with the turbulent exchange processes above and within canopies.

At stand scale, canopy stomatal and boundary layer conductances are derived as the product of the leaf conductances and the leaf area index of leaves, appropriately weighted according to the scalar (e.g. McNaughton 1994). The scaled-up leaf stomatal conductance is commonly referred to as the canopy surface conductance, or simply the canopy conductance.

Historically, resistances (the inverse of conductances) were first used but recently conductances have become more widespread. The conductance terminology is now commonly used for transfer of CO_2 and, to a lesser extent, water vapour, whereas the preferred convention for quantifying the affinity of vegetation surfaces for uptake of *reactive gases* remains the canopy or surface resistance (Fowler & Unsworth 1979), because the full range of surface affinities must be included and this would result in infinite surface conductances. The resistance approach is therefore not only conventional but also preferable on theoretical grounds.

In the cases of both HNO_3 and HCl, for example, the surface resistance is negligible and tree surfaces generally are considered to be 'perfect sinks' for these gases. There are few measurements of HNO_3 (and especially HCl) canopy fluxes, although the work so far indicates zero canopy resistance for these gases (Huebert 1983; Muller *et al.* 1993).

The combination of large atmospheric conductance (g_a) (or small atmospheric resistance, r_a) and zero canopy resistance (r_c) leads to significant inputs of atmospheric nitrogen as HNO_3 to forests even when ambient concentrations are very small and, conversely, to large losses of intercepted precipitation from wet canopies although atmospheric saturation deficits are then small.

More problematical, at least two sets of units have been, and continue to be, widely used by different sectors of the community, depending largely on whether fluxes are required in units of mass (kg), volume (m^3) or amount (mol) and whether 'concentration' differences are expressed as mixing ratios, volume fractions, mole fractions, partial pressures, etc. Conveniently, where concentrations are dimensionless, as in the case of mole fraction for example, the conductance has the same dimensions as the flux and the dimensions of the resistance are the inverse. Where the 'flux' is expressed as a volume flux density, i.e. $m^3 m^{-2} s^{-1}$, the conductance has the units of m s^{-1} and the resistance the somewhat curious units of sm^{-1}!

Aerodynamic conductance/resistance

The aerodynamic conductance/resistance should be formulated to give an accurate representation of the transfer of the appropriate scalar of interest (water vapour, CO_2 and other trace gases) from the source or sink in the canopy, across the atmospheric surface layer to the sink or source in the mixed layer. Aerodynamic conductances of canopies (g_a) have most frequently been estimated using the transfer of momentum to canopies or the transfer of water vapour away from wet canopies as tracers. The transfer of momentum is driven by pressure forces and all canopy elements provide the sink, whereas the transfer of water vapour and trace gases is by molecular or turbulent diffusion and the sources and sinks in the canopy are usually only the leaves, depending on the scalar. The difference between the two can be accounted for (Chamberlain 1975; Thom 1975) but since the aerodynamic resistance of forest canopies is generally at least one order of magnitude smaller than the surface resistance because of the strong turbulence in and near forest canopies, little is gained by this and either may be used.

Canopy aerodynamic conductance increases in proportion to wind speed. Analysis of wind profiles showed g_a for momentum to increase from 0.08 m s^{-1} (3.2molm^{-2}s^{-1}) for wind speed of 1 ms^{-1} at canopy height to 0.5ms^{-1} (20molm–^{2}s^{-1}) for wind speed of 6 m s^{-1} above a Sitka spruce stand. From a review of wind profile data, the following general relation was deduced for coniferous forest stands (Jarvis *et al.* 1976):

$$g_a = 0.1u(\mathrm{A})\mathrm{m\ s^{-1}},\ \text{i.e. } g_a = 4u(\mathrm{A})\mathrm{molm}{\sim}^{2}\ \mathrm{s}^{-1} \qquad [10.4]$$

where $u(h)$ is wind speed in ms^{-1} at canopy height.

In a Sitka spruce spacing experiment g_a for water vapour was found to increase asymptotically in relation to number of trees, and hence leaf area, per hectare, whereas the conductance on a per tree crown basis increased linearly with distance between the trees (Teklehaimanot & Jarvis 1991; Teklehaimanot *et al.* 1991). This can be attributed to enhanced ventilation of the trees and increases in a number of turbulence parameters (Green 1990). Typical values of g_a for water vapour were in the range 3-9 mol m^{-2} s^{-1} (Jarvis 1993). In a comparison between selectively logged and unlogged plots in tropical forest, Asdak *et al.* (1998a,b) found a comparable situation: the boundary layer conductance, on a per tree basis, of the trees remaining on the logged plot was higher than that of the trees on the comparable unlogged plot. It seems likely that g_a will also be influenced by vertical distribution of leaf area density in canopies: a high leaf area density in the upper layers of a multistoried tropical forest canopy inhibits penetration of downdrafts and effectively decouples the lower layers from the air above (Shuttleworth 1989; Kruijt *et al.* 1999). However, effects of crown and canopy structure on g_a have not yet been systematically investigated.

Surface conductance/resistance

Surface conductances of canopies (g_c) have frequently been estimated using water vapour transfer from dry canopies as a tracer and scaled for other trace gases such as CO_2 by the ratio of their molecular diffusivities. For a range of deposition fluxes, using a resistance analogy allows the aerodynamic resistance to be subtracted from the total transfer resistance to give the surface resistance. The absence of a residual term implies very efficient exchange and large deposition rates (velocities). However, more commonly a residual or surface resistance is present which, in the case of reactive trace gases, may be considered as a measure of the chemical affinity of the absorbing surface for the trace gas in question. In general, highly reactive gases such as HCl or HNO_3 are characterized by very small or zero surface resistances.

Surface conductances of dry canopies for water vapour (g_c) lie in the range 0.02-2molm^{-2}s^{-1}. Despite high leaf area index in some species, very low maximum values of g_c occur in conifers, partly because the stomatal antechambers are filled with wax rods and tubules. Higher values of g_c occur in broadleaved trees, particularly in multistorey tropical forest. In addition to the area of leaves in a canopy, g_c is sensitive to the several environmental and physiological variables that influence stomatal aperture (Schulze *et al.* 1994). Stomatal conductance increases with PPFD, has a temperature optimum, and decreases with atmospheric water vapour saturation deficit and CO_2 concentration, and with shortage of soil water (Jarvis & Morison 1981). Canopy surface conductances are usually at least an order of magnitude smaller than canopy aerodynamic conductances so that fluxes from forest canopies are generally effectively constrained by g_c. In coniferous forests in particular, atmospheric conditions at the leaf and canopy surfaces are very similar to the conditions overhead so that feedbacks affecting the local atmosphere play little or no role in constraining transpiration and exchanges of non-reactive trace gases, which are highly sensitive to changes in g_c (McNaughton & Jarvis 1991).

There are several alternative models of stomatal action in relation to environmental variables and leaf properties (e.g. Jarvis 1976) and these have been incorporated into large-scale soil-vegetation atmosphere transfer schemes (SVATS). In due course dynamic models incorporating surface chemistry will be able to simulate surface reactive processes within SVATS, and the first steps in this process have been made (Flechard *et al.* 1999). However, for most forests and trace gases, current understanding limits the scope for such modelling to a very few specific cases.

EVAPORATION AND TRANSPIRATION

Evaporation and transpiration of water vapour from forests have major influences on forest production, local water supplies and regional climates. Depending on the precipitation climate, significant amounts of water are returned to the atmosphere by evaporation after interception by the overstorey and understorey canopies without ever reaching the soil, the so-called interception loss (Rutter 1975). A proportion of the precipitation reaches the ground by through-fall and stemflow and infiltrates the soil. Some of this water is taken up by roots of the trees and understorey vegetation, and having traversed from roots to leaves is returned to the atmosphere in transpiration, defined as evaporation of water from within the leaves and its subsequent diffusion and turbulent transfer from the sites of evaporation to the air above (Jarvis 1976; Whitehead & Jarvis 1981). Total evaporation and transpiration rates from forests may reach 7 mm daily, although annual totals mostly average 1-3 mm daily (e.g. Gash & Stewart 1977).

Driving variables and constraints

The driving variables for both the evaporation of intercepted water and for transpiration are the net radiation and sensible heat absorbed by the leaves, both of which raise leaf temperature and power the phase change in evaporation from liquid water on leaf surfaces or within leaves to water vapour, together with the water vapour mole fraction or vapour pressure deficit at the sink for water vapour in the atmosphere outwith the canopy. The process is constrained by the catena of conductances or resistances along the pathway from the sources of water vapour on the surfaces of wet leaves or from within dry leaves to the sink in the atmosphere. This catena of conductances, together with the difference in water vapour mole fraction between the sources of water vapour on the surfaces of, or within, the canopy leaves and the sink in the atmosphere, determines the tendency for molecules of water vapour to escape from the canopy to the atmosphere. Surface conductances (or resistances) strongly determine the exchange of water and other scalars between vegetation and the atmosphere at leaf, stand, forest and regional scales (e.g. Lindroth 1985; Kelliher *et al.* 1994; Raupach 1995).

Evaporation of intercepted water

Although models using a statistical description of raindrop size and frequency may give a somewhat better predictive representation of the interception process (Calder 1996), the evaporation of water from wet canopies (E_i) has generally been represented using the Penman equation (Mon-teith & Unsworth 1990) in the Rutter model (e.g. Rutter *et al.* 1975; Rutter & Morton 1977; Tekle-haimanot *et al.* 1991; Whitehead & Kelliher 1991; Valente *et al.* 1997; Asdak *et al.* 1998b), i.e.

$$E_i = [e/(e + 1)](A/A) + [1(e + 1)](g_a D/p)$$

where e is a coefficient for change in the sensible and latent heat contents of air with respect to temperature, *X* the molar latent heat of vaporization of water, and *D* and *P* the ambient water vapour pressure saturation deficit and atmospheric pressure of the air at the reference location above the canopy. Both the available energy and saturation deficit of the atmosphere are usually small (< 100Wm^{-2} and < 0.1 kPa, respectively) during and immediately after rainfall events, when evaporation of intercepted water occurs. None the less, evaporation rates are high, up to 0.6 mm h^{-1} (400 W m^{-2}, 10 mmol m^{-2} s^{-1}) for short periods as measured by eddy covariance or inversion of the Penman equation (Mizutani *et al.* 1997). This is a result of the high aerodynamic conductance to sensible heat transfer towards the forest surface, and to water vapour transfer away from the source to the sink in the atmosphere above, and because the saturation deficit, although small, is maintained by advection of drier air from the landscape surrounding the area of the rainstorm (Stewart 1977; Asdak *et al.* 1998b).

The water vapour pressure at the canopy surface may fall to the saturation vapour pressure at the wet-bulb temperature (Teklehaimanot & Jarvis 1991) and then the wet canopy behaves like a large psychrometer: the rate of evaporation is balanced by the input of sensible heat and thus given solely by the second term on the right-hand side of Eqn 10.5 (Jarvis 1993), i.e. the net radiation term can be neglected, a useful convenience when deriving g_a from inversion of Eqn 10.5.

The proportion of gross precipitation that is intercepted and directly evaporated back to the atmosphere depends strongly on the frequency and intensity of the rainfall (Rutter 1975). In the tropics, where much of the rainfall comes in relatively short intense storms, interception loss may amount to no more than 11% of the gross precipitation (Lloyd *et al.* 1988; Asdak *et al.* 1998a), although some higher values have been reported (e.g. Sinun *et al.* 1992).

At the other extreme, in maritime climates where the rainfall comes in gentle showers over long periods, so that the canopy is wet for much of the time, interception loss can amount to 40% of the measured precipitation (e.g. Jarvis & Stewart 1979; Gash *et al.* 1980).

Furthermore, much of the fog and, on hills and mountains, the cloud water intercepted by the foliage of trees is not measured by conventional rain gauges and is readily evaporated back to the atmosphere, frequently leaving a nasty deposit on leaf surfaces (see section 10.8). In 'cloud forest' however, fog days may add significantly to the precipitation, although not measured as such, and consequently is known as 'occult' precipitation.

The evaporation of intercepted water is influenced by tree spacing and logging. One might expect the amount of water evaporated to decline in proportion to the reduction in number of trees because of the reduction in surface area of wet foliage. However, in a Sitka spruce spacing experiment this was found to be compensated to a significant degree by the increase in g_a on a per tree basis associated with the increase in distance between the trees (Teklehaimanot & Jarvis 1991) and similar results were obtained in a comparison between logged and unlogged areas of tropical forest (Asdak *et al.* 1998b).

Valente *et al.* (1997) added an additional coefficient to the Rutter model to take account of the wide open spaces in the sparse canopies of Mediterranean forests and Gash *et al.* (1999) have shown, by comparison with eddy covariance data, that evaporation is extremely well represented by their sparse-canopy Rutter model in combination with the *momentum* aerodynamic conductance.

Evaporation of transpired water

A forest comprises a system of parallel conduits through which water is passively transferred from soil to atmosphere as the result of evaporation of water from the leaves and the consequent development of a gradient in water potential (Jarvis 1975). Recently, attention has become strongly focused on the capacity of the liquid water conducting system and its vulnerability to cavitation and entry of air into the vessels and tracheids.

However, it is relevant to re-emphasize the point made long ago (Rawlins 1963; Philip 1966; Weath-erley 1970) that by far and away the largest drop in water potential (or equivalent vapour pressure) in the soil-plant-atmosphere continuum (SPAC) occurs across the stomatal pores, and consequently this is the one location in the SPAC where the flow of water from soil to atmosphere can effectively be regulated. Thus the conductances of the stomata in a dry canopy provide the fine-scale, variable control of the transpiration and latent heat fluxes. While the mechanism of stomatal action is still somewhat of a 'black box', one hypothesis that has been incorporated into some models (e.g. Williams *et al.* 1996, 1998) has it that stomatal conductance adjusts to minimize the risk that the conducting system is impaired through cavitation and air entry.

The driving forces and constraints on transpiration are combined in the now very familiar Penman-Monteith equation (Monteith 1965; Monteith & Unsworth 1990), which provides the basis for the representation of transpiration in most canopy models. While based on sound physics at the scales of the pore and the leaf, use of this equation at canopy scale does involve some assumptions and approximations because of the different spatial distribution of the sources and sinks for heat and water vapour in a canopy compared with a single leaf (Jarvis & McNaughton 1986; Finnigan & Raupach 1987; McNaughton 1994).

Coupling to the atmosphere

While the temperature and humidity of the air may in some circumstances be regarded as independent driving variables, vegetation influences its own local environment to varying degrees, depending particularly on its structure (McNaughton & Jarvis 1983, 1991). At one extreme, feedback from the exchanges of heat and water vapour in extensive areas of crops, for example, determines the temperature and humidity within the vegetation and in the adjacent surface layer. Equilibrium profiles of temperature and humidity develop in relation to the fluxes of heat and water vapour that are driven by the absorbed net radiation. Consider the consequences of a change in conditions that lead to an increase in transpiration, such as an increase in stomatal conductance or saturation deficit. There will be a transient increase in transpiration, but if the additional molecules of water vapour are not able to escape from the vicinity of the foliage, transpiration will subsequently be damped down and will return to its original rate, as determined by the net radiation. From an analysis of transpiration datasets obtained from extensive areas of field crops, Priestley and Taylor (1972) arrived at the following model for equilibrium transpiration:

$$Eeq = [^{£}/(^{£}+ 1)\backslash cc(A/X)$$

where a is a coefficient, in principle unity but found by Priestley and Taylor to have an empirical value of about 1.3 for field crops, that essentially takes into account effects of entrainment and advection when this equation is used alone. More recently, this model for transpiration has been shown to represent transpiration by a range of field crops reasonably well (McNaughton & Jarvis 1983) but was found to be completely inadequate for plantations of trees, for which wholly improbable values of *a* of about 11 were required (Shuttleworth & Calder 1979).

At the other extreme, consider a stand of tall trees with an irregular, 'rough' canopy surface. Partly because the foliage of tall trees is in a higher wind-speed regime but also because of the 'rough' surface, air movement and turbulence are much greater among the foliage, with the result that the ambient environmental conditions are imposed close to the leaf surfaces. Consequently, when an initial increase in transpiration occurs because of an increase in stomatal conductance or ambient saturation deficit, the additional molecules of water vapour have little difficulty in escaping so that the increase in transpiration is maintained at a new higher rate that is largely independent of the net radiation input. At this limit, leaf and air temperatures are equal and the ambient saturation deficit is imposed right up to the leaf surfaces so that transpiration is given by

$$E_{imp} = gcD/(P)$$

McNaughton and Jarvis (1983) and Jarvis and McNaughton (1986) redeveloped the Penman-Monteith equation to give expression to these two limit situations and in the process derived a decoupling coefficient, Q., that defines the extent to which actual transpiration approaches one or other of the two limits, i.e.

$E = GE_{,,}$.

. -(1-J2)E $_{im}$P

where $Q = (e+1)/(e+1+g_a/g_c)$

Q has a range of zero to 1.0, approaching zero as g_a increases relative to g_c and approaching 1.0 as g_c increases relative to g_a. Since g_a is a function of wind speed and turbulence and g_c a function of water stress, the ratio g_a/g_c is large for tall stands of trees in windy environments, particularly when saturation deficits are large and soil water stress intervenes, and is small for well-watered short vegetation in less windy conditions. The ratio also varies somewhat with stand and canopy structural features such as tree spacing and the spatial distribution of leaf area density, both of which affect g_a, and with leaf area, structure, anatomy and physiology, all of which affect g_c.

Estimates of Q are in the range 0.1-0.3 for stands of conifers and 0.3-0.6 for stands of broadleaved trees, the lower values of each range being in windier maritime climates, the higher values in less windy, more continental climates. These low values of Q show that E_{im} is the much more important component of transpiration in forests than is E_{eq} and thus that saturation deficit is a more important driving variable than net radiation, especially in conifers, and indeed that stomatal conductance is a more important constraint than is the availability of absorbed net radiation. Furthermore, E is necessarily limited by the availability of net radiation whereas E_{im} is open-ended in response to saturation deficit, unless or until stomatal closure or leaf fall intervenes.

Dynamics of transpiration

The daily dynamics of forest transpiration are driven in particular by the saturation deficit, and to a lesser extent by the net radiation, and follow very closely changes in surface conductance, which are moderated especially by the fluctuating incident PPFD and saturation deficit of the ambient atmosphere and by the availability of soil water (Fig. 10.7).

The seasonal dynamics are also strongly constrained by the surface conductance, but for rather different reasons in different localities. In the boreal forests, the stomata remain closed during the winter while the soil is frozen so that it is the timing of the thaw in the spring and the freeze-up in the autumn that determines the period over which the surface conductance can respond to the environmental driving variables.

In deciduous temperate forests, the phenology of leafing and senescence of the foliage determines the period of transpiration, and in Mediterranean climates the seasonal dynamics are determined by lack of water. In humid tropical forests, the seasonality is much less evident, although even here periods of water stress occur and the canopy leaf area also fluctuates somewhat for other reasons, thereby affecting the surface conductance.

Role of the understorey

In widely spaced open stands the evaporating surface area, and hence the canopy conductance, of the trees is less than in denser stands and it might be thought that the amounts of water returned to the atmosphere in transpiration would be correspondingly less (Whitehead *et al.* 1994). However, Roberts (1983) compiled data on annual transpiration from a number of investigations in stands of different kinds and stocking across Europe, including some of his own, and found that the annual amounts of transpiration were very similar among the stands, with an overall mean of 333+35 (s.d.) mm (*n*= 12). He drew the conclusion that strong development of the understorey in widely spaced stands compensated for the reduction in the overstorey as far as transpiration is concerned. Is this likely?

A priori one might assume that there would be little transpiration from the understorey, firstly because it is shaded from above and consequently has less net absorbed radiation, and secondly because it would be much less well coupled to the atmosphere above the stand (Baldocchi & Vogel 1996). In the latter case, transpiration would tend more towards the equilibrium rate and would thus be small because of the small input of net radiation.

However, measurements of vertical profiles of air temperature, water vapour pressure, CO_2 and other trace gas concentrations, particularly in coniferous stands, show only very small differences with height at any one time and measurements of these variables in the trunk space differ little on average from those above the canopy. The explanation for this lies in the frequent penetrating downdrafts of air from above every few minutes (Denmead & Bradley 1987). In other words, the understories of coniferous stands are surprisingly well coupled to the atmosphere above. The combination of good coupling with the comparatively high stomatal conductances in understorey foliage seems to be sufficient to account for the compensation noted by Roberts (1983). The degree of coupling of the understorey to the atmosphere above is somewhat less in stands of broadleaved trees, possibly because of less deep canopies with higher leaf area density, and is very much less in multistoried, humid, tropical forest stands where there are bands of high leaf area density in the upper canopy (e.g. Shuttleworth *et al.* 1984; Shuttleworth 1989; Kruijt *et al.* 1999).

Bowen ratio

As discussed earlier, *[3* is a functional descriptor of the partitioning of energy between warming or cooling the forest and evaporating water, and varies widely depending on forest type and climate. Analysis of *[3* in terms of the likely variables (Jarvis *et al.* 1976) shows that these observations are explicable in terms of the so-called 'isothermal' or 'climatological' resistance of Monteith (1965) and Stewart and Thom (1973). Combining this resistance with the Penman-Monteith equation (Jarvis *et al.* 1976) leads to the following expression for the Bowen ratio

$$p+1 = (e+1 + gag_c)/(e + gag_i)$$

where the climatological conductance, g_i, is given by:

$$g_i=(AfD)-(P/X)$$

It is apparent that *p* is approximately proportional to the climatological conductance, g_i, essentially the ratio *A/D*, and inversely proportional to the stomatal conductance, becoming larger in a predictable manner as *D* declines relative to *A*, or as g_c changes with vegetation type and structure and as stomata close. In the case of different climates cited earlier, it is the differences in g_i that are important; in the case of different forest types (see Fig. 10.4), it is the differences in g_c among the stands that account for the different values of *p*.

Equation 10.10 can be rearranged to provide a simple direct means of deriving the canopy conductance from a knowledge of *p*, g_a and g_i as follows (Thom 1975; Jarvis *et al.* 1976):

$$g_c =1[(\#-1)/g_a+(/J+1)/g_i]$$

This is not only a useful means of derivation of g_c (e.g. Gash & Stewart 1975) but also provides a practical description of the interrelationships among energy partitioning, the pathway properties and the driving variables of available energy and saturation deficit. In essence this expression encapsulates the most significant functional attributes of forest canopies with respect to the exchanges of heat and water vapour with the atmosphere.

Some conclusions

There are some paradoxes evident here with respect to water use by forests. Canopy aerodynamic conductances are generally high, especially so in comparison with crops, grassland and heath-land, decreasing somewhat from coniferous boreal forest, through mixed broadleaved temperate forest to multistorey, humid, tropical forest. Conversely, canopy surface conductances are generally low in coniferous boreal forest, close to zero during the period of frozen soils in winter; somewhat higher in broadleaved temperate forest, at least during the foliated period; and possibly somewhat higher still in humid tropical forest, the year round. In general, forest canopies, particularly coniferous forest canopies with large g_a/g_c, are extremely well coupled to the atmosphere.

High g_a leads to high rates of evaporation of intercepted water from canopy surfaces; low g_c leads to low rates of transfer of transpired water vapour from canopies to the atmosphere. Thus in climates where a large proportion of the precipitation occurs during long periods of low-intensity rainfall, such as in temperate maritime regions, evaporation of intercepted rainfall, particularly from coniferous forest, can amount to a very large direct return of water to the atmosphere. On the other hand, the low g_c of temperate and boreal coniferous forest results in low transpiration rates from dry canopies. Thus the local forest water budget depends on the balance between the periods of time that the canopy is wet or dry and thus on the precipitation regime in a particular area (Jarvis & Stewart 1979).

Because of low g_c, forest canopies, even when not superficially wet, present a particularly dry surface to the atmosphere. High g_a/g_c also leads to relatively high rates of sensible heat transfer and to large Bowen ratios which drive regional climate. However, the magnitude of this effect is moderated by another aspect of local climate, the relative size of g_i, the climatological conductance. At identical g_c, p increases as g_i increases and transpiration is inhibited by small saturation deficits.

We conclude this section on evaporation and transpiration, with its emphasis on Q and p, by suggesting that these two coefficients are useful summarizing descriptors of the functional properties of forest stands and could well form the basis for a classification of forest stands into functional types.

CARBON DIOXIDE EXCHANGE

The policy imperative

The exchange of CO_2 between forests and the atmosphere has become a topic of intense interest over the past 3 years as the role of forests in the global atmospheric CO_2 budget has become more widely appreciated. The Kyoto Protocol, arising from the Third Conference of the Parties (COP3) of the United Nations Framework Convention on Climate Change (UNFCCC) held in Kyoto in December 1997, explicitly implicated forests as agents in the net removal of CO_2 of anthropogenic origin from the atmosphere. The developed countries of the world were assigned legally binding targets for the reduction of their industrial emissions of CO_2 to the atmosphere, a part of which could be offset against the net uptake of CO_2 by new, young forests. The Intergovernmental Panel on Climate Change (IPCC) was commissioned to produce a special report on 'Land Use, Land Use Change and Forestry' for submission to the UNFCCC at COP6 in November 2000 and there is an expectation that 'full accounting' of all forests may then be included. The overall result of these developments has been a major upsurge of interest and concern regarding the exchanges of CO_2 between forests and the atmosphere on stand, forest, national, regional and global scales, as is happening now and is likely to eventuate over the next 100 years.

Forests as a carbon pump

Forests are the major terrestrial interface for C transfer between the atmosphere and the soil. Like the net exchange of short- and long-wave radiation and the balance between precipitation and evaporation, the NEE of CO_2 between forests and the atmosphere is a balance between two largely simultaneous, co-located, opposed sets of processes. In all three cases it is the balance between the inflows and outflows that is of major consequence. We are concerned with the small shift in the radiation balance responsible for global warming, with changes in the spatial and temporal balance between precipitation and evaporation that may lead to water shortage and, in forest stands, with the size and permanence of the balance between the inflows of C in photosynthesis by the trees, understorey and ground vegetation and outflows resulting very largely from the heterotrophic respiration in the soil and from the corresponding autotrophic respiration of the trees.

We may regard the trees in forests as 'pumps' that effect a net transfer of C from the atmosphere to the soil where it is sequestered. The large amounts of C that have accumulated in forest soils in the Northern Hemisphere since the retreat of the ice sheets after the last glaciation are evidence of this. While the trees in a forest are juvenile and growing rapidly, they may also accumulate significant amounts of C in the wood; however, even when the trees 'mature' and are growing very slowly, if at all, they none the less continue to transfer C from the atmosphere to the soil where it accumulates. This transfer is effected through leaf and branch fall, internal translocation of assimilate to the root system and fine-root turnover. For example, trees in large areas of the boreal forest today are small in diameter (e.g. stands of black spruce with a median diameter of 10 cm at 120 years old) and are growing on deep peat-rich soils, the C of which has all accumulated over the past 8000 years or so. On the basis of the 'climax concept' (Clements 1916), it was long believed that pristine forests, particularly tropical forests, were in a state of equilibrium such that over a period of several years they were C neutral, with neither a net gain nor loss of C. This view has been challenged in recent years with increasing evidence from eddy covariance measurements of NEE of a net gain in the exchange of CO_2 (Malhi *et al.* 1999) and from sample plot studies of NPP which show that tree growth in undisturbed tropical moist forests continues to sequester C (e.g. Lugo & Brown 1992; Phillips *et al.* 1998).

Regarding forests as a pump transferring C from the atmosphere to the soil in this way is closely analogous to the 'biotic pump' in the photic zone of the oceans, which transfers C from the atmosphere to long-term sequestration in the deep ocean.

Dynamics of carbon dioxide exchange

Daily dynamics

Over the course of a day, C sequestration essentially follows solar radiation (provided there is no major constraint such as frozen or dry soil), with C being accumulated during the daylight hours and lost at night. For example, large daytime gains by tropical forest stands are offset by large night-time losses (Malhi *et al.* 1999). Depending on the balance between these hourly gains and losses, for any stand there may be a net gain or loss of C over any 24 h in the year. Typically, through a growing season, there may be a net gain of C on about three-quarters of the days but a loss on days of particularly low solar radiation input (i.e. with cloud and rain, or smoke in the atmosphere) and high temperatures (e.g. Jarvis *et al.* 1997).

Seasonal dynamics

Over a year, the length of the photosynthetic season has a major influence on C transfer (e.g. Berg *et al.* 1998). In boreal coniferous forest, for example, one-third to a half of the C gained in the five summer months is lost by respiration over the seven winter months, during which a small efflux of C continues although the ground is frozen. In broadleaved temperate forest the length of the photosynthetic season is determined by budburst in the spring and leaf senescence in the autumn, whereas in temperate coniferous forest the season of net photosynthetic gain is determined by daylength and daily total radiation input in the winter months and may be 10 months long for coniferous forest in maritime climates. In boreal, temperate and Mediterranean climates the vegetation is strongly seasonal and NEE may be strongly constrained by water availability for a large part of the time; only in tropical moist forests is net C gain near continuous throughout the year, being reduced by occasional short periods of low temperature and moderate seasonal water shortage.

Annual dynamics

Transfer of CO_2 to young forest stands regenerating after disturbance such as fire or harvesting is critically dependent on the phase of the succes-sional cycle. During the first 5 or 10 years the disturbed area of young trees is likely be losing C to the atmosphere; subsequently, as the trees come to occupy the site fully, the area will accumulate C strongly during a phase of rapid growth that may last for decades, depending on the species of trees and site conditions. Mature forests take up C from the atmosphere at much slower rates, but even as the growth increment of the trees declines towards zero, C continues to be transferred from the atmosphere to the soil via the trees in the form of above- and below-ground detritus. None the less, old-growth forests do become net sources of C to the atmosphere under some circumstances, for example if the forest soil becomes warmer or more aerobic, thus promoting oxidation of the soil organic matter (Lindroth *et al.* 1998).

Net transfer of carbon dioxide from the atmosphere to forests

Tropical forests

So far there are few C flux measurements over periods long enough to give annual estimates of NEE in tropical forests, although they are likely to increase appreciably over the next 5 years with the onset of the LBA experiment. Eddy covariance measurements indicate an annual net C sink of about 1.0 Mg ha^{-1} in pristine, sparse, dry, rain forests in Amazonia (Fan *et al.* 1990; Grace *et al.* 1995a,b, 1996) and about 5.5 Mg ha^{-1} for dense, moist, rain forest (Malhi *et al.* 1998, 1999).

Temperate forests

Forests in the temperate region are virtually all managed to a greater or lesser extent and there are but few patches that might be regarded as pristine. Recent measurements of NEE by eddy covariance over a year or more in Europe in the EUROFLUX experiment (Fig. 10.16) and in North America (e.g. Goulden *et al.* 1996; Greco & Baldocchi 1996; Valentini *et al.* 1996; Baldocchi 1997; Anthoni *et al.* 1999) indicate rates of C sequestration in the range 1.5 to 7 Mg ha^{-1} over about 20 sites differing in latitude, altitude, climate (continental vs. maritime), species, sparseness of cover and degree of management. The values at the lower end of the range derive from sparse sites where lack of water is a major factor or from northern sites where length of growing season, lack of nutrients and low temperatures are major factors. Estimates of NPP of sample plots indicate annual carbon sequestration of approximately 3 Mg ha^{-1} (range 1 to 8 Mg ha^{-1}) based on numerous yield tables (e.g. Spiecker *et al.* 1996). A preliminary scaling-up exercise of the EUROFLUX measurements suggests that the largely temperate forests of the European Union are a current annual C sink of 0.17 to 0.35 Gt (Martin *et al.* 1998).

Boreal forests

The extensive boreal forests across Siberia and Canada are fire-driven climax forests, the near end-point of succession following retreat of the ice after the last glaciation about 10 000 years ago. These forests have been subject to increasing exploitation over the past 150 years but much of the area standing can be regarded as largely pristine. Measurements of C sequestration by eddy covariance on a campaign basis in Siberia (Hollinger *et al.* 1994, 1995, 1998; Kelliher *et al.* 1997;

Schulze *et al.* 1999), over periods of several months up to 5 years in northern Canada, in the BOREAS experiment (Sellers *et al.* 1997) and in northern Europe (Valentini *et al.* 2000) have demonstrated old-growth spruce stands that are C neutral in Canada (Goulden *et al.* 1998) and a C source in Sweden (Lindroth *et al.* 1998), losing C at an annual rate of up to 1 Mg ha^{-1}. However, the majority of boreal forest stands investigated, some 12 or more, are C sinks sequestering C at annual rates of up to 2.5 Mg ha^{-1} (Black *et al.* 1996; Blanken *et al.* 1997, 1998; Jarvis *et al.* 1997; McCaughey *et al.* 1997; Chen *et al.* 1999; Schulze *et al.* 1999). Estimates of NPP from sample plots also indicate that boreal forests are weak C sinks of about 2.5 Mg ha^{-1} (range 1 to 6 Mg ha^{-1}) (Gower *et al.* 1997; Jarvis *et al.* 2000).

Carbon balance components

Carbon stocks and flows in forest biomes

To understand the magnitude of the net transfer of CO_2 between stands and the atmosphere at a particular stage in a succession and to appreciate its sensitivity to current conditions, disturbance and climate change, it is helpful to consider the principal component processes within the stand that add up to give the overall net exchange. The feedbacks among these processes, their speed of response and their sensitivity to environmental change determine the present and future flows of CO_2 and the C sequestration capacity of the stand.

It is evident that the annual NEE is the difference between a very large gain term (i.e. photosynthesis of the foliage) and a very large loss term dominated by respiration of heterotrophs in the soil (see Fig. 10.8). Thus the net exchange is particularly sensitive to relatively small proportional changes in the opposed gain and loss terms, particularly if they are out of phase.

A mass balance of the component fluxes above ground (photosynthesis; foliage, branch and stem respiration; leaf, branch and stem litter of all kinds, i.e. detritus; and above-ground NPP) enables an estimate to be made of the amount of C internally translocated below ground. A mass balance of the component fluxes below ground, comprising the inputs from above (i.e. the detritus and translocate), root and heterotrophic respiration, fine-root turnover, and mycorrhizal and root system NPP, enables an approximate estimate to be made of net changes in the pool of soil C.

In principle, summation of the component fluxes over a year should add up to the independently measured annual NEE. However, there are appreciable errors in measuring the below-ground components in particular, so that close agreement between measurements or estimates of the components of the budget is not as yet to be expected.

Exchanges of volatile organic compounds and methane

The net exchange of C between forests and the atmosphere also includes the emission of bio-genic volatile organic C compounds (VOC) such as isoprene and terpenes from the tree canopy (Baldocchi *et al.* 1995). Simple algorithms have been developed to calculate emissions of individual compounds from individual tree species based mainly on PAR and leaf temperature (Guenther *et al.* 1991). The emissions of VOC increase with temperature and PPFD and it has been argued that the emissions of certain VOC compounds, notably isoprene, reduce the physiological effects of water stress (Sharkey & Loreto 1993). The absolute magnitude of C exchange represents a small fraction of the total. Emissions of terpenes from Norway spruce in Denmark (Christensen *et al.* 1997) amount to no more than 0.3% of the annual C assimilated, but short-term losses from the Mediterranean species *Quercus ilex* may exceed 6% at high temperatures (Staudt & Bertin 1998) Globally emissions are small, around 0.1% of annual carbon emissions from vegetation (Guenther *et al.* 2000).

Undrained peatlands in high latitudes have accumulated appreciable amounts of C from the atmosphere since the retreat of the ice and are currently significant annual CO_2 sinks (0.2-

0.5Mgha^{-1} of C) but are also small annual sources of methane (CH_4) (0.03-0.3 Mgha^{-1} of C). By contrast, drained peatlands, whether intended for agriculture or afforestation, release C as CO_2 because of accelerated decomposition of the aerobic peat (Cannell *et al.* 1993) but no longer release CH_4 in significant amounts. Peatlands drained for agriculture continue to be a sustained C source while the peat remains. Depending on species of tree and time in the rotation, peatlands drained for afforestation may continue to be a source of C in spite of forest biomass growth (Zoltai & Martikainen 1996; Cannell *et al.* 1999). Thus drainage and afforestation of peatlands reduces CH_4 emissions and provides a larger CO_2 sink than the peatland plant community. However, the net exchange of C by peatlands is an upward flux for some years, until the C fixed by the canopy exceeds the losses of C from the oxidizing peat with the lower water table. The primary interest in forest-atmosphere C fluxes is the contribution to the global atmosphere C budgets and the consequent radiative forcing of climate. As CH_4 on a per molecule basis in radiative equivalents has a global warming potential 30 times that of CO_2, it is not simply the mass fraction that should be used to identify priorities. The change in the net direction of CH_4 flux from emissions to deposition needs to be included in C budgets and the overall net radiative forcing calculated.

Future carbon sequestration potential

Across Europe forests are now growing faster than previously (Spiecker *et al.* 1996) and similarly in the tropics (Phillips *et al.* 1998). We currently seem to be in a period of especially strong C uptake by forests, although it has been suggested that this will not continue indefinitely, and indeed there is concern that the rate will diminish significantly as the 21st century proceeds (Walker *et al.* 1999).

It has frequently been suggested that the present rates of CO_2 uptake and growth are the combined result of the recent global increases in atmospheric CO_2 concentration (e.g. Jarvis

1998), N deposition (e.g. Kauppi *et al.* 1992; Hudson *et al.* 1994) and temperature. Quantitative evaluation of the relative impacts of all three of these factors is a focus of current research.

CO_2*-stimulated carbon sequestration*

It is difficult to measure the impact of the slow progressive rise in atmospheric CO_2 concentration on the C sequestration capacity of stands of trees but some relevant indications can be obtained from recent experimental programmes to evaluate the impacts of elevated atmospheric CO_2 concentration on the growth, development and physiology of young trees.

Doubling atmospheric CO_2 concentration speeds up development, photosynthesis and growth by up to 60% in a wide range of species of young trees grown rooted in the ground in the field over periods of up to 5 years in both North America and Europe (Curtis & Wang 1998; Medlyn *et al.* 1999; Peterson *et al.* 1999). Moderate lack of nutrients and of water reduce growth but have little adverse effect on the *relative* impact of the increase in CO_2 concentration. To all intents and purposes the impact of the increase in CO_2 concentration is that trees get bigger quicker but otherwise remain similar in most respects to trees of the same size in the current conditions. Meta-analysis of the results from many experiments shows that the key physiological parameters defining capacity for photosyn-thetic CO_2 uptake by trees, V_{cmax} and J_{max}, are downregulated on average by no more than 12% and stomatal conductance by 15% as a result of growth in elevated CO_2 concentration (Curtis & Wang 1998; Medlyn *et al.* 1999).

A key question, as yet unresolved, is to what extent will the responses of key parameters to increased CO_2 concentration change when a stand of young trees reaches canopy closure. This is not readily solvable other than by long-term, free air elevated CO_2 concentration exposure experiments (FACE), starting with seedlings or clonal propagules. So far, the few FACE experiments in progress in forests have been imposed on existing stands (e.g. Ellsworth 1999), which are unlikely to acclimate fully over, say, a 5-year period of exposure. Thus major uncertainties remain as to the likely long-term effects of the rise in atmospheric CO_2 concentration on C sequestration and the contribution of CO_2 fertilization to the global terrestrial C sink (Friedlingstein *et al.* 1995).

Temperature-stimulated carbon return to the atmosphere

Photosynthesis is particularly dependent on solar radiation, CO_2 concentration and N availability and thus is likely to be reduced by increase in cloudiness but increased by elevations of the global atmospheric CO_2 concentration and by N deposition. All respiratory processes are very sensitive to temperature, as is the multiplication of the populations of respiring organisms, particularly the fine roots and heterotrophs in the soil. Thus soil respiration increases strongly in boreal and temperate forests in relation to the rise in soil temperature as the spring progresses (Boone *et al.* 1998; Rayment & Jarvis 1999) and consequently is likely to be very sensitive to the increase in global temperature. Increase in soil temperature leads to enhanced mineralization of soil organic matter and release of N, which feed back to stimulate photosynthesis, tree growth and transfer of CO_2 from atmosphere to forest (Bergh & Linder 1999; Jarvis & Linder 2000). The balance between these conflicting effects of rising temperature on the net exchange of CO_2 (enhanced respiration and enhanced photosynthesis) is only now being resolved experimentally in the short term, although models indicate a potentially complex time-course in the long term (Dewar *et al.* 2000).

Carbon sink saturation

It has been proposed that on time-scales of decades to centuries saturation of C sinks will occur and that existing C sinks will become significant C sources (Scholes 1999; Scholes *et al.* 1999). This effect, it is suggested, arises from a difference in phase and functional relationship between the responses to global climate change of the principal gain and loss terms in NEE. The CO_2 stimulation of photosynthesis increases with increasing atmospheric CO_2 concentration (the CO_2-fertilization effect) but does so at a diminishing rate. On the other hand, heterotrophic respiration (decomposition of litter and soil C, resulting in emission of CO_2 to the atmosphere) increases somewhat later in time as detritus production builds up and increases exponentially with increasing temperature (Boone *et al.* 1998; Rayment & Jarvis 1999).

Because so much C is stored in forest soils, and because this C is potentially vulnerable to climate change, it is essential to take full account of the C stocks in soil. It has been postulated on the basis of models (e.g. Cao & Woodward 1998; Scholes *et al.* 1999) that changes in climate, particularly the increase in temperature, will lead to higher rates of heterotrophic respiration and oxidation of the C stock in the soils, it is presumed without acclimation. Thus, as both atmospheric CO_2 concentration and temperature rise, the rate of heterotrophic respiration may be expected to increase relative to the rate of photosynthesis, and the overall capacity of the terrestrial biosphere to take up C from the atmosphere to diminish. However there are a number of possible feedbacks not included in these model analyses. These include the effects of rising CO_2 and temperature on:

1 litter quantity, which may increase as a result of any short-term CO_2-fertilization effect and may lead to enhanced nutrient availability and C storage in soils;
2 litter quality (i.e. the C:N ratio), which may decrease and retard decomposition and nutrient release;
3 allocation of C below ground, which may well increase and lead to increased production of roots, mycorrhizae and exudates;
4 increased nutrient availability and temperature leading to higher photosynthetic rates and NPP; and
5 longer photosynthetic and growing seasons.

These feedbacks raise major uncertainties, currently being addressed by soil-warming experiments and modelling. The results of recent modelling analyses that have taken these feedbacks into account (McMurtrie & Dewar 1999; McMurtrie *et al.* 2000a,b; Medlyn *et al.* 2000) suggest that the dominant *short-term* constraint on the CO_2-fertilization effect is an increase in litter quantity. On the other hand, *long-term* increases in C sequestration are possible as atmospheric CO_2 concentration increases, if the net N input also increases (either through fixation or deposition) or if the N : C composition of newly formed litter substantially decreases. If below-ground C allocation increases, as observed in many experiments, and leads to increased production of roots, mycorrhizae and exudates, with consequent increase in N fixation, a large long-term increase in NPP and C sequestration is likely (Medlyn *et al.* 2000).

The simulated *long-term* effect of rising temperature is a large increase in NPP, and hence litter production, as a result of enhanced N mineralization and consequent increased photosynthesis, whereas *short-term* effects of temperature on photosynthesis and respiration are relatively unimportant (Dewar *et al.* 2000).

These simulations highlight the importance of litter production on the one hand and turnover processes in the soil on the other, the former being strongly constrained by N availability and air temperature, the latter by soil microbiological processes and soil temperature. One cannot escape the conclusion that more emphasis needs to be placed on understanding better the processes in the soil, and the link between soil and atmosphere through the medium of the trees.

Indications from soil-warming experiments are that after an early initial flush of CO_2, the CO_2 efflux is similar in the heated and unheated control plots; furthermore, the feedbacks are actually increasing the efficiency of the 'forest pump' through the release of N (Lückwille & Wright 1997; Ineson *et al.* 1998) and may override the initial losses of C (Jarvis & Linder 2000). The effect of climate change on the efficiency of the pump in transferring C from the atmosphere to the soil via enhanced nutrient availability, photosynthesis and detritus production needs to be evaluated in addition to the effect of climate change on the return of C from the soil to the atmosphere, in order to obtain a complete picture of the net change in C sequestration by forests in a warmer climate.

A further key question is whether the current annual rate of N deposition (= 20kgha–^{1}) adequately balances the current annual rise in atmospheric CO_2 concentration (= 1.5mmolmol^{-1}) to sustain the NEE over the next 50 years. This is addressed in section 10.9. As things are at the present, the possibility of C sinks becoming sources in the mid twenty-first century remains highly speculative.

TRACE GASES, AEROSOLS AND CLOUD DROPLETS

The interactions between forests and the atmosphere outlined so far identify the key role of forests in carbon exchange between the global atmosphere and the biosphere, in regulating regional climates and in the exchange of water vapour. These interactions have drawn attention to forests as a central issue within the global warming debate. The loss of forest through biomass burning, especially in tropical regions, is closely associated with global carbon emissions but is also a major contributor to regional air pollution through the production of photochemical smog, with important consequences for human health.

Forests have been at the centre of earlier environmental issues, for example the acid rain debate, a major issue of the 1970s and 1980s throughout Europe and North America (Last & Watling 1991). Forests were regarded as one of the ecosystems most sensitive to deposited acidity and 'forest decline' was widely associated with air pollutants derived from anthropogenic emissions of oxides of sulphur and nitrogen

(Ulrich *et al.* 1980; Schulze & Freer-Smith 1991). Multinational research programmes investigated the underlying processes in field and laboratory studies and many important links between the pollutants and effects were established. It is notable that these links often proved subtle and complex, and some of the more obvious connections that were anticipated were never established.

For example, deposited acidity has been shown to be associated with the decline of red spruce in the Appalachians of North America (De Hayes 1992); however, the mechanism involves susceptibility to winter injury and frost damage (Sheppard 1991) and is restricted mainly to stands at moderate or high elevations that are subject to orographic cloud containing large concentrations of NO_3^-, SO_4^{2-} and H^+ (Fowler *et al.* 1989). There is also evidence that the same high-elevation stands of red spruce have been influenced by photochemical oxidant pollutants (McLaughlin & Kohut 1992). Other examples include induced magnesium deficiency in European silver fir stands on acidified soils (Roberts *et al.* 1989).

Forests are efficient 'scavengers' of pollutants from the atmosphere as a result of their low canopy aerodynamic resistance. The term 'filtering effect' has been extensively used to emphasize the relative efficiency of capture of pollutants by trees relative to shorter vegetation (Johnson *et al.* 1991). It has also been suggested that trees provide an effective means of reducing urban air pollution, largely as a consequence of the assumed 'filtering effect' (Freer-Smith *et al.* 1997), although field data in support of such claims are scarce. There are, therefore, effects of reactive atmospheric pollutants on forests and effects of forests on the atmosphere.

In this section we examine the underlying mechanisms that control the interactions between the major groups of trace gases and aerosols and forests. Particles are present in sizes ranging from a few nanometres to 10mm, and the aerosols contain many further minor and trace plant nutrients. This list is far from exhaustive, and within the scope of the chapter a complete and detailed treatment of each pollutant is not possible. In the following sections the pollutants are classified largely by environmental issue, which in the majority of cases also groups them by their general chemical properties. Deposition of all the compounds on forest canopies therefore contributes to biogeochemical cycling at regional scales.

Acid gases: HC1, $HN0_3$, HF

For the very reactive gases, including HNO_3, HCl and HF, forests represent an important sink, even when ambient concentrations are small. The highly reactive nature of these gases causes them to be removed rapidly at terrestrial surfaces.

The canopy or surface resistance can be derived as the residual when the aerodynamic turbulent transfer and boundary layer resistances have been subtracted from the total resistance to transfer from a reference height in the atmosphere to the effective surface within the forest canopy.

The presence of atmospheric aerosols, clouds and rain provide additional atmospheric sinks for these gases and, as a consequence, their lifetime in the atmosphere and their ambient concentrations are small. In the case of HCl and HNO_3, there are both natural and anthropogenic sources, whereas HF is largely anthropogenic in origin and is of importance only at local scales.

Ambient HNO_3 concentrations in Europe vary from 0.1 / *ig m*$^{-3}$ in the maritime regions of northern and western Europe to 1-5 */ig m*$^{-3}$ in polluted areas of central Europe (Erisman *et al.* 1998). For a forest with an atmospheric resistance of 10sm^{-1} such concentrations would lead to N inputs ranging from 0.7 to 70kgha^{-1}. Clearly, forests exposed to large ambient HNO_3 concentrations will receive appreciable atmospheric inputs through dry deposition. Such areas include substantial areas of southern Europe and the forests in southern California. The use of mean values, for example, is appropriate for rough approximations such as these but in practice ambient HNO_3 concentrations are closely coupled to the synoptic meteorological conditions, being largest during periods of persistent anticyclonic weather in which the sources of primary pollutants (NO_x and VOC) are processed through photochemical reactions to generate significant HNO_3 concentrations, and smallest in cyclonic conditions with wind and rain (PORG 1997; Kley *et al.* 1999).

Concentrations of HNO_3 are monitored at few locations and we currently rely primarily on long-range transport models for regional concentration fields and estimates of deposition. The large atmospheric conductances of forests relative to shorter vegetation (or open water or soil surfaces) make the trees the primary sink for dry deposition in a mixed land-use landscape. It is of interest to calculate the fractional cover within the landscape necessary for the woodland to 'capture' say 50% of the dry deposition. As the relative deposition rates to forest and short vegetation differ typically by a factor of 5, then in a landscape containing 20% woodland the cumulative input to the woodland would be similar to the combined input to the remaining 80% of the land cover. In practice, the concentration fields are not spatially uniform, but the general point is clear, and the importance of forests as a sink for fixed N.

While the current uncertainty in estimating inputs of HNO_3 (or HCl) to forests lies primarily in knowledge of the ambient concentrations of the two gases, there are aspects of the underlying deposition process that remain poorly understood. The exchange of momentum between forests and the atmosphere is both well described and easily measured, and forms the basis of our understanding of forest-atmosphere exchanges. However, the exchange processes at the surface differ in an important way as there is no equivalent in mass transfer to the transfer of momentum by form drag (Thom 1975). The conventional practical solution used to overcome this problem is to introduce a further resistance (r_b) in series with the aerodynamic resistance (r_a). Many different formulations for r_b may be found in the literature, and are discussed by Brutsaert (1991) and, in the case of HNO_3 deposition, have been considered by Muller *et al.* (1993). However, the available field data over forest are too limited to be able to identify the most appropriate of the formulations. These uncertainties will remain until a substantial quantity of flux measurements with much smaller uncertainties in the measurement become available. Such developments await an instrument able to detect fluctuations in ambient HNO_3 with similar accuracy to the instruments used to measure atmospheric CO_2 fluctuations.

This section has focused on HNO_3 rather than HCl or HF because HNO_3 represents a much more important component of the trace gas climate above forests and constitutes an important source of N deposition in the warmer polluted regions of the planet. However, both the two other gases are believed to behave in broadly similar ways.

Ammonia

Gaseous NH_3 is a trace gas that interacts with vegetation in similar ways to CO_2, even though the two gases differ greatly in their chemical properties and roles in plant biochemistry. Both gases are processed through all plants and animals, play a major role in plant biochemistry and physiology, exhibit bidirectional exchange between the atmosphere and terrestrial ecosystems, and exhibit a 'compensation point', i.e. a surface concentration at which no net surface-atmosphere exchange occurs. Both CO_2 and NH_3 are also important atmospheric pollutants, their emission as a consequence of anthropogenic activities representing an important driver of the change in the chemical composition of the atmosphere.

These similarities have largely been overlooked because knowledge of NH_3 is much more recent, the gas is more difficult to measure and, most important of all, NH_3 has a very short atmospheric lifetime relative to CO_2. This highly soluble reactive gas readily undergoes gas to particle formation and is a major component of aerosols over the mid-latitude continental regions (Dentener 1993). Ammonia also deposits rapidly on vegetation, soil and water surfaces (Sutton *et al.* 1993). The atmospheric lifetime and fate of NH_3 and is generally considered to be of the order of 0.5-2 h, depending on the presence of acidic aerosols and wet surfaces (Erisman *et al.* 1998). Ambient concentrations of NH_3 are therefore small, generally in the range 0.1-3.0,ugm^{-3}. However, close to major sources, such as intensive livestock units, mean ambient NH_3 concentrations can reach 30,ugm^{-3} (Pitcairn *et al.* 1998).

The exchange of NH_3 between forests and the atmosphere is bidirectional. Within foliage, the presence of NH_4^+ in the apoplast (the liquid phase within cell walls) leads, via Henry's law, to a potential equilibrium gas-phase NH_3 concentration. The partial pressure of NH_3 within the substomatal cavity drives the exchange with the atmosphere within or above the forest canopy. The net transfer of NH_3 molecules through the stomata represents uptake or loss from the foliage and is regulated by the direction of the concentration gradient. However, the uptake of NH_3 is not limited to stomatal exchange and the primary sinks in forests for NH_3 are the external surfaces of the foliage (Wyers & Erisman 1998). Unlike the very reactive HNO_3, the forest canopy is not a perfect sink for NH_3. The magnitude of the surface resistance is regulated by a combination of chemical processes on the external surfaces and the net exchange between apoplastic NH_4^+ and substomatal gaseous NH_3 (Flechard & Fowler 1998). The effect of a forest on net annual inputs of NH_3 may be quantified from recent studies of NH_3 concentration and deposition at three European sites: Auchencorth in southern Scotland, Speulde in the central region of The Netherlands, and Melpitz in south-east Germany close to Leipzig.

By applying a constant value ($37sm^{-1}$) for canopy resistance (r_c) at all three sites, based on continuous measurements of r_c over a year, the net sink strength of terrestrial surfaces may be quantified using data from the three sites. The enhancement in NH_3 deposition by a forest relative to short vegetation is 65%. The problem with presenting comparisons between different surfaces using measured variables is that there are no field data available for both forest and short vegetation at the same location. Furthermore, it is clear from the studies to date that the concentrations of major pollutants present, in this case SO_2 and NH_3, interact with one another on the surfaces of vegetation (Flechard *et al.* 1999). The local meteorology at the site, especially the frequency of wet surfaces, and the N status of the canopy, and hence apoplas-tic NH_4^+ and H^+, also influence r_c and no rigorous comparison based on measurements has been attempted to date. The main point of this exercise is that NH_3 inputs to forest may be large, even at sites unaffected by large local sources of NH_3, and are larger than inputs to short vegetation (Erisman *et al.* 1998).

Canopy-atmosphere exchange of NH_3 and interactions with other pollutants

The preceding arguments may be formalized within a model that simulates the interaction of turbulent exchange processes with leaf surface chemistry and exchange between apoplastic NH_4^+ and the ambient NH_3 concentration with plant canopies.

The first dynamic canopy-atmosphere NH_3 exchange model, developed by Flechard (1998) and described in Flechard *et al.* (1999), is outlined in diagrammatic form in Fig. 10.21. The leaf surface solution chemistry is simulated using the Henry and solution equilibria for the trace gases NH_3, SO_2, CO_2, HONO and HCl. Oxidation rates for SO_2 in solution and ion exchange between the leaf surface and the interior of the leaves characterized by apoplasm solution are also simulated. As the detailed chemistry simulated is limited to bulk solution phase processes, the model is designed to describe the exchange processes for a wet (or partially wet) canopy, and activity coefficients are included within the modelling scheme for pH and solute concentrations up to ionic strengths of 0.3 $moll^{-1}$. For higher concentrations and for 'dry surfaces', which are assumed at relative humidities less than 70%, simple transfer resistances are applied. The site used to provide test data for the model (Auchencorth) is 'wet' within the definition applied by the model for almost 70% of the time.

The model is initialized using measured precipitation chemistry and ambient concentrations of the trace gases, and fluxes and surface concentrations simulated for periods of 2 to 11 days. The results of the comparison of 1629h of flux measurements with the model show the net NH_3 deposition over the period (68 days) to be within 3% of the measured fluxes (i.e. -6.3$ngm^{-2}s^{-1}$ vs. -6.1 $ngm^{-2}s^{-1}$). This represents a major improvement over application of a simple canopy resistance model, which overestimated the net deposition flux by 27%, largely because such models are unable to simulate emission fluxes. The limitation of this approach is the requirement for extensive chemical data as input variables. However, the successful simulations show that the major processes that regulate NH_3 fluxes into and out of forests are now understood and can be quantified for situations where the major gases and the precipitation chemistry are continuously monitored.

One important consequence of the recent long-term flux measurements and dynamic modelling is that interactions of pollutants on the external surfaces of vegetation have now been recognized as important. In particular, the interaction of NH_3 with SO_2 effectively regulates the canopy resistance for SO_2. In effect the presence of sufficient NH_3 prevents the pH of the leaf surface water falling to values that would suppress further SO_2 uptake, just as NH_3 in the boundary layer maintains the pH of cloud water sufficiently high to promote heterogeneous SO_2 oxidation by O_3 in low-level stratiform cloud.

A consequence of the chemical control of forest-atmosphere exchange of pollutants is that control strategies to regulate effects of one pollutant may inadvertently influence the deposition footprint and effects of another pollutant, and this has already introduced non-linearity into the relationship between sulphur emission and deposition at a regional scale (RGAR 1997).

Local influence of forest on NH_3 deposition and dispersion

The rapid deposition of NH_3 on forest leads directly to large inputs of fixed N in forests in areas with large ambient concentrations. Such inputs may represent a valuable nutrient supply and contribute, at least in the short term, to net sequestration of atmospheric CO_2 (see section 10.7). The rapid 'sequestration' of NH_3 from the atmosphere may also be regarded as an opportunity to use forest or woodland cover as a means of reducing the impact of NH_3 from intensive livestock sources on the local environment. In principle, a shelterbelt plantation of woodland surrounding a ground-level source of NH_3 from an intensive livestock unit would capture gaseous NH_3 more rapidly than shorter seminatural vegetation and much more rapidly than heavily fertilized grassland or arable crops. The latter would simply introduce a surface with a much higher compensation concentration, and hence reduce net NH_3 deposition.

The preceding section shows that a rough estimate of local NH_3 deposition can be made from first principles using the dispersion equations on the assumption that forests have a constant canopy resistance (and compensation concentration) at all distances from the source. However, recent field data are now available to examine the NH_3 concentration profile downwind of an NH_3 source surrounded by woodland and also the influence of ambient NH_3 concentration on r_c for NH_3 (Pitcairn *et al.* 1998). The field data obtained from transects of

NH_3 concentration downwind of a poultry farm show a rapid decline in NH_3 concentration, from almost 30,ugm^{-3} at a distance of 15 m from the source to 2,ugm^{-3}, effectively background, at 270 m from the source. The relationship between canopy resistance and ambient concentration from measurements at a site in the same region allow concentration-specific values of r_c for NH_3 to be applied in order to calculate the local dry deposition rates for surfaces that are wet approximately 60% of the time. The resulting local mass balance is illustrated in Fig. 10.22 (from Fowler *et al.* 1998a).

The local mass balance shows large annual N inputs within 20 m of the source (42 kg ha^{-1}) yet the total deposition within 270 m of the source represents only 3.2% of the annual source of NH_3. The quantity deposited is subject to considerable uncertainty but even taking quite generous estimates of the likely errors in the estimates, local removal is unlikely to capture more than 20% of the emissions from the source within this zone. The conclusion therefore is that the use of woodland to capture even rapidly deposited pollutants such as NH_3 must be regarded as only a partial solution, unless very large areas of woodland are used or methods of introducing the NH_3 within the trunk space are developed.

Sulphur dioxide

The deposition of SO_2 on forests has been one of the most intensively studied aspects of atmospheric trace gas deposition. The interest stems from two quite different requirements. Firstly, there was the need to parameterize the regional deposition fluxes in long-range transport models for both Europe and North America, where forests represent a substantial fraction of the land cover. Secondly, and equally important, was the interest in the potential effects of sulphur on forest health and productivity. The concern during the early years (1970-80) of the acid rain issue was centred in Scandinavia on the effects of deposited acidity on freshwater ecosystems and forests (SNSF 1981). This early work identified clear effects on fish and fresh water but effects on forests remained equivocal. However, within the last decade the limited understanding of SO_2 transfer to forests has been enhanced by the development and application of continuous SO_2 flux measurement stations over forests (Erisman & Wyers 1993).

The deposition of SO_2 on forests is regulated by a combination of surface chemical processes within surface moisture on the external surfaces of foliage and by stomatal uptake in parallel. However, for regions with significant NH_3 concentrations, the processes on leaf surfaces represent the primary sink and provide effective control over the overall rates of exchange.

The chemistry regulating SO_2 canopy resistance is primarily the ratio of the NH_3 concentration and the sum of the acid gases present ($SO_2 + HNO_3 + HCl$); because SO_2 is the dominant acid gas present in most of the polluted regions of northern Europe, it is the NH_3/SO_2 ratio that regulates r_c for SO_2.

At Speulde Forest in The Netherlands, the r_c value for SO_2 obtained from continuous flux monitoring (32 s m^{-1}) for a site with an NH_3/SO_2 molar ratio of 3.7 is much smaller than the corresponding r_c value at Auchencorth Moss (240 s m^{-1}) where the NH_3/SO_2 ratio is 2.0.

These observations show that the sink strength of forests for SO_2 depends on both the physical and chemical climatology (Erisman *et al.* 1998). Thus, as emissions and concentrations of SO_2 have declined, the canopy resistance for SO_2 has also changed as a consequence of changes in the NH_3/SO_2 concentration ratio, and the direction of the change has led to an increase in the deposition velocity (of canopy conductance) of SO_2 with time. However, ambient concentrations of NH_3 have only recently been monitored continuously anywhere in Europe and both emissions and concentrations are very poorly known for periods prior to 1995.

The practical consequences of the new understanding of

SO_2 dry deposition have yet to find their way into the policy forum. However, the international protocols developed within Europe to regulate emissions of SO_2 will further increase the NH_3/SO_2 concentration ratio throughout the region and accelerate the dry deposition and near-field removal of SO_2. Such effects will increase non-linearity in the spatial patterns of the deposition footprint.

Forest canopies remain the surfaces with the largest sink capacity given a constant chemical composition, and in the source regions especially will continue to receive large dry deposition inputs of SO_2 and NH_3.

The areas of greatest interest for SO_2 deposition globally are the rapidly expanding zones of China and South-East Asia, which experience large ambient SO_2 concentrations (Galloway & Rodhe 1991). It has been estimated that the areas of forest subject to sulphur inputs equivalent to 2 keq ha^{-1} will increase by a factor of 6 between 1985 and 2050, and that the largest increases will be in southern and eastern Asia (Fowler *et al.* 1999).

Nitric oxide and nitrogen dioxide

Exchanges of these gases between forests and the atmosphere are closely linked, at least in polluted regions. The respective sources and sinks are well defined and reasonably well understood but there are complexities that have made progress towards a complete understanding of overall rates of exchange of the individual gases and their interactions rather slow.

NO is not deposited at significant rates within forests but is generated within soils largely by nitrification processes (Davidson & Kingerlee 1997). The emission fluxes from forest soils range from 0.1 to 50 ng m^{-2} s^{-1}, increase with soil N and temperature, and are optimal at intermediate water-filled pore space (WFPS) values (Skiba *et al.* 1997).

NO_2 is readily taken up by leaves via the stomata and detailed laboratory studies show no evidence of internal resistances to uptake (Thoene *et al.* 1991). The rates of stomatal uptake of NO_2 are therefore readily quantified from a knowledge of ambient NO_2 concentrations within the canopy and the canopy conductances for NO_2. This relative simplicity in the NO_2 exchange process is complicated by gas-phase processes within the canopy in which emissions of NO from the soil are readily oxidized to NO_2 by O_3.

A consequence of these interactions is that while NO_2 is possibly being absorbed by the tree canopy, the source of the NO_2 molecules is ambiguous: a significant fraction may result from cycling between forest soils and the foliage. Furthermore, in warm summer conditions, a forest may be a net source of NO_x ($NO + NO_2$), while NO_2 is being absorbed by the canopy as a consequence of a substantial soil NO flux (Pilegaard *et al.* 1995). This may arise as a consequence of the rapid increase in soil emission of NO with soil temperature and relatively small rates of NO_2 uptake by the canopy and is therefore characteristic of locations with small ambient NO_2 concentrations.

At a global scale, emissions of NO from soil have been estimated to range from 6 to 20 Tg of N annually. The larger values (Davidson & Kingerlee 1997) are based on the assumption that a negligible proportion of the soil emission flux is captured as NO_2 by canopy uptake; similarly, the smaller values assume that the canopy captures a substantial proportion of the soil NO emission (Yienger & Levy 1995). The current uncertainty in the net forest-atmosphere exchange of NO_x is therefore large and there are clearly important feedbacks between the NO soil flux and the overall quantity of N cycling within forests as NO and NO_2 (Skiba *et al.* 1997).

The direct measurement of NO_2 deposition using micrometeorological approaches is further complicated by photochemical processes, notably the photolysis of NO_2 above the canopy. Such effects have been simulated and incorporated within models of NO_x exchange between plant canopies and the atmosphere (Duyzer *et al.* 1995). Overall, uptake by forest of NO_2 is similar to uptake by shorter vegetation with relatively small average fluxes. Current interest in NO_x and forests centres on the interactions of soil sources of NO with canopy sinks of NO_2 and their influence on the net surface-atmosphere exchange of NO_x.

Ozone

Deposition on to natural surfaces represents the major sink for O_3 within the convective boundary layer. Quantifying the magnitude of the sink and understanding the underlying mechanisms are essential for modelling regional and global concentrations and budgets (Stevenson *et al.* 1998). Ozone is also recognized as the major regional phytotoxic pollutant globally and has been identified as an important contributor to forest decline in Europe and North America (McLaughin & Kohut 1992; Chappelka & Samuelson 1998; Skarby *et al.* 1998).

The O_3 flux from the atmosphere to forest canopies may be partitioned between stomatal uptake and an external surface flux. The available literature suggests that physiological damage and growth and yield reductions are caused almost entirely by stomatal uptake. However, it is also important to understand and quantify the overall flux in order to be able to define the fate and atmospheric residence time for O_3, because over seasonal time-scales the non-stomatal flux is the largest component of the total flux to semi-natural vegetation (Fowler *et al.* 1998b).

The available literature for both agricultural crops and forests has identified an ambient concentration above which accumulated exposure to O_3 leads to growth reductions (Skarby *et al.* 1998). The concentrations used in experiments on the effects of O_3 have been used to develop simple linear relationships between accumulated exposure to O_3 over a threshold concentration and reductions in dry matter yield. The concentration threshold used (40ppb) is arbitrary and there may be physiologically important effects at concentrations less than 40ppb. However, the concentration of 40ppb is quite close to the free tropospheric background O_3 concentration in northern mid-latitudes during spring and summer (Roemer 1996).

Ozone concentrations in Europe have increased from about 10 ppb around 1900) to values in excess of 20 ppb, but early measurements are few (Voltz & Kley 1988). Application of three-dimensional chemistry-transport models to simulate global concentration fields of O_3 provide an alternative measurement. The United Kingdom Meteorological Office unified model, used at climate resolution with a full description of the atmospheric chemical processing of the pollutants leading to O_3 formation (Collins *et al.* 1997), shows the increase in surface concentrations during the last 240 years and may be used to quantify the exposure of forests to O_3.

The magnitude of the effects of elevated O_3 concentrations on forest health or productivity remains uncertain but there are areas of forest that have clearly been damaged visibly by O_3, especially in the San Bernadino Mountains in southern California (Miller *et al.* 1963). There is also substantial evidence of regional effects of O_3 on tree growth and productivity in the southeastern states of the USA (especially *Pinus taeda, Pinus echinata, Pinus virginiana* and *Pinus strobus)* (Chappelka & Samuelson 1998). Data from similar studies are available in Europe, with beech, spruce and poplar species all showing reductions in the biomass of saplings (Skarby *et al.* 1998). The index of exposure currently used is the cumulated exposure above an arbitrary threshold, in this case 40 ppb, i.e. AOT_{40}, which provides a measure of the dose, even though dimensionally it is simply the product of concentration and time and is not a flux. The dry matter reduction found in many of the studies to date declines linearly with increasing AOT_{40}

and has been used to define critical levels of O_3 in Europe (Fuhrer *et al.* 1997). An AOT_{40} of 10^4 ppb·h has been set as the critical level for forests.

While it is not possible to quantify the current magnitude of yield loss in global forests attributable to O_3 with current AOT_{40} procedures, it is possible to quantify the area of forest that is exposed to O_3 concentrations in excess of 60 ppb, where reduced productivity or physiological injury may occur. This is a somewhat larger ambient O_3 concentration than the threshold used for definition of the critical level but has the advantage that it is substantially larger than background (which has not been shown to be causing damage to forests) and is more likely to identify the key areas in which O_3 presents a potential problem for forest health. The global surface O_3 concentrations for 1990 were provided by the STOCHEM model (see Stevenson *et al.* 1998).

The 1990 area of forest exposed to O_3 concentrations in excess of 60 ppb represents 18% of the total global forest area (Table 10.5). This large area of exposure is a consequence of the extensive zones in both the tropics and mid-latitude regions over which elevated O_3 concentrations occur. Table 10.5 also illustrates the increase in exposure to these large concentrations since 1860 and provides very speculative estimates of possible exposure in the year 2100.

To quantify the magnitude of loss of forest production, the relationship between O_3 dose and forest productivity must be defined. As the available evidence shows that uptake through the stomata is the primary cause of physiological effects, a relationship between the stomatal dose above a threshold and the dry matter loss per unit uptake is required. Such an approach has been proposed by many.

The concept of a threshold is necessary because O_3 is a natural component of surface air and there is no evidence that the preindustrial concentrations or fluxes were damaging to vegetation. A rough estimate of the likely threshold flux below which no damage is likely to occur may be obtained from the maximum concentration at which no effects have been observed and the canopy conductance. While very approximate, this approach indicates a likely threshold flux of O_3 of about 0.5^igm^{-2}s^{-1} (Fowler *et al.* 1998b). A quantitative basis for estimates of forest yield loss, therefore, seems a reasonable goal provided that there are properly replicated field studies to provide the necessary validation.

The conclusion is that O_3 appears to present a threat to forest productivity on a global scale and the current global models suggest that concentrations and exposure may progressively increase over the coming decades.

The simplistic approaches adopted to date are not adequate to quantify yield loss. Many feedbacks have been ignored and some may play an important part. In particular, interactions between drought stress and the effects of O_3 may be expected (Mansfield 1998). In drought stress conditions the reduced stomatal conductance to water vapour reduces stomatal O_3 influx and the overall deposition flux, and this would be expected to feed back to generate larger O_3 concentrations in the convective boundary layer (CBL). There is evidence that peak O_3 concentrations in the UK occur in precisely these conditions, yet the response of vegetation to these peak concentrations is largely unknown.

Volatile organic compounds

Terrestrial vegetation represents a major global source of the primary reactants required for production of photochemical oxidants including O_3, H_2O_2 and peroxyacetyl nitrate (PAN). The compounds emitted by trees include isoprene, terpenes (including a-pinene, /3-pinene and A^3-carene) and alcohols and organic acids (Stein-brecher *et al.* 1997a). While emissions of VOC from anthropogenic sources dominate the source inventory in small heavily industrialized countries such as the UK or The Netherlands, in remote areas biogenic sources dominate production of precursors of photochemical oxidants. Globally, vegetation contributes more than two-thirds of total VOC emissions (Guenther 1997). The spectrum of organic compounds emitted is very specific to plant species and to environmental conditions (Guenther *et al.* 2000). The options for agencies wishing to regulate ambient O_3 concentrations must therefore be tailored to the region and the relative magnitudes of the anthropogenic and vegetation sources.

Aerosols and cloud droplets

Atmospheric aerosols contain a substantial fraction of the reaction products of the pollutant gases and therefore include a wide spectrum of ions from the acid gases, including SO_4^{2-}, NO_3^-, Cl^-, the base cations Ca^{2+}, Na^+ and Mg^{2+}, and H^+, as well as the ubiquitous NH_4^+. Aerosols also contain the majority of the heavy metals in the atmosphere (Pb, Cu, Zn, Cr) and a wide range of other trace metals. Organic compounds are also present in substantial quantities in aerosols. These elements and compounds are returned to the surface in rain and by dry deposition. The rates of dry deposition on forest are strongly influenced by particle size and the characteristic dimensions of the foliage, with the most effective sinks being conifer forests with large leaf area indices. Wind tunnel studies show a very striking relationship between particle size and deposition velocity. There is a minimum deposition velocity for aerosols in the range 0.3,um to 0.5,um diameter, but at sizes both above and below this deposition velocity increases, for rather different reasons (Chamberlain 1975).

However, recent field data obtained by a wide range of methods, including eddy covariance flux measurements using active scattering laser spectrometers, passive flux measurement techniques and leaf washing methods, all imply much larger aerosol deposition rates on forests than the wind tunnel studies indicated (Gallagher *et al.* 1997a). A physical model to provide a mechanistic interpretation of extensive field data is currently lacking but it is clear that forests capture aerosols much more effectively than short vegetation. For example, the inventory of aerosol-deposited ^{210}Pb beneath shelterbelt woodland is 40-50% larger than that under grass. The filtering effect is clearly, therefore, also a feature of forest canopies in the case of atmospheric aerosols, and aerosol, deposition inputs to catchments are greatly reduced following clearfelling.

Cloud droplet deposition

Unlike the bulk of atmospheric aerosols, in which the mass is contained primarily within a diameter range 0.5-1.5 /m, the cloud droplets present in orographic cloud and coastal and radiation fcgs are much larger, typically 3-10^im in diameter. Such droplets are too large to follow the stream-

lines of airflow around leaves or branches and are very efficiently captured by a forest canopy. In fact the deposition of cloud water is similar to that of momentum, when expressed as conductivities (or, more commonly, as deposition velocities) for the canopy (Beswick *et al.* 1991). The efficiency of cloud droplet capture by forests leads to two important ecological consequences. Firstly, and very widely known, are the cloud forests throughout the world, which receive an important water supply directly through the capture of cloud water; such a water supply frequently maintains a unique ecosystem.

100 —

10 —

Secondly, and potentially much less beneficial, is the capture of orographic cloud in polluted regions. In polluted air the oxidation product of SO_2 oxidation is ultimately aerosol SO_4^{2-}, which is generally accompanied by variable amounts of NH_4^+ (depending on available NH_3), NO_3^- and H^+ as the four dominant ions. These aerosols are readily activated into cloud droplets as moist air is advected up hillsides. The droplets formed grow rapidly with height to provide typically 200 mg m^{-3} of liquid water at heights 100 m above cloud base (Fig. 10.26). The effective capture of this cloud water by forest represents a major input to high-elevation forests in windy, polluted regions. Measurements, especially in Europe and North America, show inputs of N to high-elevation forests in the range 20-50 kg ha^{-1} annually and even larger inputs of sulphur in polluted regions (Unsworth & Fowler 1988; Crossley *et al.* 1992). Even in the relatively unpolluted areas of southern Scotland the N input to a Sitka spruce forest at an elevation of 600 m is approximately 50 kg ha^{-1} annually, of which 60% is NH_4^+-N and 40% NO_3—N (Crossley *et al.* 1992). A further property of cloud droplets is that the concentrations of the major ions may be sufficiently large to cause foliar injury or reduction in frost hardiness (Leith *et al.* 1989; Cape *et al.* 1991; Sheppard *et al.* 1993).

Diurnal and seasonal cycles

The reactive gases that are primary pollutants exhibit marked diurnal cycles in ambient concentration. In part these cycles are generated by diurnal changes in the sources of the pollutants. For example, sources of the oxides of nitrogen are closely coupled to sources of combustion and anthropogenic activity. Sources of these gases within the boundary layer also lead to marked diurnal cycles through the daily growth and decay in boundary layer depth. The forest-atmosphere exchange of NH_3 would also be expected to exhibit a marked diurnal cycle because the partitioning between liquid-phase NH_4^+ concentrations and gaseous NH_3 is strongly coupled to temperature, with the result that vegetation may change systematically from a sink to a source as temperature increases during the day. This effect is further enhanced by leaf surface humidity and/or surface water. In this case the sink presented by high humidity at night is removed as the canopy dries and warms during the day. Thus marked diurnal cycles in the exchanges of NH_3 and NO_2 have been widely reported (Sutton *et al.* 1995; Hargreaves *et al.* 1992).

The reactive gases that are secondary pollutants, such as HNO_3 or PAN, also show marked diurnal cycles of concentration as a result of depletion at the surface during the night, and reduced downward transport from the free troposphere. These two gases also show marked seasonal cycles, with pronounced maxima coinciding with a broad seasonal peak in photochemical activity during the summer months.

The seasonal cycles in the exchanges of SO_2 and NH_3 with forests are controlled more by the relative frequency of surface water and its effect on canopy resistance than by the ambient concentrations. As the frequency of wet surfaces and ambient concentrations is at a maximum in the winter months, the deposition rates of SO_2 and NH_3 show strong seasonal patterns with a winter maximum and summer minimum. While the close link between deposition rates and surface wetness in the control of SO_2 and NH_3 fluxes generates both diurnal and seasonal cycles in the net exchanges between forests and atmosphere, it also leads to different geographical patterns in the seasonality of trace gas exchange. For example, the pronounced wet and dry seasons of South-East Asia almost certainly influence the wet and dry deposition rates of SO_2 and its atmospheric lifetime, although these seasonal changes are quite different from those in Europe and North America. Generalizations at a global scale about the seasonality of these fluxes is, therefore, inappropriate.

Spatial variability in forest-atmosphere exchange of trace gases and aerosols

This discussion of trace gases according to their chemical properties identifies a range of chemical affinities, ranging from HNO_3 and HCl, which are captured by forest canopies as rapidly as atmospheric conductivity permits, to N_2O, which is entirely unreactive in the troposphere (Wayne 1991). Spatial variability in the deposition or emission of the reactive gases results from spatial variability in canopy conductance. For example forest edges, which are particularly well coupled to the atmosphere with very efficient exchange at all heights within the canopy, represent hot-spots of deposition within the landscape. Likewise hilltops, where wind speeds are substantially enhanced and which are frequently in cloud, represent areas in which inputs are enhanced (Fowler *et al.* 1989; Crossley *et al.* 1992). It is relatively straightforward to quantify the local enhancement in the deposition field for these reactive pollutants at a site, given appropriate measurements of the gas concentrations and meteorological variables. However, to quantify the cumulative effects of edges and exposed hilltops and ridges on the deposition field at a regional scale is a more complex task, and there is evidence that current regional deposition amounts are underestimated for this reason. The magnitude of edge effects has been examined in a range of studies of NH_3 deposition (see Fig. 10.22) and aerosol deposition of ^{210}Pb and has been found to range from an enhancement of 30 to 50% (Fowler *et al.* 1998c) to up to a factor of 4 for hilltops or woodland close to point sources of NH_3

ECOLOGICAL EFFECTS OF NITROGEN DEPOSITION

In areas of the world in which HNO_3 concentrations are enhanced by anthropogenic emissions of NO_x, the atmospheric inputs of fixed N may represent an important contribution to the N economy of the forests. Similarly, the annual inputs of fixed N as NH_3 to forests in regions with elevated ambient NH_3 concentrations range from 10 to 50 kg ha^{-1} and the areas of Europe and North America with large inputs is extensive and increasing. The high-elevation forests enveloped in orographic cloud for a significant fraction of the time are also subject to large inputs of ions within the cloud water, including NH_4^+ and NO_3^-. These areas are also hot-spots of N deposition and occur widely in polluted regions of North America, Europe and South-East Asia.

Rather than considering broad regional N deposition values for forests, as has been the focus within global analyses, consideration should be given to the effect of the spatial variability in N deposition on forests at much smaller scales. In this way we may be able to show whether the effects of the deposited N are simply proportional to the total input or whether there are threshold separating effects that are beneficial (e.g. in C sequestration) from those we may regard as damaging. Indicators of negative effects may include NO_3- leaching, stimulation of N_2O and NO production, or a reduction in CH_4 oxidation. Such approaches have commonly been applied in the development of *critical load* concepts (Hornung *et al.* 1995), which have been very useful in the development of control strategies for pollutants in Europe.

To put this argument into perspective, consider the atmospheric budget of fixed N over the UK. The annual emissions of oxidized N within the UK are 780 Gg, of which 150 Gg is deposited on terrestrial surfaces within the UK. For reduced N the annual emission is much smaller at 260 Gg and the annual deposition larger at 230 Gg. Thus the deposition budget is dominated by reduced N even though these emissions represent only 25% of the total fixed N emissions (Fig. 10.27). The 380 Gg of N deposited in the UK is equivalent to an average deposition of $16kgha^{-1}$, although the input to forests ($33kgha^{-1}$) exceeds that to non-forest-land by a factor of 2 (Table 10.6).

These averages also conceal a substantial range in annual N deposition, which from the measurement networks may be roughly estimated to be 3 to $90kgha–^1$ at 5 x 5 km resolution (Fig. 10.28). There is substantial evidence that at the upper end of this distribution there are clear effects on the forest, including increased leaching loss of $NO_3–$, increased emissions of both NO and N_2O, and loss of species diversity in the ground flora (Pitcairn *et al.* 1998).

This approach can be extended to other European countries on the basis of measured data, although insufficient measured data are available to provide more extensive regional or global analysis and we must rely entirely on models to estimate budgets of net deposited N. It is probable that the relative deposition inputs of forest vs. non-forest are similar in many parts of the world simply because the enhancement in deposition to forests includes HNO_3, NH_3, aerosol NO_3^- and NH_4^+ and cloud droplet inputs of NH_4^+ and NO_3^-, and is not limited to a single compound or geographical area. The exception is NO_2, which appears to be deposited on short vegetation and forest at broadly similar rates.

Nitrogen-stimulated carbon sequestration

In general, the forests of the world are chronically deficient in nitrogen (or in some cases phosphorus), particularly the extensive forests in the northern temperate and boreal regions from where the glacial ice cover has retreated relatively recently.

In general, annual total wet and dry deposition of N (oxidized and reduced) to forests in rural areas is in the range 5-40 kg ha^{-1}. (Exceptions are forests close to industrial sources and in the near vicinity of intensive agricultural pig and poultry enterprises, where deposition may be substantially larger.) It is likely that such inputs are supporting the rapid growth and C sequestration of young temperate forests, of particular relevance to the Kyoto Protocol (Cannell *et al.* 1999; Valentini *et al.* 2000), but the causal link remains to be firmly established.

A number of experiments over the past 60 years have demonstrated that the growth of forests in northern Europe is very responsive to application of fertilizers, particularly nitrogen (Tamm 1991). Recent long-term experiments in Sweden have shown a fivefold increase in growth of Norway spruce in response to annual fertilizer N applications of 75kgha–^{1} at 64° N over the past 12 years and a threefold increase at 57°N over the past 10 years (Bergh *et al.* 1999).

In northern Britain, growth of commercial forest is also responsive to applications of N (Taylor & Tabbush 1990; Wang *et al.* 1991). Separate consideration of daytime and night-time C fluxes of an 18-year-old maritime forest of Sitka spruce, now at canopy closure (yield class 16 m^3 ha^{-1}) and initially fertilized with urea, indicates a large annual gross primary production of about 19Mgha^{-1} and a large autotrophic plus heterotrophic respiration of about 13Mgha^{-1}, i.e. an annual NEE of approximately 6Mgha–^{1}.

The extent to which N deposition is currently maintaining high rates of C sequestration by forests requires more thorough study, including hypothesis testing with field experiments and modelling (Vitousek 1994). On balance, of the current hypotheses to explain the observed rapid growth of European forests (increases in N deposition and CO_2 concentration and changes in climate), N deposition appears to be more consistent with spatial patterns in the observed increases in growth. The forward projection of these effects will rely heavily on models of N deposition to forests over the coming decades.

There are control strategies for oxidized N emissions in Europe and North America but controls on NH_3 emissions are very limited. The expansion of fossil fuel combustion elsewhere in the world more than compensates for the reductions in Europe and North America. Thus we can anticipate further increases in N deposition on to global forests through the coming decades.

The net result of interactions between the effects of N deposition and changes in climate and CO_2 concentration on the net land-atmosphere exchange of C are unknown and present a major challenge. Current approaches to quantify the effects rely on models that are somewhat simplistic and lacking in relevant feedbacks. As the questions are very important, both scientifically and politically, it is necessary to develop experimental studies to test hypotheses developed from the models. Field experiments in this area have very largely been limited to the short term and to one or two of the variables. There is a clear requirement to develop large-scale field experiments in order to track the fate and effects of deposited N, its effect on ecosystem function and the interactions with ambient CO_2 concentration and temperature.

FORESTS AND REGIONAL CLIMATES

The potential migration of treelines in response to changes in global climate may also significantly change the regional exchange of C as CO_2 and CH_4. In the high latitudes, the peatlands have steadily accumulated C since the last ice age but at modest rates (Clymo 1984) relative to net C sequestration by young forests. However, if forests migrate into peatlands, the effective lowering of the water table will suppress CH_4 emission and lead to oxidation of the surface organic layers to CO_2. While supporting forest growth, such changes may represent a large net source of CO_2 in the atmosphere over substantial areas, as currently observed when peat wetlands are drained and planted with trees. The extent to which these changes may occur at the northern boundary of the boreal forest during the coming decades will be controlled by the changes in climate at these high latitudes, and on the balance between precipitation, and evapotranspiration and the length of growing season. At present the possible role of changes in nutrient inputs from the atmosphere remain very uncertain at these remote locations and the major controls are likely to be driven by climate.

It came as a considerable surprise when Bowen ratios with values of 2 or more for coniferous forest, measured by flux-gradient methods, were first reported in the 1960s because virtually all previous measurements over agricultural crops had resulted in values between about -0.5 and +1.0, except in a few cases of extreme water stress. Suspicion was placed on the methods being used, particularly on the problems of measuring with sufficient accuracy over sustained periods the very small gradients of temperature and humidity that occur in the surface layer over forests and which are required for the so-called Bowen ratio, flux-gradient method (Stewart & Thom 1973; Thom *et al.* 1975; Jarvis *et al.* 1976).

For those who had worked previously only with prairie grasslands and crops, it still came as a surprise 25 years later to discover that values of *p* measured by eddy covariance for stands of black spruce and jack pine, which comprise the most extensive areas of the Canadian boreal forest, were frequently larger than 2 (Goulden *et al.* 1997; Jarvis *et al.* 1997; Baldocchi *et al.* 2000), and this has revolutionized thinking with respect to climatic process at larger scales in the boreal region (Sellers *et al.* 1995, 1997). The significance of a large Bowen ratio at regional scale lies not so much in the transpiration rate but in the large sensible heat flux which, in extensive continental areas drives the CBL up to heights of 3000 m during just an hour or two in the morning, with consequent entrainment of cold dry air rich in CO_2 from above the capping inversion which, as it warms up, strongly forces evaporation and transpiration and replenishes CO_2 over cropping areas as well as the forest within the region (Nobre *et al.* 1996; Barr & Betts 1997) (for further discussion see McNaughton 1989; Betts *et al.* 1996; Pielke *et al.* 1998; Raupach 1998).

CONCLUSIONS

Drawing brief conclusions from the diversity of forest interactions with the atmosphere considered in this chapter seems bound to oversimplify reality. However, there are several scientific and political issues that merit emphasis here. In considering a relatively short list of the trace gases and aerosols and their interactions with forest there are common threads and important exceptions.

These new developments in understanding result directly from recent large-scale field studies that, while readily incorporated into models of land-atmosphere exchange, were not expected. Such lessons are common in the development of understanding environmental issues and include the serendipitous route to the discovery of acid rain by Swedish scientists during the 1960s (Oden 1968) and, more recently, to the discovery of the ozone hole from a long series of direct measurements (Farman *et al.* 1985). The lesson from such examples is that the important new signals arise largely from measurement-based research rather than from models. The developments in measurement methods to study the net exchange of CO_2, heat and water vapour continuously over years has already revealed much in understanding the coupling of forest ecosystems to short-term variability in climate and has shown the need for long-term measurements (> 10 years) to separate real trends in the annual net forest-atmosphere exchange from the effects of seasonal variability in the weather.

2

Environmental Stresses to Forests

INTRODUCTION

The physical environment determines growth rates, the survival of individual trees and thus the type, structure and extent of forest ecosystems. For managed forest stands, we can manipulate some of the abiotic factors that control growth rate. In plantations, we also specifically control species composition, spacing and other factors. At its simplest, environmental stress can be considered to occur when one or more environmental factors are present at levels that lie outside the range tolerated by an individual species or forest stand. Where tree growth has been checked or dieback or decline are occurring we are seeing the effects of environmental stress, that is unless fungal pathogens or insect pests are a clear primary cause of damage.

However, foresters and forest ecologists are also concerned when abiotic factors, particularly anthropogenic factors, are at values that, although not apparently detrimental, may be suboptimal for growth and biodiversity of the forest ecosystem. Worries over the slow imperceptible deterioration of forest ecosystems and of possible crises led to consideration of forest 'stability' even before 'sustainability' came to prominence as a concept after the United Nations Conference on Environment and Development in Rio de Janeiro in 1992. Furthermore, experience has shown that there are few forests where temporary or chronic stress does not occur due to limitations of water or nutrient availability and commonly both.

Forest managers require an understanding of the ecological processes that occur in order to be confident that their intervention will achieve the desired objectives. Stress occurs in forests but how detrimental is it to growth, sustainability, conservation, recreational value and other benefits? What actions can be taken to minimize adverse impacts, particularly those resulting from anthropogenic factors? Indeed, most forest ecosystems are influenced by human activities, in many cases severely, and remaining areas of 'pristine' forest are small. The largest areas of relatively undisturbed forest occur in the boreal regions, although even here logging and mining affect a significant area. Many tropical forests are generally severely disturbed and the effects of pollutants are clear in many temperate forests and also in the Pacific Rim. Finally elevated CO_2 concentrations and climate change will have a widespread effect. Thus human influence is a major factor.

Since we are concerned here with the response of forests to environmental stresses and these responses are not simple, it is necessary to give brief consideration to definitions. Levitt (1972, 1980) derived a definition of biological stress and strain from physical science. Physical stress is force applied to an object and strain is the change in that object caused by this stress. Levitt suggested that biological stress is the change in environmental conditions that reduce or adversely affect plant growth or development, biological strain being the reduction of, or change in, function. Levitt also distinguished elastic and plastic biological strain on the basis of whether plant function returned to its normal level when conditions returned to initial conditions (elastic) or did not (plastic). Interestingly, Levitt's definition applies the term 'stress' to factors that result in adverse effects alone. In forest ecosystems a change of environmental conditions may have adverse effects on one species but beneficial impacts for a second, i.e. species composition may alter.

The effect or 'strain' may be succession or evolutionary adaptation. Biological systems are complex and the physical analogy has clear limitations. Perhaps more usefully, Levitt also distinguished 'stress avoidance' from 'stress tolerance', stress avoidance being typified by responses like exclusion of toxic metals or pollutants. An example might be closure of stomata to exclude the entry of gaseous air pollutant. In contrast, stress tolerance is exemplified by a plant that allows uptake into the substomatal cavity and responds by chemical detoxification mechanisms. It is worth noting at the outset that the detailed interactions between the plant and the environment will differ for trees and forests compared with herbaceous plants. This is because of the size, longevity and anatomy (i.e the presence of the tall woody stem) in trees.

In this chapter I have interpreted Levitt's 'environmental conditions' as meaning changes to the physical conditions experienced by plants. Biotic factors, such as pests, pathogens, genotypes (species and provenance) and grazing by animals, are clearly important to forest ecosystems and their effects are known to interact with those of the key abiotic factors; however, they have not been my primary concern here.

Plant growth is influenced fundamentally by availability of nutrients, light and water and, at the practical level, by climatic and soil conditions, which determine the availability of resources (nutrients, light and water) and also influence forests directly. In plantation forestry, the intention is to select species and provenance suited to the particular conditions of a site and/ or to manage conditions of the site so that they favour the selected species.

Stress should not be present or at least can be considered to be present at low enough levels that it is 'tolerated' by the system, to the extent that there are not changes in the relative competitive ability of species leading to species decline or creation of new niches that enable new species to gain a foothold.

In unmanaged forest ecosystems, plant competition and, in the long term, natural selection will control species composition. Disturbance by wind, fire and, in some instances such as *Metrosideros* forests of Hawaii (Hüttl & Mueller-Dembois 1992), nutrient limitations are a normal part of succession in unmanaged forest ecosystems. However, after the climax high forest has been established, species composition and ecosystem structure should be such that they are suited to the prevailing environmental conditions.

Undisturbed first-growth forests have evolved over millennia and are considered to be stable; they are well suited to the environmental conditions in which they grow except perhaps for species at the edge of their natural distribution, or where occasional infrequent extreme events occur which damage or even kill trees that have become established in benign intervening years. Ecosystem productivity is still limited by the availability of light, water and nutrients or temperature, but changes in these factors do not elicit ecosystem responses. Thus, Levitt's definition helps us in that it draws attention to *change* in environmental conditions. Of the abiotic factors that influence plant growth, light is perhaps the least likely to be changing at the ecosystem level.

Competition for light is an important factor within forest ecosystems. However, except in the equatorial zone where daylength does not vary seasonally, daylength and light quality are important mechanisms by which plants respond to season; tree response to photoperiod is thus of major importance when introducing trees to new latitudes. However, in the sections that follow I have chosen to focus on climate, pollution, water deficit (drought), and soil conditions, nutrient deficiency/enrichment and soil degradation as factors which are now subject to change to the extent that forest ecosystems could experience stress on a worldwide basis. On the time-scales with which we are concerned, humans are the major cause of these changes.

CLIMATE

Climate is the dominant control factor in the distribution of the world's main vegetation types or biomes. Biomes are defined as a distinctive ecological system, characterized primarily by the nature of their vegetation (Houghton 1997). On a global scale and in a historical and geological time frame, response to climatic stress is of overriding importance. The relevance of understanding tree and forest ecosystem response to climatic stress has increased because we are currently experiencing an unprecedented change of global climate which is, at least in part, the result of anthropogenic factors.

Most contemporary texts on the influence of climate and vegetation date our understanding of the relationship between climate and the distribution of vegetation from the work of Von Humboldt at the beginning of the nineteenth century (Woodward 1987; Landsberg & Gower 1997). Holdridge (1947 and subsequent work) demonstrated a strong correlation between the main groups of life form or biomes (e.g. deserts, grasslands, deciduous or coniferous forests) and two major climatic characteristics, temperature and water availability. These climatic factors are the main influence at the biome scale, while soil type (nutrient availability) topography and anthropogenic factors are major influences on vegetation patterns within biomes on a smaller local scale.

It is of considerable interest and relevance that where temperature and moisture availability or moisture budget (defined as precipitation-evapo-transpiration) are similar, the same tree species or similar species of one tree genera are present or prove to be satisfactory forestry species if introduced. This reflects the relationship between climate and suitable physiology and anatomy, and also the pattern of species' evolution and migration. The timing of the separation of the earth's present-day continents relative to the evolutionary history of tree species and taxa determines presence or absence of particular species within suitable climatic zones. Eventually the land bridges between the continents became impassable to tree species during the period of their rapid evolution in the Cretaceous Era (Daubenmire 1978). In the absence of human influence, the geographical extent (natural distribution) of the various forest biomes is thus determined mainly by climatic conditions and the natural species composition will be further influenced by evolutionary and geological factors.

There are several critically important temperature thresholds that affect physiological processes and thus define the environmental limits of the major forest biomes (Woodward 1987). The first threshold is a critical minimum temperature in the range +12 to 1°C, which results in chilling injury to plant membranes (Larcher & Bauer 1981). The next critical threshold is at about -15°C and roughly corresponds to the temperature at which frost damage occurs to leaves and buds (depending on the degree of frost acclimation).

The leaves of broadleaved species with a damage threshold at about -15°C are less resistant to frost than coniferous needles (Woodward 1987). The buds of broadleaved and coniferous species have similar minimum temperature thresholds but the xylem of broadleaved trees (angiosperms) is more susceptible to ice formation than that of conifers. This is because coniferous xylem is made up of tracheids, which have a smaller lumen diameter than the vessels that make up the xylem in broadleaved trees. Similarly broadleaved species with diffuse-porous xylem, which is of smaller diameter than ring-porous xylem, are more resistant to ice-induced xylem damage. Broadleaved trees with ring-porous xylem are notably absent from boreal forests.

The next critical temperature threshold is at -39 to -40°C, below which only a few boreal tree species can survive (e.g. *Picea glauca, Larix laricina* and *Larix sibirica*) because this temperature will freeze the xylem and buds. At their extreme northern limits, these cold-tolerant species often have a parenchyma pith cavity beneath the crown of the primordial bud that prevents ice formation from spreading from the xylem to the bud (Richards & Bliss 1986).

It has been argued that in harsh climates, particularly low temperatures, the evergreen habit gives a more favourable carbon balance (Schulze *et al.* 1997) and thus we see the dominance of coniferous evergreens in cold montane and boreal forests. Climates with ample rainfall, well distributed throughout the year and with rare frosts, as experienced in temperate regions (30-55° of latitude), also favour evergreen rather than deciduous forests. This is considered to have led to the dominance of broadleaved evergreen forests in the temperate regions of the Southern Hemisphere, with the notable exception of southern Chile where deciduous broadleaved forests occur. Broadleaved deciduous tree species predominate in the northern temperate regions.

The distribution of the various forest biomes is thus determined by climatic conditions. However within the major biomes individual species gradually decrease in numbers near their altitudinal or latitudinal limits. Woodward (1987, 1995) attributed this more to increasingly non-competitive carbon balance rather than to direct damage from low temperatures. Although the tree species present within the various forest biomes should not normally be experiencing climatic stress, climate remains of major importance to forestry and to the conservation of forest ecosystems for three main reasons. First, within a climatic region foresters are able to select species that grow better (faster) or provide other desirable benefits for particular sites, as influenced by local conditions of topography and soils. Second, the effect of climate on tree species limits the use of introduced or exotic species, which otherwise has proved a very successful strategy for improving yields in commercial forestry worldwide. Third, and perhaps of greatest interest, is that climate changes, not only naturally on a geological time-scale but also rapidly as a result of human activity, i.e. global climate change.

Landsberg and Gower (1997) followed Melillo *et al.* (1993) in adopting a classification of forest biomes based on major climatic region (tropical, temperate and boreal) and tree physiognomy (broadleaved, evergreen, broadleaved deciduous and needle-leaved evergreen conifer). Seven forest biomes were identified as follows: boreal, temperate deciduous, temperate coniferous, temperate mixed, temperate broadleaved evergreen forest, tropical evergreen and tropical deciduous. Of these, the boreal and tropical evergreens cover the greatest area. Forest biomes are covered in detail in Chapter 2.

The increase of global surface land and ocean temperatures that has been observed during the last 100 years (see Chapter 10) is faster than that observed during the geological past. Predictions of future climate indicate that some tree species, and some parts of the forest biomes, will experience climates outside those of their natural range. Over significant areas climatic stress will occur and dieback is likely. A number of authors have used existing relationships (correlations) between climatic factors and biome distribution to predict the future distribution of terrestrial biomes from the climate predictions provided by general circulation models (e.g. Woodward 1987; Landsberg & Gower 1997). Changes in biome distribution might be expected to occur by migration, although migration at rates of 5 km annually will be required and palaeoecological records indicate postglacial migration rates of tree species of only 40-150 m annually. Thus migration rates are likely to be insufficient, resulting in significant areas of stress and dieback, or rather, that stress and dieback will be part of the process of migration. A recent example of such predictions is that of Friend *et al.* (1997) who mapped the global distribution of eight biomes and of desert for existing (today's) climate and for climate predicted for the year 2080.

This model, called 'HYBRID', predicts vegetation type at any particular location on the basis of the outcome of competition for light, nitrogen and water and of the plants' ability to survive extreme conditions. Unlike earlier, less sophisticated work of this type, HYBRID predicts that tropical forests will decline in area, with dieback beginning in the 2050s as a result of decreased rainfall and increased temperatures. Temperate and mixed forests are likely to move northwards and increase their total area. Boreal forest area is predicted to change very little provided that these forests can establish in more northern areas with shallow poorly developed soils (Plate 1, facing p. 298). The palaeoecological records show that the species composition of forest ecosystems varied during their postglacial advance so we could also predict some changes of species composition as a result of the stress caused by climate change.

These predictions suggest that forest managers will need to plan for, and respond to, climate change if extensive areas of forest dieback are to be avoided; some such problems are likely to occur in any event. Indeed, there is firm evidence that climatic conditions have been a major, or perhaps *the* major, factor responsible for forest dieback in Europe and the north-eastern USA (Johnson *et al.* 1994). Changes of species choice will be an obvious course of action in plantation forestry. The successful use of 'exotics' in commercial forestry, for example Sitka spruce *(Picea sitchensis)* in western Europe, *Pinus radiata* in New Zealand and Chile, and *Eucalyptus* in Portugal and South America, indicates that forest managers can, in any event, achieve increased yields by planting species outside their current natural distribution.

Species choice and the use of the 'right tree for the site' has long been recognized as a very effective mechanism of avoiding stress to plantations and of optimizing yield (Anderson 1950). Various systems of biogeoclimatic ecosystem classification (BEC) have recently been adopted in different parts of the world (Pojar *et al.* 1987; Pyatt & Suárez 1997). Essentially such systems provide site classification based on our understanding of the influence of environmental factors on forest ecosystems and thus allow sound management of plantation and seminatural stands for timber production, conservation or other benefits.

The basis of BEC, and the UK equivalent, ecological site classification (ESC), is consistent with our understanding of the climatic control of biome distribution and the influence of other factors, particularly nutrient availability (but also topography and windiness), on species composition within the major biomes. Sites are classed on the basis of three principal factors considered to control site quality: climate, soil moisture regime (on which climate exerts a significant influence) and soil nutrient regime. Choice of species is arguably the most important management and silvicultural decision. ESC provides a list of species suited to the climatic and soil qualities and capable of producing good-quality timber. Tree species are listed as *optimal* if they will grow at the upper rate given by models of general yield class (GYC) without undue risk of disease and pest attack. Species are rated as *suitable* if they will grow on the lower part of GYC curves. Where ESC predicts increased risk of injury from pests, diseases or drought species are considered *unsuitable*. Predictions of GYC can be made for a particular species.

Growth rates and productivity are influenced by climatic stress, although current indications are of increased growth prior to dieback, perhaps even prior to catastrophic decline. The important study by Spiecker *et al* (1996) indicated that the growth rates and timber yields of European forests are currently increasing relative to those achieved in earlier rotations. This is probably the result of better silviculture and planting stock, the use of fertilizers and suitable thinning regimes. However, the effects of warmer weather, nitrogen depositions and elevated CO_2 have almost certainly also contributed to this effect. Perhaps hard to believe is the prediction of the HYBRID model that the potential biomass between latitudes 30° and 60° N will increase by 70% by the year 2080 *cet. par.*

Biogeoclimate classifications can be developed further to provide advice on other aspects of management, in particular risk from windthrow, ground preparation, regeneration techniques and management of open space. Currently, historical climatic data (weather records) are used to 'par-amaterize' these systems of site classification; however, consideration of rotation length relative to the predicted rates of climate change indicates that the use of predicted climate of the site might provide more accurate advice on species choice and future management. Over a number of years, the evidence from average global surface temperatures has become increasingly clear and 1997 was the hottest year on record to date.

Average global temperatures have risen by 0.6°C in the last 130 years and general circulation models are now able to predict the impact of increasing greenhouse gas concentrations on global temperatures. It is now accepted that anthropogenic climate change is occurring, with the UN Intergovernmental Panel on Climate Change (IPCC) concluding in its 1995 report that 'the balance of evidence suggests a discernible human influence on global climate' (Houghton *et al.* 1995). To understand the potential impacts of climate change on forests it is essential to have accurate predictions of future climate at the regional scale. Internationally, predictions or scenarios have been provided by the IPCC; within the UK, they have been provided by the Meteorological Office based at the Hadley Centre, Reading, at a spatial resolution of 10min (i.e. 10 km grid squares). Mean winter temperatures and average precipitation (mm daily) are available for the 1961-90 baseline period and for the years 2025, 2050 and 2100. Relatively small changes in temperature (+1.0-1.8°C) and rainfall (-9% in summer to +10% in winter) will lead to much larger changes in potential evapotranspira-tion (40% increase predicted for southern England by 2050), while the annual distribution of rainfall and the occurrence of storm events may also change. Projected temperature increases should therefore not be viewed in isolation.

The changes predicted for the UK would have very important implications for forestry.

The occurrence of late spring frost is already a problem in forestry and restricts the use of some tree species and provenances (Murray *et al.* 1995). Similarly, increased windiness and particularly storms could have devastating effects (e.g. the 1987 storm in southern England). Two important features in forestry are that a number of introduced species are used because they grow rapidly over short rotation lengths and, secondly, that native species have ranges which span considerable climate differences. Seed origins (provenance) are used to select the most appropriate genotype to maximize growth potential.

Therefore, sourcing seeds from different origins is a possible proactive response to climate change: for example for Sitka spruce it is suggested that more Oregon or Washington provenances should be planted in place of those from the more northerly Queen Charlotte Islands. Similarly, species choice could be adjusted, with species such as *Eucalyptus* and *Nothofagus*, natives of regions in warmer climates, becoming suitable for Europe (for further discussion see Broad-meadow & Freer-Smith 1998).

In addition to temperature and extremes of climate (unusually late spring frosts, storms and drought), there are a number of other environmental factors that are changing as a result of human activities. These include UV-B radiation and air pollutant concentrations and depositions. Such factors and their interacting effects on trees and forest insects and pathogens are likely to have significant effects on tree growth and forest productivity.

POLLUTION

During the last 20 years it has become clear that vegetation, soils and the aquatic environment are more important sinks than the atmosphere for many pollutants. Pollutants are transferred from the atmosphere to the terrestrial environment by three processes. Dry deposition: the movement of particles and gases by molecular diffusion and turbulent transfer to wet and dry surfaces.

1 Wet deposition: the movement of particles and dissolved gases in rainfall.

2 Occult deposition: the movement of particles and dissolved gases in cloud water, fog and mist. For particles (dust, smoke and smaller material), impaction and gravitational deposition (sedimentation) are also important processes. Additionally, tree roots show preferential and active uptake of some pollutants. Trees and forests are more effective at removing pollutants from the atmosphere because of their high leaf areas and because their height increases turbulent mixing, enhancing the deposition of those pollutants for which surface resistance does not limit deposition (i.e. SO_2, O_3, NO and NO_2). Pollutant flux by wet deposition is largely unaffected by land use, while uptake by forests will be greater via both dry and occult deposition and for impaction of particles (for further details see Chapter 10). Our principal concern here is how pollutants affect trees and forest ecosystems and how foresters may be able to respond to adverse effects.

It is helpful to distinguish direct effects, resulting from the entry of the pollutant itself into the tree, from indirect effects, usually considered to be principally the result of alterations to soil quality caused by the presence of pollution.

It is logical to include pollutant effects on any other component of the ecosystem (e.g. damage to mycorrhizal fungi or insect pests and fungal pathogens) as indirect effects.

Possible pathways of exposure and uptake, as well as physiological effects, metabolic impacts and the possible outcome of both direct and indirect effects.

Direct effects

Taylor and Constable (1994) have provided estimates of the proportions of various pollutants that enter vegetation through stomata or are deposited on the leaf surface. Pollutants can damage foliage directly when deposited on leaf surfaces, the best-established impacts being surface lesions caused by highly acidic rain and the erosion of epicuticular wax structure. However, most pollutants deposited here are likely to be washed down the stem to the soil where they contribute to soil-mediated effects or are lost in water flow (surface run-off or to ground water). Clearly the potential for pollutants to have detrimental effects on plant metabolism and physiology are strong once they have entered leaves via stomata. For a number of the major pollutants, pathways through which metabolism is damaged are now well established (Wellburn 1994). Essentially, the reactions of photosynthesis, respiration, energy distribution, storage and biosynthesis are inhibited by the presence of dissolved pollutants or their dissociation products. In a number of cases, the control of pH within cell compartments is disrupted or damage occurs to cell membranes resulting in leakage of metabolites and cell death.

Indirect effects and soil acidification

Effects on epicuticular wax, litter decomposition in the upper soil horizon and cation leaching from foliage are all potentially damaging. However, for both sulphur and nitrogen pollution soil-mediated effects are probably of overriding importance. The importance of soil processes and, in particular, the concept of the 'mobile anion effect' and associated 'aluminium' toxicity were developed by Ulrich and his coworkers in the early 1980s (Ulrich 1989). It is hard to underestimate the importance of this work: it formed the conceptual basis for soil critical load calculations now used to focus scientific understanding of pollutant impacts and to guide agreed international deposition and emission targets.

In brief, the mobile anion effect suggests that soil solution pH is usually buffered or controlled by the exchange of protons (H^+) with exchangeable base cations (Ca^{2+}, Mg^{2+}, Na^+ and K^+); these are normal cation exchange processes. If strong acids (H_2SO_4) enter the system, sulphate (SO_4^{2-}) and base cations will be present in soil solution and will be lost in soil drainage water. However, if the inputs of strong acid anions (sulphate and perhaps nitrates) persist, soil acidification continues until buffering of pH in soil solution is no longer via cation exchange mechanisms but rather by exchange with aluminium ions (Al^{3+}) in the $Al(OH)_3$ pool in soil solution (Al buffering range when pH<4.2). Soils then acidify (H^+ concentrations increase), Al concentrations in soil solution increase and percentage base saturation decreases with loss of Mg^{2+}, Ca^{2+} and Na^+ along with SO_4^{2-} in soil leachate.

In even more acid conditions there is a further Al/Fe buffer range (pH< 3.8). The resulting free Al^{3+} ions are toxic to roots and the loss of base cations and overall change is destabilizing to soil nutrient cycling. Full soil chemistry models are very complex, but an insight into the fundamental process is important since it informs understanding of soil status and of suitable management. There is now a very large body of data to support these ideas and they can be regarded as established science.

It is now clear that the atmospheric deposition of sulphur and nitrogen have a strong influence on the status of soils and on forest nutrition (Schulze *et al.* 1989; Zottl & Huttl 1991). Sulphur and nitrogen depositions and forest nutrition are strongly associated globally, although depositions and soil sensitivity to damage vary geographically. Recently, policy on emission abatements has been guided by the critical loads approach rather than, as previously, by an ill-defined concept of protecting ecosystems from damage. For forest ecosystems, soil critical loads can be set using a mass balance equation such that deposition of strong acid anions does not exceed the rate of release of base cations by weathering of minerals (after allowing for cation loss from soil in nutritional uptake of cations and nitrogen) and an allowable leaching of alkalinity (Sverdrup & De Vries 1994). In acidified soils low availability and uptake of base cations may limit tree growth, and the ratio between the divalent base cations (Ca and Mg) and Al in soil solution reaches a critical value (a molar ratio of 1.0).

Below this value nutrient uptake is suboptimal, root damage can occur from free Al in soil solution, tree growth is reduced and visible forest damage may start to occur. The mass balance equation can be used to calculate S and N depositions (critical loads) below which ($Ca^{+}Mg$)/Al is greater than 1.0 so that forest soils are protected from 'damage'. Information is now becoming available on S and N critical loads throughout Europe and initial work is being done on the soils of South-East Asia where major problems may occur over the next few years (Freer-Smith 1998). The above summary is sufficient to indicate the strong link between acidic deposition, forest nutritional status and the ability of forest soils to sustain successive rotations without loss of their capacity to supply base cations and nitrogen. Evaluation of the status of forest soils and the consideration of suitable management options (e.g. liming) becomes possible when these mechanisms are understood.

Atmospheric concentrations of carbon dioxide

Increases in atmospheric concentrations of CO_2 are probably the primary driving force of the anthropogenic greenhouse effect and thus of climate change; however, the atmospheric concentration of CO_2 also directly affects plant growth. Atmospheric CO_2 is the source of the plant's carbon and its active uptake in photosynthesis depends on diffusive flux across a concentration gradient. Trees grow better in elevated CO_2 compared with preindustrial ambient values (=240 ppm) when other environmental factors, particularly nutrient and water availability, are not limiting. However, when these factors are below optimum, trees suffer from increased stress in elevated

CO_2. Furthermore, CO_2 concentrations directly affect many plant processes other than photosynthesis, including respiration, stom-atal conductance, ratio of root to shoot mass, rates of leaf emergence, leaf area index (ratio of leaf area to ground area), growth, senescence and tree phenology. The potential for the effects of elevated CO_2 concentrations to interact with those of other factors is considerable. Experimental evidence from controlled exposures is now showing that such interactions occur and can result in enhanced susceptibility to a number of abiotic stresses, particularly drought, nutrient deficiency, frost damage and damage from other air pollutants (Chappelka & Freer-Smith 1994).

Although the growth responses of trees to elevated CO_2 are more often positive than negative, they vary greatly with species (Ceulemans & Mousseau 1994) and the assumption that the overall effects of the current rise in CO_2 concentrations will be beneficial to forestry is an oversimplification that cannot be justified by detailed consideration of the evidence. The data reported by Broadmeadow and Freer-Smith (1999) are representative of similar interactions reported in the literature. Oak *(Quercus petraea)* showed a positive growth response to twice current ambient CO_2 concentrations (700 ppm); moreover, the detrimental effects of realistic peaks of ozone (O_3), i.e. a diurnal cycle peaking at 80ppb, were lost when *Q. petraea* was grown in 700 ppm CO_2. Two other European species (ash, *Fraxinus excelsior*, and Scots pine, *Pinus sylvestris)* showed no detrimental effects of O_3 exposure and smaller stimulations of growth in 700 ppm CO_2. As has been reported for most trees exposed to realistic doses of these pollutants, the stimulation of growth in oak was the result of increased photosynthesis, while the chronic growth reduction due to O_3 resulted from reduced photosynthetic capacity.

A perhaps unique feature of this particular experiment was that soil-rooted (rather than pot-rooted) plants were also grown with two different soil water regimes in all combinations of CO_2 and O_3 (droughted and irrigated). The detrimental effect of O_3 on photosynthesis was reversed by elevated CO_2 but only for plants experiencing drought. Protection by CO_2 from O_3 probably results from the increased internal leaf CO_2 concentrations, closing stomata and limiting O_3 uptake (Stitt 1991); a classic stress avoidance mechanism in Levitt terminology. In well-watered trees, elevated CO_2 failed to decrease stomatal conductance and thus failed to provide protection from O_3. Unfortunately, tree responses to CO_2 and the interacting effects of different abiotic factors are even more complicated in forest stands.

A comprehensive consideration of the biochemical and physiological effects of CO_2 is beyond the scope of this chapter. This overview is based on the recent compilation of results on elevated CO_2 effects on trees resulting from the investigation by the European Union (EU) ECOCRAFT project (Jarvis 1998). Within this programme, comprehensive studies of eight or more different tree species were conducted using a number of different techniques. The key processes affected were stomatal conductance (both stomatal opening and stomatal density), photosynthesis (ribulose 1,5-bisphosphate carboxylase oxygenase (Rubisco) content and activity, chlorophyll content and the light reactions), respiration (although CO_2 effects seem variable and small), phenology (particularly where nutrient limitations towards the end of the growing season give early bud set and senescence) and allocation.

Compiled as a single volume, the studies conducted within ECOCRAFT present a coherent picture of increased growth in elevated CO_2 and of the very major way in which nutrient availability and water deficit can modify this response. The growth increases in elevated CO_2 in all the experiments conducted varied between 5% (Sitka spruce) and 58% (beech). In forest ecosystems water and nutrient availability are closely linked and experiments have also been conducted on the three-way interactions of elevated CO_2 concentrations, nutrient availability and drought on tree growth (Heath & Kerstiens 1997). These interactions are of major significance in determining stress response and forest condition.

Nitrogen depositions

Nitrogen is important as a plant nutrient because it occurs in many plant proteins (particularly Rubisco, the enzyme that catalyses the first carbon fixation reaction of photosynthesis) and chlorophyll. Although N_2 makes up about 78% of the atmosphere by volume, this is not available to plants. Plants absorb almost all N from the soil as nitrate (NO_3~) or, in acid soils, as ammonium (NH_4^+) (see Fig. 11.4). First, atmospheric N_2 has to be fixed (reduced) to organic nitrogen by soil microorganisms or in the roots of N-fixing plants (e.g. alders, *Acacia*). Most of the N in soils is in the form of organic N, which is unavailable to tree roots. Organic N is then converted to NH_4^+ by ammonification, which in warm near-neutral soils is rapidly oxidized to NO_3~ (nitrification) by soil bacteria that derive energy from the conversion. In acid forest soils, nitrifying bacteria are less abundant and NH_4^+ becomes a more important source of N. Low temperatures in some forest soils will also lower NO_3~ availability. Ammonification consumes protons but nitrification generates protons. The net result of the conversion of organic material to NH_4^+ and then NO_3~ is acidification. As a cation, NH_4^+ can be held on cation exchange sites, while NO_3~ is more likely to be leached from soils. Nitrogen is also lost from soils by denitrification, the production of N_2, NO, N_2O and NO_2 from NO_3~ by anaerobic bacteria, often deep in soils or in waterlogged or compact soils.

Small amounts of N are also passed from the atmosphere to soil as NO_3~ and NH_4^+ in rain (up to 30 kg ha^{-1} annually) and these ions can then be absorbed by plants. Natural sources of atmospheric NO_3~ and NH_4^+ are forest fires, volcanic activity and the oceans and NO_3~ production in lightning; however, industrial processes and the agricultural use of nitrogenous fertilizers and intensive animal husbandry are major anthroresult from large NH_4^+ inputs. This will inhibit base cation uptake resulting in K or Mg deficiency. Soil acidification from NO_3~ or NH_4^+ inputs will also reduce the decomposition of organic matter so that it can accumulate in soils; litter accumulation.

There is a limit to the amount of N that a forest ecosystem can use and this limit is likely to be set by the availability of other nutrients, water, light or other environmental factors. A forest is said to be N saturated when it cannot retain any additional N and leaching occurs. The concept of N saturation has become central to discussion of forest soil critical loads.

WATER DEFICIT

Water must inevitably be lost from leaves in transpiration if stomata are to allow CO_2 to be fixed. The amount of water lost for each molecule of CO_2 assimilated into biomass is known as the water-use efficiency. Although water-use efficiency varies from plant to plant and indeed within species, larger plants with larger leaf areas require more water. Water availability (soil water potential), which for a particular soil is determined by water budget (precipitation minus evapo-transpiration, run-off and leakage below the root zone), will thus limit the type of vegetation that can grow on a site. For example, Spurr and Barnes (1980) showed that an annual rainfall of 380mm or more is required for open woodland in central areas of the USA, while over 640 mm was required for closed forest to occur.

The global distributions of forest ecotypes described at the beginning of this chapter (see Plate 1) show how, with increasing length of the dry season, rain forests give way to semi-evergreen and then deciduous types. In the strongly seasonal dry tropics, forests of simple structure and fewer woody species occur and, ultimately, closed forest is replaced by open woodland and then savannah. In many areas of the world, sclerophyllous forests give way to scrub and then desert (Mediterranean Basin,

North and South Africa, parts of South America) in a similar way. Desert, areas of sparse vegetation, have less than 200-400 mm of rain per year depending on temperature and potential evaporation. The most extensive deserts occur 20-30° north and south of the equator. However, in much of the temperate zone, climate patterns can be uncertain so that areas which normally have plenty of rain to support forest biomes may experience droughts for weeks, months or even several years. Examples are the widespread summer droughts of 1988 in the USA and of 1983 in Europe. In these areas, forest composition is controlled by these extreme events rather than the average condition.

The different physiology and anatomy of tree genera and species confer different degrees of drought tolerance, and as is the case for climate overall smaller-scale differences in water availability caused by topography and soil will influence species composition, growth rate and survival of trees within the major forest biomes. A major anatomical difference that influences drought tolerance is the presence of tracheids in conifers. Tracheids have border pits in the walls that close during drought. In contrast, the vessels of hardwood species have no tracheids so that water columns cannot be re-established after the withdrawal of water during drought.

The buffering of leaf water potential by the storage of water in the stems of conifers has also been shown to minimize leaf loss during drought (Waring & Running 1978). In hardwoods, leaf abscission is a response to drought. A number of temperate zone species (e.g. *Ulmus americana, Tilia americana, Acer platanoides, Populus deltoides* and *Fagus sylvatica)* show whole or partial defoliation during summers of extreme drought (Woodward 1987). This response is not normally seen in conifers. A number of conifer leaves have thick waxy cuticles and additional chambers (antechambers) above the pair of guard cells that control gas exchange, including water loss, between the leaf and atmosphere. Water-use efficiency is often greater in conifers than broadleaved trees, although a net uptake of CO_2 may be maintained for larger periods of the year.

The cessation of leaf growth and stomatal closure are physiological responses to drought that normally precede leaf abscission. All three responses will limit growth but can be regarded as 'elastic' since they can be reversed. Cacti show many of the anatomical characteristics generally associated with drought tolerance (thick cuticles, presence of leaf hairs, high water storage) and many of them also show the principal physiological adaptation to drought, crassulacean acid metabolism (CAM).

This is a fascinating combination of anatomical and physiological adaptations that allows stomatal opening for CO_2 uptake to occur at night but the light reactions of photosynthesis to occur during the day while stomata are shut. As a result, transpiration losses are minimized. Only one tree has been reported as showing this adaptation, the tropical *Clusia rosea* which germinates from seed on the branches of other trees and thus experiences extreme drought between rain storms. *Clusia* has been shown to be a facultative CAM plant, switching between normal C3 photosynthesis and CAM in response to changes in water availability and light (Schmitt *et al.* 1988).

Adverse effects of water deficit (drought stress) occur when trees experience levels of water deficit to which they are not adapted. Drought has undoubtedly been a major factor in many of the forest declines that have occurred across the world but its role is particularly clear in the decline of oak in eastern and central USA during the last 20 years (Ciesla & Donaubauer 1994). In Europe the good records of forest condition have resulted from the monitoring work under the EU air pollution regulations and the Forests Programme (ICP) of the Convention on Long-range Transboundary Air Pollution. These data show that there was a general worsening of forest health in Europe between 1990 and 1995, attributed mainly to a series of dry years with drought and high summer temperatures (Freer-Smith 1998).

SOIL CONDITIONS, NUTRIENT DEFICIENCY/ ENRICHMENT AND SOIL DEGRADATION

Plant nutrients are normally considered in two categories: macronutrients (N, P, K, Mg, Ca and S, to which C, H and O should be added for completeness) and trace elements or micronutrients (Mo, Ni, Cu, Zn, Mn, B, Fe and Cl). The availability of these elements varies with soil type, pH, cation exchange capacity and organic matter content, and with the exchange and other soil processes (e.g. weathering and mineralization, processes that are often rate-limiting) which determine availability from soil solution. Given the number of elements required for growth and the complexity of atmospheric and soil chemistry, it is perhaps inevitable that some degree of nutrient limitation and imbalance can result in stress to forests on a global scale.

Indeed nutrient availability can result in natural successions in forest ecosystems, as seen in the *Metrosideros* rain forests of the Hawaiian islands and in *Eucalyptus* forests of eastern Australia. In the *Metrosideros* rain forests of the Hawaiian islands, low N availability on thin volcanic soils limits forest development and decreasing availability of base cations and P become a major causal factor in stand dieback. In eastern Australia, P availability on ancient soils limits the growth of indigenous *Eucalyptus*.

Here fertilization can increase growth rates but causes increased susceptibility to insect pests which, along with other factors, cause dieback (Heatwole & Lowman 1986). There is also some evidence that the common age-related decline in forest growth may be related to increased nutrient constraints. *Eucalyptus* decline is a good example of a very common event, i.e. fertilizer application based on an identified mineral deficiency failing to alleviate decline or slow growth.

Clearly, it is important for forest managers to have a general understanding of the processes that determine nutrient availability and to be aware of the likely or actual nutrient limitations of regions and stands. Earlier sections of this chapter have already touched on a number of the key processes so that the links between water availability, climate, pollutant inputs and nutrient availability will already be clear. Pedogenesis (soil formation) occurs through the weathering of parent bedrock or deposited material, along with the decomposition and mineralization of organic matter (fallen leaves, etc.). Boreal soils are referred to as young, being postglacial and having been least weathered; temperate forest soils are moderately weathered, while warm temperate and subtropical soils have been strongly weathered. A number of the nutrients listed above are commonly available in soils and taken up by trees as positively charged cations. These are the base cations (Ca^{2+}, K^+, Mg^{2+}, Na^+) and NH_4^+, and also H^+ and Al^{3+}, which are not plant nutrients. The availability of these elements to tree roots in soil solution is determined by their release from the surface of soil mineral and organic material. Both organic material and minerals normally present negatively charged surfaces on which the cations are held and released into soil solution in exchange for H^+.

Minerals are mainly made up of aluminium octahedral and silica tetrahedral layers, making Al and Si the most common elements in most mineral soils. The minerals of most tropical soils are predominantly oxides of Al that have been strongly weathered so that the small cation exchange capacity which such soils have is provided by their organic matter. Of the macronutrients listed above, availability of N, P and S is not via cation exchange reactions (except for N uptake as NH_4^+). We have already considered the dependence of N supply on fixation, ammonification, nitrification and denitrification, processes largely determined by soil microbial activity. Phosphorus does occur in soil minerals (e.g. apatite) but it has low solubility and dissolved P is normally at very low concentrations. Plant uptake can rapidly deplete any dissolved P. The movement of P into solution is commonly the rate-limiting (perhaps growth-limiting) process.

Significant amounts of P enter soils in leaf and branch litter and, like N, availability is then strongly dependent on soil microbial activity. Phosphorus deficiency can thus be a significant stress in a number of forest systems. Like N and P, S also occurs primarily as an anion in soil solution and can be immobilized in organic matter in soils, so that the rate of microbial mineralization may determine availability for plant nutrition. Sulphur is present in soil minerals as metal sulphides (e.g. FeS_2 and ZnS), particularly in igneous and sedimentary rocks. Sulphur differs from P in that sulphate, SO_4^{2-} its common form, can be rapidly leached from soils. Even in soils not experiencing anthropogenic S inputs, SO_4^{2-} inputs in rain are commonly greater than availability from mineralization of organic S.

Nutrient cycling is known to be 'tight' in forest ecosystems (Miller 1989), meaning that availability is commonly limiting or close to it and reuse following litterfall, decomposition and mineralization is rapid and efficient. Leaching of nutrients (loss in soil water movement) is uncommon in natural ecosystems and leaching is commonly an indication of stress and disturbance. The quantification of elemental sinks and fluxes, particularly atmospheric inputs and losses from forest ecosystems, is thus of major importance. Understanding the importance of atmospheric inputs has occurred only relatively recently (see for example Ulrich 1989). In the last 20 years there have been a number of major forest catchment-scale studies that provide valuable data on forest nutrient budgets, on elemental losses from forest ecosystems and thus on the biological sustain-ability of the systems. The development of this 'ecosystem approach' can be directed at understanding and indeed treating specific nutritional problems (see Zöttle & Hüttl 1991). The mass balance and critical load approach to acidification has developed from the understanding of nutrient cycling and leaching and has drawn on the datasets provided.

We have already seen that deposition of anthropogenic S and N can result in soil acidification, raised Al concentrations in soil solution and loss of base cations through leaching. Magnesium deficiency has commonly been seen as the first nutritional imbalance to occur in this sequence. Nitrogen, like P and K, can limit productivity in forests. As with S, human activities have resulted in substantial increases in the deposition of inorganic N from the atmosphere. Smith (1999) estimated that the global fixation of atmospheric N_2 for use in fertilization in agriculture rose from less than 10Tg annually (1Tg=1Mt) to 80 Tg annually in 1980, and this value is likely to rise to 135 Tg annually by 2030 with an estimated additional 20 Tg annually being added through the deposition of pollutant N from the burning of fossil fuels. Thus, human activity adds as much N to the terrestrial ecosystems as natural sources. It is not surprising then that some forests are showing clear symptoms of excess N and, furthermore, that anthropogenic N inputs have been proposed, along with rising CO_2 concentrations and warming temperatures, as a major cause of increased forest growth throughout Europe.

CONCLUSIONS

In many ways the last two sentences of the preceding section would have made a suitable closing statement: the deposition of elements derived from anthropogenic emissions (S and N) are linked with changes of atmospheric chemistry (CO_2) and climate to produce an impact on forests (decreased or increased growth rate, declines, etc.). However this statement places too much emphasis on nutrient enrichment. In many parts of the world forests persist on poor soils where nutrient availability is a common limitation and anthropogenic inputs are likely to be of limited relevance. In such systems, sensitive management is essential if productivity is to be sustained over successive rotations (Evans 1999). Furthermore, consideration of the four abiotic factors in this chapter has also illustrated a number of more fundamental and overarching points.

Firstly, when abiotic stress is sufficient to cause system shifts (increased growth, decline, biome migration, etc.) it is often, perhaps always, associated with changes in environmental conditions. These may be natural, resulting from extremes of climate (ice ages or droughts), or anthropogenic, caused by the introduction of exotic species, repeated rotations of fast-growing plantations, pollutant deposition or greenhouse gas emissions. Secondly, forest ecosystems and the effects of the interactions of abiotic factors on them are complex. Interactions in effects and causal chains are the norm not the exception.

Faced with this, the objective of providing an understanding of ecological processes on which forest managers can make decisions that achieve the desired objectives proves difficult but not impossible. In many cases our understanding can be aided by the construction of conceptual and mathematical models and a number of these have been mentioned, for example Levitt's conceptual model of stress, general circulation models, models linking climate to vegetation (e.g. HYBRID, BEC, ESC), pollutant deposition and soil acidification models, critical load models, plant growth models and stand nutrient models. Today, modelling is often an effective way forward and we see the development of increasingly sophisticated forest growth models and decision support systems. We are fortunate to be at a stage in the development of forest science where such approaches are possible. Such models provide mechanisms by which we can integrate and draw on our complex knowledge of processes and of key interactions when making policy and management decisions.

3

Forest Hydrology

INTRODUCTION

Scientists and the public alike have long appreciated that a forest cover influences climatic and soil conditions and therefore the amount of water flowing from forested areas. In one of the earliest reviews of forest influences, Zon (1927) stated that 'forests increase both the abundance and frequency of local precipitation over the areas they occupy'. Furthermore it was not only claimed that 'forests increase underground storage of water' but also that 'forests tend to equalize the flow throughout the year by making the low stages higher'. Even after several catchment experiments completed during the next few decades had shown that both annual and summer flows increased after forest clearing (Hoyt & Troxell 1932; Hoover 1944), the classical text on forest influences by Kittredge (1948) still concluded that 'forests prolong increased flow in low-water periods'.

Moreover, the belief that forest removal automatically results in diminished dry-season flows and increased flooding is still regularly encountered today, particularly in the tropics (cf. Hamilton & King 1983; Bruijnzeel 1990). Whilst the current wealth of experimental evidence on the hydrological role of forests may have revealed some serious shortcomings in these earlier beliefs, it basically confirms the contention of Zon (1927) that 'of all the direct influences of the forest the influence upon the supply of water in streams and upon the regularity of their flow is the most important in human economy'.

With populations rising explosively in some parts of the world, and per-capita demands increasing in others as living standards continue to improve, optimization of water resources (both streamflow and groundwater reserves) is becoming increasingly important, particularly during the dry season. Similarly, the rising demands for industrial wood (pulpwood, saw and veneer logs), fuelwood and charcoal (mostly in the tropics) require the establishment of large areas of fast-growing plantation forests, often on land that is currently not forested (Brown *et al.* 1997). Coupled with the continued indiscriminate clearing of the world's forests (Jepma 1995; Nepstad *et al.* 1999), which in many areas serve as the traditional supplier of high-quality water, the associated deterioration of soil and water quality due to erosion and pollution (cf. Oldeman 1994) and the possibility of gradually less dependable precipitation inputs due to global change (Wasser & Harger 1992), a sound understanding of the hydrological functioning of forests is arguably even more important now than ever before.

A classic example of the conflicting interests of wood producers and water supply institutions is provided by the controversy following the finding of Law (1956) that a spruce plantation in the British Pennines consumed almost 300 mm more water per year than an adjacent grass sward. He concluded, on the basis of a lysimeter experiment, that if the whole catchment had been afforested with spruce this might have led to a reduction in water yield to a downstream reservoir by as much as 42%. The debate that followed the publication of these results was so heated that it not only began to threaten upland afforestation plans in the UK but also stimulated a major forest hydrological and micrometeorological research programme (see summaries by Rutter 1968; Shuttleworth 1989; Calder 1990). Results from these programmes both confirmed Law's original findings and greatly increased our understanding of the underlying hydrological processes.

The first part of this chapter reviews the current state of knowledge with respect to the major hydrological processes that occur in forests and how these processes affect amounts and timing of streamflow. The second part of the chapter discusses the effects of (i) various forest management options (thinning, selective logging, clearfelling) and (ii) replacement of forest by grass or crops, and vice versa. The principal focus is on the more humid parts of the world (both temperate and tropical).

FOREST HYDROLOGICAL CYCLE

Rain *(P)* is the main precipitation input to most forests, supplemented by snow at higher altitudes and latitudes and by 'occult' precipitation (fog) in coastal or montane fog belts. A small part of the precipitation reaches the forest floor directly without touching the canopy, the so-called 'free' or 'direct' throughfall. Another (usually small) part travels along the branches and trunks as stemflow *(Sf)*. A substantial portion of the precipitation intercepted by the canopy is evaporated back to the atmosphere during and shortly after the storm (called interception loss, E_i), whereas the remainder reaches the soil surface as crown drip after the storage capacity of the canopy has been filled. Because direct throughfall and crown drip cannot be determined separately in the field, the two are usually taken together and referred to as through-fall *(Tf)*. However, the distinction between the two is useful in modelling the interception process. The sum of through-fall and stemflow is commonly called net precipitation and is usually substantially smaller than amounts of incident precipitation unless there are significant (unmeasured) contributions by fog precipitation:

$$P = Tf + Sf + E_i$$

and

$$E_i = P - (Tf + Sf)$$

If the intensity of the total throughfall and stem-flow reaching the forest floor exceeds the infiltration capacity of the soil, the unabsorbed excess runs off as 'Hortonian' or 'infiltration-excess' overland flow (HOF). Due to the generally very high infiltration capacity of the organic-rich topsoil in most forests, this type of flow is rarely observed in undisturbed forest unless there is an unusually dense clayey substrate (Elsenbeer *et al.* 1992) or an excessive concentration of stemflow (Herwitz 1986). Not all of the water infiltrating into the soil emerges as streamflow.

A large part is taken up by the vegetation and returns to the atmosphere via the process of transpiration (£$_t$). The term 'evapotranspiration' *(ET)* is used to denote the sum of transpiration (evaporation from a dry canopy), interception loss (evaporation from the exposed surfaces of a wet canopy) and evaporation from the litter and soil surface (£$_s$). The latter term is often small, especially in dense forests where little radiation penetrates to the forest floor, humidity is high and the air virtually stagnant. It is essential to distinguish between E_t and E_i because the former is strongly governed by stomatal control and the latter mostly by the aerodynamic properties of the vegetation (Jarvis & Stewart 1979). Thus:

[12.3]

$$ET = E_i + E_t + E_s$$

The remaining soil moisture drains towards the nearest stream via 'throughflow', the result of downward-moving water meeting an impermeable layer of subsoil or bedrock and being deflected laterally.

Such water drains slowly and steadily, thus accounting for the 'baseflow' of streams. In humid temperate climates, baseflow generally reaches a minimum in the summer period, whereas under seasonal tropical conditions this occurs during the dry season. These low flows are usually referred to as 'minimum flow', 'dry-season flow' or simply 'low flow'. During rainfall, infiltrated water may take one of several routes to the stream channel, depending on soil hydraulic conductivity, slope morphology and the spatial distribution of soil moisture. 'Saturation' overland flow (SOF) is caused by rain falling on an already saturated soil.

This situation typically occurs in hillside hollows or on concave foot-slopes near the stream where throughflow tends to converge and maintain near-saturated conditions. Occasionally, widespread hillside SOF (i.e. outside concavities and depressions) has been observed during and after intense rainfall in the tropics in places where an impeding layer is found close to the surface (Bonell & Gilmour 1978; Elsenbeer & Cassel 1990). Rapid through-flow during storms (subsurface stormflow, SSSF) usually consists of a mixture of 'old' (i.e. already present before the start of the rain) and 'new' water travelling through 'macropores' and 'pipes' (Bonell 1993; Brammer & McDonnell 1996).

As a result of contributions by SOF, SSSF and, in extreme cases, HOF, streamflow usually increases rapidly during rainfall. This increase above base-flow levels is called 'stormflow' or 'quickflow'. The highest discharge observed in association with a precipitation event is referred to as 'peak flow'. Peak discharges may be reached during the rainfall event itself or as late as a few days afterwards, depending on catchment characteristics, soil wetness and the duration, intensity and quantity of the rainfall (Dunne 1978; Pearce *et al.* 1982;

Brammer & McDonnell 1996). The total volume of water produced as streamflow from a catchment over a given period of time (usually a month, season or year) is called 'water yield'.

The interrelated character of the chief components of the hydrological cycle is summarized by the catchment or site water budget equation:

$$P = E_i + E_t + E_s + Q + AS + AG$$

where Q is streamflow or drainage to deeper layers, AS change in soil water storage and AG change in groundwater storage, with the remaining terms as defined previously. All values are expressed in millimetres of water per unit of time (hour, day, week, month or year). Note that *AS* and *AG* may assume positive (gain) or negative (loss) values. In view of the seasonal cycle of soil water and groundwater storages in many areas, the values of *AS* and *AG* tend to approach zero on an annual basis (Lee 1970). Therefore, the annual water balance is often simplified to:

$$P=ET+Q$$

FORESTS AND 'OCCULT' PRECIPITATION

Forest-climate interactions in general have been dealt with in Chapter 10. Therefore the present discussion does not focus on the extent to which a forest cover generates its own rainfall (and over what scale) but rather on the importance of fog and other forms of cloud moisture ('occult' precipitation) as an additional input of water. Wherever fog impacts a forested area, particularly where the fog occurs in the form of an orographic cloud belt or advective coastal fog, additional moisture is intercepted by plant surfaces (or indeed any other obstacle) and precipitation may occur in the form of 'occult' precipitation or 'fog drip', even if no rainfall is recorded on adjacent open ground (Zadroga 1981).

An extreme example has been described by Aravena *et al.* (1989) whose isotope studies have demonstrated that the frequent occurrence of advective sea fogs along the arid coast of northern Chile has given rise to a patchy forest that, in the almost complete absence of ordinary rainfall, thrives primarily on fog. Several studies of fog drip beneath trees along the US Pacific Coast have shown that the amount is directly related to the area and density of the tree profile and to the degree of exposure of the trees to windblown fog. During times of fog, fog drip at the edge of a forest may be several times the rainfall in the open. However, amounts often decrease sharply towards the forest interior.

Therefore, reports of increased net precipitation beneath vegetation need to be considered carefully in terms of gauge positions with respect to the edge of the forest (Grünow 1955; Weathers *et al.* 1995). At favourably exposed locations the extra inputs stripped from the fog by trees (conifers especially) may be considerable. Examples include 425 mm in 46 rainless summer days below 18-m tall Douglas fir in northern California (Azevedo & Morgan 1974), 760 mm annually measured in Hawaii below *Araucaria* by Ekern (1964) and 880 mm annually for tall old-growth Douglas fir in Oregon by Harr (1982). Bruijnzeel and Proctor (1995) and Bruijnzeel (2000) recently reviewed the hydrological characteristics of 'cloud forests' found in orographic cloud belts on wet tropical mountains and reported extremely variable net precipitation fractions for these forests (55-130% of incident rainfall).

As such, although tropical montane cloud forests are supposedly exposed to frequent fog (Zadroga 1981), the associated amounts intercepted by the trees are not always sufficient to raise net precipitation totals significantly above the 70-80% commonly recorded for montane rain forests on cloud-free locations. Such variations may be interpreted in terms of exposure to and persistence of fog, as well as to contrasts in canopy epiphyte biomass (Bruijnzeel & Proctor 1995).

Quantification of the amount of fog intercepted by a forest is difficult, particularly if the fog occurs together with rain. The usual approach is to compare amounts of net precipitation (often throughfall only) beneath the forest with the rainfall measured in the open (e.g. Harr 1982) or to subtract the latter from the catch obtained with some kind of fog gauge placed next to an ordinary rain gauge. A number of different fog gauge designs have been proposed, including wire harps (Goodman 1985), cylindrical screens (Russell 1984), $1m^2$ polypropylene screens (Schemenauer & Cereceda 1994) and louvered metal gauges (Juvik & Nullet 1995).

The through-fall method essentially gives an estimate of 'net' fog drip since it includes an unmeasured amount of water lost to evaporation from the wet vegetation (i.e. E_i, see also next section). In addition, the result is site specific.

The use of a fog gauge (regardless of the type adopted) also requires a site-specific conversion factor to relate the catch of the gauge to that of the actual forest canopy. Some progress has been made with physical fog deposition models (Joslin *et al.* 1990; Mueller 1991; Walmsley *et al.* 1996, 1999) but the data requirements of these models are such that their use at remote forest locations must remain limited to a few well-researched sites.

Therefore there may be some merit in alternative approaches to the quantification of fog contributions, such as the sodium/chloride budget method (Hafkenscheid *et al.* 1998) or the contrasting stable-isotope signatures of rain and fog water (Dawson 1998; Ingraham 1998).

For example, by comparing the stable isotope compositions of rain, fog, soil moisture and groundwater with those of xylem water in the dominant species of a Californian redwood forest, Dawson (1998) was able to demonstrate the importance of fog to the different plant groups. During a year with average climatic conditions, 25-50% of the water uptake by the tall redwood trees was shown to consist of fog whereas these figures roughly doubled during a drought year. Under-storey herbs were even more dependent on fog water: 19-50% in an average year and 28-100% in a drought year.

As discussed more fully, transpiration (£$_t$) ceases whenever the canopy is fully wetted. Because of this and the reduced radiation and high relative humidity normally associated with such conditions, E_t of trees exposed to frequent fog is low (Hutley *et al.* 1997). Together with the additional inputs via occult precipitation, this makes for an especially favourable water balance, i.e. amounts of stream-flow or groundwater recharge will be comparatively high. For these reasons Zadroga (1981) expressed the fear that clearing tropical montane cloud forest could well result in substantially reduced water yield, especially during the dry season. Some support for this contention could come from the contrasting dry-season flows emanating from two pairs of cloud-forested and cleared catchments in Guatemala and Honduras reported by Brown *et al.* (1996).

However, both catchment pairs were too different in size and elevational range (and therefore exposure to fog and rainfall) to be sure that the approximately 50% reduction in flow was entirely due to the replacement of the forest by vegetable cropping.

A more convincing case was provided by Ingwersen (1985) who observed a (small) decline in summer flows after a 25% patch clearcut operation in the same catchment in the Pacific North-west region of the USA for which Harr (1982) had inferred an annual contribution by fog of about 880mm. The effect disappeared after 5-6 years.

Because forest cutting in the Pacific North-west is normally associated with strong increases in water yield (Harr 1983), this anomalous result was attributed to an initial loss of fog stripping upon timber harvesting, followed by a gradual recovery during regrowth.

Interestingly, the effect was less pronounced in an adjacent (but more sheltered) catchment and it could not be excluded that some of the condensation not realized in the more exposed catchment was 'passed on' to the other catchment (Ingwersen 1985). The observation of Fallas (1996) of enhanced throughfall in patches of forest surrounded by pasture in the montane cloud forest belt of northern Costa Rica is probably pertinent in this respect. Further (process-based) work is needed to decide on the importance of occult precipitation for water yield from fog-affected areas (cf. Bruijnzeel 2000).

THROUGHFALL, STEMFLOW AND INTERCEPTION LOSS

Amounts and measurement of rainfall interception

Arguably, no subject in (temperate zone) forest hydrology has received as much attention as the measurement of throughfall (*T/*), stemflow *(Sf)* and derived estimates of interception loss (E_i). Yet, until the pioneering work of Rutter and colleagues in the 1960s (Rutter 1967; Rutter *et al.* 1971, 1975) the increase in understanding of the underlying processes was not commensurate.

Before then, interception was mainly studied in terms of tree species and age, or the amount, intensity and duration of the rain. For example, in a review covering more than 50 interception studies in the USA spanning half a century, Zinke (1967) arrived at essentially the same generalizations as Kittredge (1948) and Horton (1919) had before him. These can be summarized as follows:

1. E_i is a function of incident rainfall *(P)* and typically declines more or less hyperbolically when expressed as a percentage of *P*;
2. both E_i and the canopy storage capacity *(S)* are generally larger for coniferous forests (E_i = 15-40%; *S* = 0.5-3.0 mm; average ~2mm) than for deciduous forests (growing season, £$_i$ = 20-25%; *S* = 0.5-2.0 mm; average =1.0 mm);
3. winter values of E_i and *S* for deciduous forests are roughly half to two-thirds of summer values;
4. *Sf* generally constitutes only a modest fraction of *P* (typically < 3%), with the exception of smooth-barked species such as beech or maple (5-12%) or young trees;
5. E_i increases with stand density;
6. snowfall interception storage by coniferous canopies exceeds that for rainfall.

The extensive reviews of early European work by Delfs (1955) and Molchanov (1963) and of British studies by Hall and Roberts (1990) broadly support the above generalizations obtained for forests in the USA.

The main contribution by Rutter and coworkers to our current, improved, understanding of the rainfall interception process has been to move away from the empirical site-specific approach of the past to a more explicitly physical description of the process. Central to the Rutter approach is a running canopy (and trunk) water balance in which hourly inputs (rainfall) and outputs (drainage, evaporation) determine the amount of water stored on the canopy (and the tree trunks). The latter governs both the rate of drainage from the wet canopy and the rate of evaporation (for storage less than *S*) (Rutter *et al.* 1971, 1975).

Usually, the results of interception studies are expressed in relation to gross rainfall, either as a ratio, percentage or through various types of regression equations. Comparisons between different studies, even for the same species and age class, are rendered difficult because of the more-or-less unique character of each forest stand in terms of density, presence or absence of undergrowth, exposure to prevailing air streams, and rainfall regimes. In addition, there is a methodological problem in that the notoriously uneven distribution of *Tf* (both in space and time) requires a rigorous sampling strategy that not all studies have achieved. In general, the spatial variability of *Tf* increases with forest density, i.e. it is greater in summer than in winter for deciduous stands (Helvey & Patric 1965) and much larger in tropical rain forest than in temperate plantations.

The vegetation in most natural forests is made up of a mosaic representing different stages of growth, ranging from young rapidly growing trees in gaps to old-growth emergents on the decline. Burghouts *et al.* (1998) reported an inverse relationship between amounts of *Tf* and litterfall in a spatially heterogeneous lowland rain forest in Borneo. Delfs (1955) observed a gradual decrease in *Tf* over an age sequence from young regenerating spruce in the sapling and pole stages to mature stands.

At the microscale, Eschner (1967) reviewed a range of studies in deciduous and coniferous forests showing that beyond the immediate sphere around the trunks (where *Sf* and drip from the points of juncture of branches and bole tend to concentrate), *Tf* often increases away from the trunks to reach a maximum just within the perimeter of the crown. Hutchinson and Roberts (1981) reported that 98% of all *Sf* generated by a 9-m tall Douglas fir originated in the upper half of the tree, whereas the sheltered and more depressed branches of the lower half (representing 31% of total branch interception area) contributed little to stemflow production.

Czarnowski and Olszewski (1970) demonstrated that using up to 30 fixed standard gauges gave different average *Tf* values for a natural deciduous forest in central Europe, whereas the estimate stabilized after using 30 gauges or more. Helvey and Patric (1965) suggested that six gauges during the dormant season and 15 during the growing season would be sufficient for a proper estimation of *Tf* in mixed hardwood stands in the eastern USA, provided the gauges were relocated regularly. Other investigators relied on increasing the sampling surface area, be it through the use of large metal plates (Crockford & Richardson 1990), elongated gutters (Rowe 1983) or plastic sheets (Calder & Rosier 1976). However, the use of a large collecting surface *per se* is not a guarantee of a good estimate of E_i.

For example, Bruijnzeel and Wiersum (1987) used 10-12 trough-type *Tf* gauges (with a total surface area equivalent to 140-168 standard gauges) in an *Acacia auriculiformis* plantation in Indonesia. Measurements were made during two consecutive rainy seasons with fixed trough arrangements that differed between the two periods because the gauges were removed during the dry season. Although both estimates of seasonal *Tf* had a standard error of less than 5%, the mean values were very different.

Because the difference was only partially explicable in terms of increases in canopy development and differences in rainfall patterns, it had to be concluded that the two fixed trough configurations sampled the spatial variation in *Tf* differently. Such findings indicate the need for a sufficiently large sampling plot commensurate with the heterogeneity of the forest under study.

A 10 x 10 m sampling plot could be sufficient for a uniform tree plantation of high stem density but entirely inappropriate for a heterogeneous species-rich lowland rain forest (Roberts 1999). Lloyd and Marques (1988), using a 100 x 4m sampling transect in a central Amazonian rain forest, showed that about 40 fixed standard gauges would be needed to sample *Tf* with a standard error of 10% but that the same result could be achieved with only 10 'roving' gauges.

Interestingly, Lloyd and Marques (1988) obtained an E_i of only 9% using 36 roving bottle gauges where Leopoldo *et al.* (1982) had previously reported a value of 19% for the same forest on the basis of 20 fixed collectors. The large difference between these two estimates may well be caused by a more representative sampling of so-called 'drip points' (i.e. $Tf > P$) by the roving-gauge arrangement. Not many studies have used a roving-gauge approach and published estimates of E_i must therefore be viewed with caution.

Despite the large variation encountered in the deciduous group, E_i in deciduous stands is invariably lower than in coniferous forest for the same amount of *P* (Hall & Roberts 1990; Roberts 1999; cf. Zinke 1967). A similar contrast was noted for coniferous (E_i > 20-25%) and (semi)deciduous plantations such as teak and mahogany in the tropics (£^20%; Bruijnzeel 1997). Although evergreen, the relatively light crowns and smooth stems of (young) eucalypt plantations intercept only modest quantities of rainfall (typically about 10-15%), both in the tropics (Bruijnzeel 1997) and in their native Australia (Dunin *et al.* 1988; Crockford & Richardson 1990).

However, recent work in south-eastern Australia has shown that E_i in an age series of natural eucalypt forest may rise to a peak of 25% at age 30 years after which it declines to about 15% at age 235 years (Haydon *et al.* 1996). Although some of the variation in E_i between different deciduous forests in Fig. 12.5 may be related to the presence or absence of a well-developed understorey, little is known of the intercepting capacity of the latter. Noirfalise (1959) obtained values of 10.4 and 12.6% for E_i below bracken fern *(Pteridium aquilinum)* between late May and mid September and between mid September and mid November, respectively. Using rather more indirect means, Gash and Stewart (1977) derived a value of 12.3% of *P* for bracken fern below Scots pine in the eastern UK between mid May and early October, representing 12.6% of the annual E_i of the forest.

Bruijnzeel (1990) derived an average *Tf* of 85% (range 77-93%) from 13 investigations conducted in tropical lowland rain forest that used either a roving-gauge arrangement or more than 20 fixed gauges. Stemflow in these forests was usually less than 2%. Corresponding average values for tall montane forests experiencing little to no cloud incidence are 75% (range 67-81%) and less than 1%, respectively (Bruijnzeel 2000). As discussed in section 12.3, net precipitation in mossy montane cloud forests may be much higher due to the effect of 'occult' precipitation. The most stunted forms of ridge-top montane cloud forest, which frequently have crooked stems and trees with multiple stems, may exhibit exceptionally large amounts of *Sf* (up to 18%; Bruijnzeel 2000).

It should be noted that no distinction was made by Bruijnzeel (1990) between forests at mid-continental vs. continental edge and island locations. Shuttleworth (1989) advanced the idea that forest evaporation (notably E_i) may be much greater in the latter situations compared with the former.

He based his contention on a comparison of the micrometeorology of a lowland forest in central Amazonia (Shuttleworth 1988) and a spruce plantation in Wales, UK (Shuttleworth & Calder 1979), as well as on the reported contrast in E_i between the Amazonian forest (Lloyd & Marques 1988) and a secondary lowland rain forest on the island of Java, Indonesia (Calder *et al.* 1986). The argument was rendered inconclusive at the time because of the use of markedly different methodologies for the estimation of E_i in Indonesia and Amazonia. However, since the late 1980s a number of rainfall interception studies in tropical forests located at continental edge and island locations with high rainfall (>3000mm annually) have confirmed the possibility of very high E_i under such wet 'maritime' tropical conditions, both in the lowlands (Scatena 1990; Dykes 1997) and at higher elevations (Cavelier *et al.* 1997; Clark *et al.* 1998).

Litter interception

Helvey and Patric (1965) argued that evaporation from the litter layer ($£_s$) may constitute a significant component of the overall interception loss and should therefore be determined separately. When measured *in situ* (as opposed to using litter trays which tend to give overestimates), $£_s$ was shown to reach 2-5% of incident P in hardwood stands in the eastern USA (=50mm annually). Interestingly, litter drying rates in winter were higher than in summer, presumably because the leafless condition of the forest permitted increased ventilation and irradiation of the forest floor at a time of maximum Tf (Helvey & Patric 1965). Later micrometeorological work by Black and Kelliher (1989) in Douglas fir forests confirmed the importance of radiant energy and degree of turbulence to forest floor evaporation.

These authors also showed that $£_s$ and under-storey ET are largely complementary processes, with high values of $£_s$ occurring in stands having little to no understorey vegetation and vice versa. Using weighing lysimetry Schaap (1996) showed

$£_s$ in a dense but well-ventilated Douglas fir forest in The Netherlands to be mainly dependent on forest floor moisture content, with (modelled) average annual values ranging from 0.21 mm daily on drier microsites to 0.38 mm daily on wetter sites. The corresponding stand-averaged annual total of 112mm represented about 12% and 22% of incident *P* and *Tf*, respectively. Similar values (9.5-11% of *P*, or = 155 mm yearly) were obtained for plantations of *Pinus caribaea* under warm non-equatorial tropical conditions in Fiji (Waterloo *et al.* 1999). Conversely, much lower annual totals (50-70 mm) have been reported for dense equatorial rain forest (Jordan & Heuveldop 1981; Roche 1982).

Interception modelling

Despite the numerous studies of rainfall interception conducted prior to the 1960s, little progress had been made in understanding the physics underlying the observed contrasts and inconsistencies in E_i, both between and within species and events. Explanations offered in the early literature were usually worded in terms of differences in canopy storage capacity (in turn related to canopy density, deciduousness, etc.) or the intensity and duration of the rain. However, by the mid 1960s profound changes were to occur. In the same year that Helvey and Patric (1965) still suggested that two simple linear *Tf-P* regression equations were sufficient to adequately quantify E_i for hardwoods in the eastern USA under a wide range of conditions, Monteith (1965) advanced a more physical description of the process of evaporation from a vegetation cover while Rutter (1967) presented a process-orientated approach to the study of E_i at the 1965 International Symposium on Forest Hydrology (Sopper & Lull 1967).

The regression approach of Helvey and Patric (1965) was later criticized by Jackson (1971, 1975) for not incorporating rainfall intensity and duration or the length of intervals beween storms. However, Jackson himself was not very successful in raising the coefficients of determination (R^2), and therefore the predictive capacity, of his own more elaborate regression equations, thus illustrating the limitations of the empirical approach. Arguably therefore the two papers by Monteith (1965) and Rutter (1967), complemented by the interception modelling work of Rutter *et al.* (1971, 1975), mark a turn from the previous largely empirical experimental approach to a more physically orientated, process-based, approach (see below).

Monteith (1965) showed that the latent heat flux density (evaporation) from a vegetated surface could be described by:

$AA + pC\ {-VPD}/r_a$

XE

$A + y(1+r_s/r_a)$

where XE is latent heat flux flux density (Wm^{-2}), A available energy (Wm^{-2}), A slope of the saturation vapour pressure curve at air temperature T ($PaKr^1$), p density of air ($kgmr^3$), C specific heat of air ($Jkg^{-1}\ Kr^1$) ypsychrometric constant ($PaKr^1$), VPD vapour pressure deficit (Pa), r_a aerodynamic resistance (sm^{-1}) and r_s surface resistance (sm^{-1}).

where r_{sto} is the stomatal resistance to evaporation at the leaf level (sm^{-1}) and LAI is leaf area index (m^2m^{-2}).

In the absence of advected heat, the energy available for evaporation *(A)* is considered equal to $(R_n - G)$, i.e. the flux density of net radiation minus the heat flux density into the ground. For a wet canopy the surface resistance r_s becomes zero (Monteith 1965) and Eqn 12.6 reduces to:

$AA + pC\ {-VPD}/r_a$

$A + Y$

$^{\wedge £}wet =$

The aerodynamic resistance r_a, whose magnitude is critical to the outcome is ideally derived from the wind speed profile as measured above the canopy under (near)-neutral conditions of atmospheric stability (Thom 1975) according

to: 2^

ln

$z - d$

z_0 r_a zz k^2-u

where z is observation height above the ground surface (m), d zero-plane displacement height (m), z_0 roughness length (m), k von Kàrmàn's constant (0.41) and u wind speed as measured at height z (ms^{-1}). In the absence of above-canopy wind data, d and z_0 are often assumed to be equal to 0.75 and 0.1 times the canopy height (i_v) (Brutsaert 1982). Alternatively, Eqn may be solved inversely when $A£_{wet}$ is known by other methods:

pC -VPD

r_a =

although this method requires highly precise measurements of the atmospheric VPD under near-saturated conditions and is thus prone to errors (Gash *et al.* 1980).

With increasing vegetation height there is a corresponding increase in roughness length d and displacement length z_0 and thus, for a given wind speed, a decrease in r_a. Also, r_a decreases with wind speed; approximate values for different vegetation covers at a wind speed of 2.5 m s^{-1} measured at 10m above the surface are 115, 50 and 10-15 sm^{-1} for short grass, field crops and forest, respectively (Pearce & Rowe 1979). Because values of the surface resistance to evaporation from a dry canopy (r_s) for grass and forest are much more similar (50-90 and 70-120 sm^{-1} respectively; Pearce & Rowe 1979),, the magnitude of r_s/ra in Eqn 12.6 is larger for a forest cover. This would lead to lower values of forest *XE* were it not for the compensating effect of the lower albedo and thus R_n of the forest. As a result, as long as soil water is not limiting and atmospheric humidity deficits remain low, transpiration rates for grass and forest do not differ much (Fig. 12.6). This is in great contrast to the finding that as a result of the much lower r_a of the forest, evaporation from a wet forest canopy will proceed much faster than from a wet grassland.

Wet canopy evaporation rates of 0.2-0.5 mm h^{-1} have been observed under temperate conditions, even in cloudy winter weather when XE_{wet} must greatly exceed net radiant energy (Rutter 1967, 1968; Shuttleworth & Calder 1979). Under maritime tropical conditions, values as high as 0.7-1.2mmh^{-1} have been inferred from measurements of net precipitation (Dykes 1997; Schellekens *et al.* 2000; Waterloo *et al.* 1999). As shown by Rutter (1967) and Stewart (1977), temperatures of wet forest canopies may be slightly cooler than the air passing overhead.

This, together with the low aerodynamic resistance conducive to rapid evaporation, allows the development of a downward sensible heat flux capable of maintaining evaporation rates well in excess of available radiant energy. The degree to which the phenomenon influences annual E_i obviously depends on the frequency of wetting of the canopy (i.e. rainfall regime) and thus on the overall setting of the forest. For a pine plantation in the relatively dry eastern part of the UK, Stewart (1977) measured instantaneous rates of XE_{wet} of 127% of net radiant energy but on an annual scale E_i was modest at 214 mm or 38% of total forest *ET* (Gash & Stewart 1977).

For a spruce plantation in the more maritime setting of wet central Wales with frequent passage of warm frontal rain, Shuttleworth and Calder (1979) reported instantaneous rates of XE_{wet} of about five times the available radiant energy. Annual *ET* exceeded R_n by 12%. Not surprisingly, E_i made up a large portion (61%) of total forest *ET* (Calder 1990). Recently, Schellekens *et al.* (2000) reported an even more extreme example from eastern Puerto Rico, where annual E_i from a colline rain forest varied between 1365 and 1790mm (39-49% of *P*). Although no direct measurements were made of a downward sensible heat flux, there were strong indications that non-radiant energy dominated wet canopy evaporation. Not only were net precipitation fractions not statistically different for daytime and night-time events but also the average evaporation equivalent of net radiant energy ($0.11 mmh^{-1}$) was far smaller than the value of XE_{wet} as inferred from measurements of E_i ($0.93\text{-}1.13 mmh^{-1}$). In addition, annual *ET* as estimated from the water budget of a small watertight catchment exceeded R_n by 42%.

The origin of the extra energy is still a matter of speculation. Advected warm air from the nearby Atlantic Ocean is a likely source (cf. Shuttleworth & Calder 1979) although, unlike the situation in Wales, wind speeds in eastern Puerto Rico are generally low. Another possible energy source may be heat released upon condensation of water vapour in the air above the forest. Some support for this contention comes from the observation that *Tf/P* was independent of storm size, i.e. larger rainfall events were accompanied by higher interception totals (Schellekens *et al.* 2000). This would suggest a positive feedback of rainfall amount (and thereby condensation) on the magnitude of E_i. Further work is needed to test these speculations.

However, even if it is accepted that for situations like those encountered in Wales and Puerto Rico, where the total energy available for evaporation during rain can be much larger than provided by radiant energy alone (Shuttleworth & Calder 1979; Schellekens *et al.* 2000), it is not clear how the aerodynamic resistance of the forest can be so low as to enable these high wet canopy evaporation rates. For the spruce plantation in Wales, Calder (1990) required an optimum value for r_a of $3.5 sm^{-1}$ (vs. a theoretical value of $5.4 s.m^{-1}$ using Eqn 12.9 at an average wind speed of $3.75 ms^{-1}$).

Using Eqn 12.10, Schellekens *et al.* (2000) obtained values of $2.1\text{-}3.2 s m^{-1}$ (depending on VPD) vs. $18\text{-}22 sm^{-1}$ when using Eqn 12.9. Whilst in the Puerto Rican case r_a may be lowered somewhat by the irregular character of the canopy due to former hurricane damage, Calder (1990) and McNaughton and Laubach (1998) have pointed to the possibility of enhanced upward transport of evaporated moisture (i.e. low r_a) by wind gusts and eddies. Such gusts would assume extra importance under conditions of relatively low wind speeds such as in Puerto Rico.

Determination of A£$_{wet}$ using eddy correlation equipment in combination with an energy budget approach (Gash *et al.* 1999) recently confirmed the basic soundness of the momentum transfer theory underlying More work is needed to resolve the matter.

Physically-based models may help to elucidate the relative importance of different factors in the interception process, which are difficult to assess from an actual interception record. Two well-known models are the dynamic model developed by Rutter *et al.* (1971, 1975) and its simpler derivative, the analytical model of Gash (1979).

The Rutter model calculates a running water balance for the canopy (and trunks). It requires hourly rainfall and meteorological data as inputs, as well as values of four parameters describing the forest (free throughfall and stem-flow coefficients, canopy and trunk saturation values). In addition, it uses an empirical expression to compute drainage from the canopy. The Rutter model has been used successfully for such contrasting environments as coniferous plantations in the UK (Gash & Morton 1978) and tropical rain forest in central Amazonia (Lloyd *et al.* 1988).

However, it greatly underestimated E_i under wet maritime tropical conditions (Java, Puerto Rico) where unrealistically high canopy storage capacities or very low aerodynamic resistances were required to match predicted and measured E_i (Calder *et al.* 1986; Schellekens *et al.* 1999). Valente *et al.* (1997) used a reformulated version of the model to predict rainfall interception by sparse canopy forests in Portugal.

The effect of varying rainfall intensities and evaporation rates, canopy storage capacity and the distribution of rain (continuous vs. intermittent) on the magnitude of E_i using the. The limiting effect of low rainfall intensity at faster evaporation rates is clearly borne out by the simulations, as is the increase in E_i at higher rainfall intensities and for higher canopy storages, especially in the case of intermittent rain.

A major practical drawback of the Rutter model is its high data requirement. The analytical model of rainfall interception developed by Gash (1979) is conceptually similar to the Rutter model but much less data-demanding.

It is usually applied on an event basis and uses average instead of hourly rates of rainfall on to, and evaporation from, a saturated canopy. Apart from evaporation from a saturated canopy, the model computes the evaporation before the canopy is fully wetted and after rainfall has ceased, the effect of small storms insufficient to saturate the canopy, and evaporation from trunks.

Total E_i is then estimated as the sum of the respective interception components. The analytical model and a derivative for sparse canopies developed by Gash *et al.* (1995) have been applied to a wide range of environments, ranging from temperate coniferous and deciduous forests (Gash *et al.* 1980; Carlyle-Moses & Price 1999) to sparse Mediterranean pine and eucalypt forests (Valente *et al.* 1997) and tropical rain forests (Lloyd *et al.* 1988; Hutjes *et al.* 1990). As in the case of the Rutter model, predicted amounts of E_i under more maritime conditions were underestimated by the model when evaporation from a saturated canopy was computed. For example, Gash *et al.* (1980) had to roughly double the average value of XE_{wet} to match measured and predicted E_i in a spruce plantation in Wales whereas Schellekens *et al.* (1999) required a fourfold to fivefold increase for the Puerto Rican case discussed above (cf. Pearce *et al.* 1980a; Bruijnzeel & Wiersum 1987; Dykes 1997). A much better match of cumulative $T/$was obtained in the latter case by optimizing for XE_{wet} than for canopy storage capacity S (cf. Calder *et al.* 1986).

In the Rutter and Gash models the canopy capacity is treated as a fixed parameter but in a more recent development in interception modelling (the so-called stochastic model proposed by Calder 1986) the size of the canopy capacity is allowed to vary. In the stochastic model the (repeated) wetting of the canopy is described in terms of the probability with which raindrops of different sizes strike the canopy. Larger drop sizes are considered less efficient at wetting the canopy (i.e. filling the storage capacity) than smaller drops.

Therefore, for the same depth of rain, larger drops will not only take longer to (re)fill the canopy capacity but also the amount of water retained on the canopy will be smaller when drops are larger. In a recent modification of the model (Calder 1996), the wetting functions were adjusted to include the possibility of wetting of lower canopy layers by secondary drops falling from the upper layers. Although the two-layer version of the model was applied successfully in the simulation of E_i from a forest in Sri Lanka (Hall *et al.* 1996), the precise physical meaning of some of the model parameters remains somewhat vague.

In this respect it is pertinent that Uijlenhoet and Stricker (1999) recently pointed out that the stochastic model employed an erroneous rainfall intensity vs. drop size relationship. In theory, however, the stochastic approach holds considerable promise for use in humid tropical situations where raindrop sizes tend to be larger than in the temperate conditions under which the Rutter and Gash models originated. It would be interesting therefore to examine the performance of the (improved) stochastic model under the contrasting climatic conditions prevailing in central Amazonia (mid-continental equatorial conditions with relatively high rainfall intensities where the Rutter and Gash models gave satisfactory predictions; Lloyd & Marques 1988; Lloyd *et al.* 1988) and eastern Puerto

Rico (maritime tropical site with frequent low-intensity rain where the Rutter and Gash models produced large underestimates; Schellekens *et al.* 1999, 2000).

Models describing rates of £$_s$ (evaporation from the forest floor) range from site-specific exponential drying curves (Helvey 1964; Waterloo *et al.* 1999) to a more explicitly physical approach that is conceptually similar to the Rutter canopy interception model (Schaap 1996).

TRANSPIRATION

Amounts and measurement of transpiration

With few exceptions (e.g. Gash & Stewart 1977; Dunin & Greenwood 1986; Shuttleworth 1988), forest hydrological studies before the end of the 1980s generally evaluated forest transpiration (£$_t$) as a residual term in the water budget equation (Eqn 12.4) by subtracting streamflow (or drainage), soil water storage changes and rainfall interception from incident rainfall. Estimates of E_t based on the catchment or site water balance approach are prone to considerable uncertainty because of the possibility of error accumulation.

Moreover, there is the danger of ungauged subterranean water transfers in the case of catchments (Lee 1970) and, for site water balances, extraction by deep roots beyond the range of the soil water measurements (Hodnett *et al.* 1996; Calder *et al.* 1997) as well as problems related to spatial variability of soil hydraulic properties and soil water contents (Cooper 1979; Rambal *et al.* 1984).

The widespread application of micrometeorologi-cal approaches such as the Bowen ratio-energy balance method (Angus & Watts 1984) and eddy correlation techniques (Shuttleworth 1992) is limited not only by their requirement of homogeneous, smooth and even fetch conditions but also by the fact that the measurements need to be made above the forest canopy. Similarly, attempts to obtain *in situ* estimates of leaf transpiration using porometers to determine leaf stomatal resistance to evaporation (r_{sto}), and the extrapolation of such results to entire canopies using Eqns 12.6 and 12.7 (Monteith 1965), have met with mixed success because of in-canopy variations in water use that require adequate characterization of climatic gradients and leaf age distribution within the canopy (cf. Schulze *et al.* 1985; Roberts *et al.* 1993; Dawson 1996).

An additional problem relates to the often poorly quantified influence on whole-plant transpiration of the diffusive resistance of the boundary layers surrounding each leaf and the canopy. The sensitivity of leaf or canopy transpiration to a marginal change in r_{sto} has been described in terms of a dimension-less 'decoupling coefficient' (Q) by Jarvis and McNaughton (1986). The value of Q ranges between 0 (full stomatal control) and 1 (no stomatal control). Decoupling of transpiration from stomatal control increases sharply with increasing leaf size, both because larger leaves are associated with lower boundary layer conductance (i.e. higher r_a) and because r_{sto} tends to be smaller for large-leaved species than for fine-leaved species such as conifers (Jarvis & McNaughton 1986).

Therefore, porometric measurements of transpiration in coniferous forests having low values of Q (high stomatal control) may be interpreted as actual canopy-scale fluxes (Schulze *et al.* 1985), although reliance on porometric data alone for such large-leaved (tropical) species as *Tectona grandis* and *Gmelina arborea* (Q values of 0.87-0.94; Jarvis & McNaughton 1986) could lead to misinterpretation of the significance of stomatal activity to transpiration (Wullschleger *et al.* 1998).

Partly in response to the limitations of conventional measuring techniques, efforts to determine forest transpiration via extrapolation to stand level of single-tree estimates of water use have been stepped up considerably, especially since the arrival of thermally based methods in the last two decades (see reviews by Swanson 1994; Smith & Allen 1996; Wullschleger *et al.* 1998; Grime & Sinclair 1999). Although estimates of water use derived from heat-balance, heat-dissipation and heat-pulse techniques suffer from uncertainties because of empirical calibrations, thermal gradients and variation in water flux with sapwood depth, these systems are relatively inexpensive, easy to use and readily linked up with data loggers for remote operation (Wullschleger *et al.* 1998). In addition, relatively good agreement has been reported between estimates of stand water use based on whole-tree measurements and eddy correlation methods in several cases (Köstner *et al.* 1992; Berbigier *et al.* 1996; Dawson 1996).

Because hydrologists need stand water fluxes to be expressed on a ground area basis (L m^{-2} or mm), estimates of the water use of individual trees (usually expressed in kilograms or litres per unit of time) need to be scaled up to the stand level. A variety of scalars have been proposed to achieve this, ranging from tree domain (defined either as distance between stems or projected crown area), basal area or stem diameter at breast height, to leaf or sapwood area.

The suitability of a particular scalar can be expected to depend on the situation (e.g. even-aged plantations vs. complex natural forests) but Hatton *et al.* (1995) demonstrated that four out of five different scalars performed satisfactorily for scaling up water use in a *Eucalyptus populnea* woodland in Australia.

In contrast to the number of studies dealing with spatial aspects of scaling, there are comparatively few investigations of the temporal aspects of scaling (Wullschleger *et al.* 1998). Hatton and Wu (1995) addressed this problem in various eucalypt woodlands and found that water use of individual trees was linearly related to leaf area during periods of abundant soil water, but that the relationship broke down during periods of water stress.

Not only did large trees take up proportionately less water per unit leaf area than small trees under such conditions but also the shape of the relationship appeared to depend on soil water content and time of year, indicating that scalars like leaf area may exhibit strong short-term temporal dependence because of the possible occurrence of soil water stress.

However, similar problems may also arise in areas where water stress is uncommon. Vertessy *et al.* (1995, 1997) derived rather contrasting relationships between tree water use and stem diameter for 15-year-old and 57-year-old stands of mountain ash *(Eucalyptus regnans).* Haydon *et al.* (1996) circumvented the long-term temporal dependence of stem diameter as a scalar by using tree sapwood area instead. Other long-term changes in forest water use may be related to the development or disappearance of understorey vegetation.

In contrast to the wet canopy component of total evapotranspiration (rainfall interception, E_i), annual totals of evaporation from a dry canopy (transpiration, E_t) show comparatively little variation between species and sites within a given climatic zone. For example, Roberts (1999) lists results for 13 deciduous and seven coniferous stands in western Europe, together representing 29 years of observations. Leaving aside for the moment the high values obtained for three broadleaved and coniferous forests in southern England (possibly reflecting overestimates related to the methodologies used; cf. Jarvis & McNaughton 1986) and one excessively low value related to drought, but adding estimates for Austrian pine, Scots pine and Douglas fir in The Netherlands (Mulder 1983; Tiktak & Bouten 1984; Elbers *et al.* 1996), yields an average of 303 + 37 (range 240-360) mm year^{-1} for the E_t of deciduous forests and 334 + 37 (range 280-360) mm year^{-1} for conifers. Roberts (1999) ascribed the surprisingly similar E_t for deciduous and evergreen species of varying age and growing on different soils to three main factors: (i) the frequently observed positive correlation between atmospheric VPD and stom-atal/surface resistance; (ii) the relative insensitiv-ity of E_t to soil water availability; and (iii) the compensatory effects of the presence or absence of understorey vegetation. The respective factors are discussed briefly below.

A distinct response in stomatal/surface resistance to increases in VPD has been observed in vegetation types as diverse as northern conifers (Tan & Black 1976; Lindroth 1985) and tropical rain forests (Shuttleworth 1988; Meinzer *et al.* 1993). Coastal species seem to be more sensitive to changes in VPD than continental species, possibly because they are adapted to maritime conditions with relatively low vapour deficits (Whitehead & Jarvis 1981). Also, conifers have been reported to be more sensitive to changes in VPD than broadleaved species (at least in the Pacific North-west region of the USA), although this was to some extent compensated by a greater sensitivity of the latter to soil water deficits (Marshall & Waring 1984).

Although the precise underlying mechanism is as yet unclear (Grantz 1990; Meinzer *et al.* 1993, 1997a,b), the strong feedback response between r_s and VPD results in a significant dampening of instantaneous transpiration rates to the extent that daily totals typically remain below 4 mm in most humid climates (both temperate and tropical), even though potential evaporative demands by the atmosphere may be much higher (Roberts 1983; Granier *et al.* 1996). On a related note, Federer (1977) showed that stomatal resistances in five broadleaved deciduous species from the north-eastern USA increased more rapidly with increasing VPD when initial values of r_{sto} were low and vice versa. Roberts (1999) suggested that, as a result, values of stomatal resistance and instantaneous leaf transpiration rates for the respective species could be much more similar under conditions of intermediate ('typical') VPDs than would be expected on the basis of the contrasts in minimum resistances alone.

This in turn might constitute another reason for the similarity in E_t between species noted above. However, it is inconsistent with the considerable reductions in streamflow (up to 100 mm annually) accompanying a shift in forest composition from a dominance by (mature) maple and beech (having relatively high r_s) to pin cherry and birch (pioneer species with relatively low r_s) following clearcutting and regrowth in the same area (Hornbeck *et al.* 1993; cf. section 12.7.3).

Although most vegetation types exhibit similar increases in r_s in response to increases in VPD (Grantz 1990), there are notable exceptions. Poplars grown in a short-rotation coppice system in the UK have been reported to maintain low values of r_s and high transpiration despite increased humidity deficits as long as soil water was not limiting (Hall & Allen 1997; cf. Meinzer *et al.* 1997b). Similarly, Elbers *et al.* (1996) obtained an annual value of about 510 mm for the E_t of a poplar stand with a high groundwater table in The Netherlands, i.e. well above the 300 mm derived earlier for temperate broadleaved species in western Europe. Plantations of *Eucalyptus camaldulensis* and *E. tereticornis* in southern India exhibited similar behaviour (with transpiration values of up to 6 mm daily) when unrestricted by soil water deficits at the end of the monsoon.

However, values fell off to 1 mm daily upon reaching low soil water contents during the subsequent long dry season (Robert & Rosier 1993). Because of this regulating mechanism, the annual water use of the eucalypt plantations on soils of intermediate depth (=3 m) was not significantly different from that of indigenous dry deciduous forest (Calder *et al.* 1992). On deep soils (>8m) the annual water use of the eucalypts exceeded annual rainfall considerably, suggesting 'mining' of soil water reserves that had accumulated previously in deeper layers during years of above-average rainfall. Moreover, the rate of root penetration was shown to be at least as rapid as 2.5 m annually and roughly equalled above-ground increases in height (Calder *et al.* 1997). Similar observations have been made below *Eucalyptus grandis* in South Africa (Dye 1996).

It is pertinent that Viswanatham *et al.* (1982) observed strong decreases in streamflow after coppicing *E. camaldulensis* in northern India. Together, these findings confirm earlier contentions in the popular environmental literature that eucalypts can be 'voracious consumers of water' (Vandanashiva & Bandyopadhyay 1983). Planting of eucalypts, particularly in subhumid climates, should therefore be based on judicious planning.

Although soil water stress has been shown to have a marked effect on r_s and E_t in seasonal climates (Harding & Stewart 1986; Roberts & Rosier 1993; Hatton & Wu 1995), the modest transpiration rates effected by the r_s-VPD feedback mechanism referred to earlier normally imply that a substantial fraction of soil water reserves can be used before transpiration starts to level off due to increased stomatal resistance. A young eucalypt forest in southeastern Australia, the point at which transpiration becomes reduced tends to be reached earlier when rates of water uptake are high compared with during times of more modest uptake. Rutter (1968) presented a number of examples from the USA illustrating the same phenomenon. As such, critical soil water deficits affecting E_t will only be rarely attained in humid climates, and may therefore be expected to play only a minor role in generating differences between species and sites (Roberts 1983).

Finally, the contribution from the understorey (and to a lesser extent the litter layer) to stand transpiration constitutes a third mechanism through which differences between sites with strongly contrasting forest structures tend to be evened out. Transpiration totals for a dense forest with little to no undergrowth can be similar to those of open forests with much more vigorous understoreys (Roberts *et al.* 1982; Roberts & Rosier 1994; cf. Vertessy *et al.* 1998). Contributions by understories can indeed be substantial: Tan and Black (1976) showed how a salal *(Gaultheria shallon)* understorey of a Douglas fir forest in western Canada could account for up to 70% of the transpiration. Similarly, Roberts *et al.* (1980) reported that bracken fern *(Pteridium aquilinum)* below Scots pine in East Anglia, UK contributed up to 60% of forest transpiration during dry spells, whereas under normal conditions transpiration from the bracken still made up 25% of the total.

Further examples have been given by Black and Kelliher (1989).

A particularly powerful (and still underused) tool in the study of relative rates and sources of water uptake by the differently sized plants of the overstorey and understorey of a forest is stable isotope (8D, 8^{18}O) analysis (Jackson *et al.* 1995; Dawson 1996). For example, using naturally occurring contrasts in stable hydrogen isotope abundances in soil and groundwater below a sugar maple forest in the north-eastern USA, Dawson (1996) was able to demonstrate that the tallest trees drew their water from groundwater found at more than 3 m below a fragipan whereas smaller trees (whose roots were unable to reach the groundwater table) used soil water exclusively, except during two periods of drought stress. Interestingly, the 'groundwater' taken up by the younger trees during these drought periods had previously been lifted to the upper layers of the soil by the larger trees via a process known as 'hydraulic lift', i.e. the nocturnal uptake of water by roots from the subsoil and later released from shallow roots into the upper layers of the soil (Dawson 1993).

In contrast to the relative abundance of transpiration estimates for humid temperate forests (Roberts 1999), information on tropical rain forests is scarce and mostly based on indirect (water-budget) computations. For nine studies in lowland rain forests, Bruijnzeel (1990) derived an average annual E_t of 1045 mm (range 885-1285 mm). For montane rain forests with limited to negligible cloud incidence, Bruijnzeel (1990, 2000) reported annual values of 510-895mm (n = 8) compared with 255-315mm for montane cloud forests. There are very few direct estimates of long-term water uptake by tropical forests, be it for natural forests (Shuttleworth 1988; Roberts *et al.* 1993; cf. Granier *et al.* 1996) or plantations (Waterloo *et al.* 1999; cf. Bruijnzeel 1997).

Transpiration modelling

With the incorporation of a physiological control (represented by the surface resistance term r_s) in the energy balance cum aerodynamic transport combination equation of Penman (1948), Mon-teith (1965) established an effective framework for the quantification of evaporation from any (vegetated) surface.

Unlike evaporation from a wet vegetation, which under given weather conditions is largely controlled by the aerodynamic resistance of the vegetation (r_a), transpiration (evaporation from a dry canopy) is chiefly governed by the magnitude of r_s, which in turn is influenced by a range of environmental and plant variables, including solar radiation, leaf area, leaf temperature and leaf water potential, as well as atmospheric VPD and soil water deficit (Stewart 1988; Shuttleworth 1989). Canopy conductance g_c (i.e. the reciprocal of r_s) increases with increasing light intensity and temperature (up to a maximum value) and decreases with increasing atmospheric humidity deficit and (as mentioned in the previous section, after exceeding a threshold value) soil water deficit. Various, increasingly complex, submodels have been developed to describe the behaviour of r_s in response to ambient environmental conditions. However, field application of such models is often hampered by their need for highly detailed input data (Whitehead 1998).

TOTAL EVAPOTRANSPIRATION

Although it is beyond the scope of the present process-orientated chapter to discuss amounts of total evapotranspiration *(ET)* associated with different forest types and climatic zones, it can be concluded from the previous sections that changes in the interception component of evaporation (E_i) will be much more pronounced than those of the transpiration component ($£_t$). Taking western Europe as an example, annual totals of E_t were shown to be quite similar for deciduous and coniferous forests over a wide range of soil and rainfall conditions (reported range 240-360mm).

It is of interest to examine whether a similar contrast between variations in E_i and E_t also exists in the humid tropics where radiation loads, average temperatures and rainfall are all higher than in the temperate zone. In a survey of (mostly catchment) water budget studies in lowland tropical rain forests, Bruijnzeel (1990) encountered such large variations in annual *ET* that he was unable to detect any systematic differences between the main rain forest blocks of South-East Asia, Amazonia and West Africa. He suggested an average annual value of about 1400 mm for forests not subject to significant water stress, ascribing annual *ET* totals well above 1500 mm generally to catchment leakage rather than to specific climatic conditions favouring high evaporation (cf. Richardson 1982). More recently, Schellekens *et al.* (2000) combined amounts of *ET* and E_i as measured in 14 lowland tropical rain forests and derived approximate estimates of E_t by subtracting E_i from *ET* when direct measurements of E_t were lacking.

HYDROLOGICAL EFFECTS OF FOREST MANIPULATION

Within the limitations imposed by flow measuring techniques, the practical overall influence exerted by forests on hydrological processes is most clearly illustrated through comparison of streamflow amounts emanating from areas with contrasting proportions or types of forest. Because of the complications related to local climatic contrasts (rainfall, exposure to radiation and air streams) and ungauged subterranean transfers of water from one catchment to another, such direct comparison of results obtained for catchments with contrasting covers can be problematic (Lee 1970).

The classical answer to these problems has been the paired catchment approach in which streamflows from two (often adjacent) catchments of comparable geology, exposition and vegetation are expressed in terms of each other (using regression analysis) during a 'calibration phase'. Once a good calibration relationship has been established, one of the catchments is subjected to manipulation of its cover (e.g. strip cutting, clearfelling or afforestation) while the other remains undisturbed as a 'control'. Throughout this 'treatment' or 'experimental' phase, streamflow continues to be monitored and any effects of the treatment are evaluated by comparing actually measured flows from the manipulated catchment with those predicted by inserting the flows from the control catchment into the calibration relationship (Hewlett & Fortson 1983).

Although a more rigorous comparison between catchments is obtained in this way, an underlying assumption is that differences in leakage between the two catchments remain unchanged with time, regardless of catchment cover status. Also, to avoid overstretching of the calibration statistics during the treatment phase to accommodate extremes in streamflow resulting from excessive rainfall or drought, it is important that the calibration period includes sufficient variation in rainfall (Hornbeck 1973; Lesch & Scott 1997).

This, of course, renders the paired catchment method a time-consuming (>5-10 years) and expensive affair. In addition, the method is essentially a black-box technique requiring additional process research to reveal the relative importance of different causative factors to explain the obtained results (Lesch & Scott 1997). All this, plus the limited resolution afforded by the paired catchment approach (usually more than 20% cover change is required for effects on streamflow to be detectable), has led to a general decline in the number of such studies in the last two decades and a gradually greater emphasis on physically based modelling.

In the following sections the hydrological effects of:

(i) forest manipulation (thinning, selective logging, undergrowth or riparian vegetation removal, clearcutting followed by regrowth or conversion to other land uses) and

(ii) (re)forestation are reviewed from the experimental manipulation and modelling perspectives.

Effects of forest thinning on rainfall interception

It has long been recognized that amounts of throughfall tend to be inversely related to the stocking of a forest, be it in the context of thinning or logging operations (Wilm & Dunford 1948; Rogerson 1967; Teoh 1977; Aussenac *et al.* 1982; Teklehaimanot *et al.* 1991; Asdak *et al.* 1998) or forest age (Delfs 1955; Helvey 1967; cf. Haydon *et al.* 1996). However, the steady increase in rainfall interception with age observed for coniferous forests (Delfs 1955; Helvey 1967) is not paralleled in deciduous forest. Helvey and Patric (1965) reported that E_i in 11-year-old oak coppice in the south-eastern USA did not differ from that observed in 30-year-old and 50-year-old mixed poplar-hickory forests in the same area.

Apparently, the oak coppice had already acquired leaf biomass and roughness characteristics similar to those of the much older forests. As indicated earlier, interception by deciduous forests during the dormant season is lower than during the growing season. Usually, an increase in throughfall of 5-10% occurs during winter (Helvey & Patric 1965). This increase is by no means proportional to the reduction in LAI, which can be up to sixfold (Monk & Day 1988). Similarly, the observed decrease in rainfall interception following forest thinning is often not commensurate with the degree of canopy opening. For example, a 50% reduction in basal area of a Douglas fir forest in France resulted in only a 13% drop in E_i (Aussenac *et al.* 1982). An even smaller effect was noticed in a regenerating eucalypt forest in south-eastern Australia, where E_i was reduced by as little as 4% following a uniform thinning operation that removed 50% of the overstorey biomass (Jayasurya *et al.* 1993).

Likewise, a 13-fold reduction in basal area (corresponding to a change in planting interval from 2 x 2 m to 8 x 8 m) in a dense Sitka spruce plantation in Scotland was accompanied by only a 3.7-fold reduction in E_i (Teklehaimanot *et al.* 1991) who explained this phenomenon not so much in terms of decreases in canopy cover *per se* but rather as a function of a gradually decreasing turbulent exchange between the trees and the surrounding air after opening up the canopy.

Evidence for this contention came from a strong negative correlation between rainfall interception and aerodynamic resistance (r_a), with r_a increasing linearly as the spacing between the trees increased up to 8 x 8m (Teklehaimanot *et al.* 1991; cf. Gash *et al.* 1995, 1999).

Research results from the humid tropics largely confirm the above findings. Veracion and Lopez (1976) and Florido and Saplaco (1981) found negligible increases in throughfall after thinning 30-50% of the biomass of 10-15-year-old and 30-year-old natural pine forests in the Philippines.

Significant increases were obtained only after 70% of the trees had been removed. Ghosh *et al.* (1980) applied a 20% thinning treatment to a broadleaved *(Shorea robusta)* forest in northern India and found that throughfall increased from 72 to 81%. However, because of a concurrent reduction in stemflow of about 4% (and not necesssarily related to the thinning), the overall change in intercepted rainfall was a modest 5%.

Recently, Asdak *et al.* (1998) compared rainfall interception from undisturbed and heavily logged lowland rain forest plots in central Kalimantan, Indonesia. Interception from the logged forest was 6% of gross rainfall compared with 11% in the unlogged forest. However, because the comparison did not pertain to the same forest before and after logging, it is not possible to assess to what extent the observed reduction in E_i reflects the change in canopy cover or pre-existing structural differences between the two stands (cf. Lloyd & Marques 1988).

Effects of thinning and selective logging on transpiration and water yield

Whilst the effect of thinning on E_i is rather limited, effects on soil water (and ultimately streamflow) are even smaller. Opening up of a stand not only enhances the penetration of radiation to the understorey vegetation and the forest floor, but also the remaining vegetation will start competing for the extra moisture supplied by the initially increased throughfall (Aussenac *et al.* 1982; Stogsdill *et al.* 1992). The magnitude and the duration of such effects will differ among locations, depending on the vigour of overstorey and understorey vegetation, climatic conditions (including site exposure) and the configuration of the cutting.

No changes were detected in the streamflow from a deciduous hardwood forest catchment of south-easterly exposure at Coweeta (southeastern USA) after selective logging removed 27% of the basal area; only a 4.3% increase occurred after a 53% selective cut. Also, removing the entire understorey (representing 22% of forest basal area) from a 28-ha catchment of northwesterly exposure in the same area produced an equally modest change (Johnson & Kovner 1956). Similarly, in a Douglas fir forest on the west coast of Canada where substantial soil water deficits develop over the summer, Black *et al.* (1980) observed 'remarkably similar' transpiration rates for unthinned stands with little or no salal *(Gaultheria shallon)* undergrowth and thinned stands with a well-developed understorey. In a related study, Kelliher *et al.* (1986) reported that following removal of the salal transpiration by the Douglas fir trees increased by 30-50%, with the greatest increases noted for the plots where the leaf biomass of the salal had been highest.

The overall effect of the removal of the undergrowth on soil water content was therefore a mere 1-3% increase (cf. Adams *et al.* 1991). In the northern UK, Whitehead *et al.* (1984) compared the transpiration patterns of two 40-year-old Scots pine plantations of similar average height but with a more than fivefold difference in stocking. Transpiration in the widely spaced plantation averaged 67% of that of the denser stand, reflecting differences in canopy resistance and LAI at stand level. However, relative transpiration rates *per tree* were 3.3 times higher in the thinned plot and were intermediate in magnitude between the relative increases in average basal sapwood area per tree (2.9 times) and leaf area per tree (4.2 times), compared with the unthinned stand.

Therefore, although the thinned plantation had not re-equilibrated completely to prethinning conditions at the time of the measurements, the clear increases in leaf and sapwood areas of the remaining trees could be seen as representing a tendency towards complete re-equilibration following a set of homeostatic relationships aimed at maximum site utilization (Whitehead *et al.* 1984). Lesch and Scott (1997) described an extreme case from South Africa where the rate of growth of young *Eucalyptus grandis* trees under seasonal rainfall conditions was such that any positive effects on streamflow of three rounds of thinning (46, 34 and 50% at age 3, 5 and 8 years) were masked entirely by the steady reduction in flows resulting from the overall vigorous growth of the trees.

Working under wet tropical conditions, Gilmour (1977) was unable to detect any changes in streamflow after 'lightly' logging a rain forest in northern Queensland, Australia. More substantial timber extractions from hill rain forest in Peninsular Malaysia, equivalent to the removal of 33 and 40% of the commercial stocking, affected overall water yield positively, with increases of 40 and 70% respectively. However, during a 7-year postlogging observation period there was no sign of a decline in the streamflow gain, suggesting that the regrowth in the gaps created by logging remained well below that of the remainder of the forest (Abdul Rahim & Zulkifli Yusop 1994).

This result is contrary to expectation in that soil water levels in gaps, although initially higher than in the surrounding undisturbed forest, tend to decline very rapidly as the regrowth is reestablished. Such findings illustrate the limitations of paired catchment studies if these are not complemented by detailed process studies (cf. Bruijnzeel 1996; Vertessy *et al.* 1998).

The influence of the configuration of the cutting on the magnitude and duration of any increases in flow has been investigated in some detail in the eastern USA.

The removal of 24% of the basal area from catchment LR2 at Leading Ridge (Pennsylvania) incurred a nearly twofold larger increase in flow than cutting 33% on catchment HB4 at Hubbard Brook (New Hampshire) or catchment FEF2 at Fernow Experimental Forest (West Virginia). The cutting at Leading Ridge consisted of a single block on the lowest portion of the catchment, whereas the cutting at Hubbard Brook took the form of a series of strips situated halfway up the catchment, and that at Fernow Experimental Forest involved harvesting trees from all over the catchment (Hornbeck *et al.* 1993). Therefore, increases in streamflow associated with strip cutting are smaller than for single blocks, which is in line with the idea of increased transpiration by surrounding trees upon opening up of the canopy (Stogsdill *et al.* 1992). No significant differences were found between the cutting *en bloc* of the upper half of a catchment (such as Catchment 7 at Fernow) or the lower half (catchment FEF6) (Hornbeck *et al.* 1993).

Of particular interest to water managers is the role of riparian vegetation which, in contrast to trees growing further upslope, generally has ready access to the groundwater table. Elimination of the riparian vegetation at Coweeta produced a decrease in diurnal fluctuations of baseflow, although the associated increase in water yield was not greater than that associated with the removal of an equal area of forest elsewhere in the catchment (Dunford & Fletcher 1947; cf. the similarity in results for catchments FEF 6 and 7).

Apparently, the riparian effect is negligible in areas where soil moisture remains readily available in all parts of the catchment, such as at Coweeta with its well-distributed rainfall.

A similar result was obtained for a catchment with deep soils in the summer-rainfall zone of South Africa (Smith & Bosch 1989; Scott & Lesch 1996), but not for an area in the winter-rainfall zone where streamflow gains after cutting pine trees in the riparian zone exceeded those associated with the harvesting of pines away from the stream by 30% (Dye & Poulter 1995).

Effect of forest clearfelling on water yield

A basic summary of short-term results obtained from paired catchment experiments conducted before 1980 was given by Bosch and Hewlett (1982). Hornbeck *et al.* (1993) and Swank *et al.* (1988) discussed longer-term results, including the effects of multiple treatments, for catchments in the north-eastern and south-eastern USA respectively. Generally, increases in water yield during the first year after treatment are roughly proportional to percentage reductions in stand basal area, provided the latter exceed a threshold of 20-25%. Bosch and Hewlett (1982) made a distinction between coniferous and deciduous hardwood forests, suggesting that increases in flow associated with the cutting of conifers were higher (40mm per 10% change in cover) than for hardwoods (25 mm per 10% change in cover).

However, the scatter around the two tentative regression lines was large, coefficients of determination modest (at 42% and 26% respectively) and no confidence limits were provided. In a later analysis of the same dataset plus an additional 50 studies (mostly from the tropics and Australia), Sahin and Hall (1996) used fuzzy linear regression analysis and obtained the following average changes in flow per 10% change in cover: conifers, 23mm; mixed hardwoods-conifers, 22mm; and hardwoods, 17-19 mm (depending whether annual precipitation exceeded 1500mm or not). Based on this fuzzy regression approach, the overall differences between the respective vegetation groups were therefore smaller than suggested earlier by Bosch and Hewlett (1982). Stednick (1996) approached the problem of the heterogeneity in results for 95 paired catchment studies from the USA by deriving separate regression equations for each of eight geographically homogeneous regions.

In doing so, a clearer picture was obtained of the regional variation in yield increases, which ranged from about 10mm per 10% change in cover in the Rocky Mountains to over 60mm in the Central Plains. Also, some of the regionally applicable regression equations had substantially higher coefficients of determination (e.g. 0.65 for the Pacific Northwest or Appalachia, which both had the largest number of experiments), although correlations for other regions were extremely low (e.g. 0.01 for the Rocky Mountains). As such, there is something to say for the approach of Trimble *et al.* (1987) who simply pooled the coniferous and mixed hardwood data of Bosch and Hewlett (1982) and added 10 data points of their own, representing reductions in annual flow from large non-experimental ('real world') catchment areas in the Piedmont of the south-eastern USA that had undergone 10-28% reforestation.

The overall coefficient of determination for the combined dataset attained the reasonable value of 0.50 by the inclusion of the Piedmont subset, with 8 of 10 data points from the latter falling within half the standard error of the estimate (compared with only 22 of 55 data points in the Bosch and Hewlett set). This finding is all the more remarkable because half the additional data involved a change in cover of less than 20%, a value below which Bosch and Hewlett (1982) had considered effects on streamflow to be more or less non-detectable (at least on small headwater streams).

Apart from contrasts in tree species and age of the vegetation (see below), much of the variability in the change in stream-flow observed for different sites and years after a change in cover relates to differences in climate, catchment exposure and soil depth. The climatic aspect is aptly summarized by the classic statement of Hewlett (1966) that 'it takes water to fetch water' (cf. Stednick 1996; Bruijnzeel 1990).

The importance of catchment exposure is illustrated by the difference in first-year streamflow gain after cutting differently exposed deciduous hardwood forest catchments at Coweeta in the south-eastern USA.

Flows from northerly exposed catchments increased by about 130mmyear^{-1} but increases from southerly exposed catchments could be as high as 410mm year^{-1} (Swank *et al.* 1988). As for the effect of soil depth, Trimble *et al.* (1963), when discussing differences in duration of the changes in streamflow following forest clearing in West Virginia, stated that 'the deeper the soil, the longer it takes roots of new growth or the expanding root systems of residual plants to occupy the soil mantle. When the soil mantle is reoccupied, transpiration reaches maximum levels again, and increases in streamflow disappear'. The role of soil depth can be illustrated further by examining the timing of the maximum and minimum increases in flow after forest clearance during the year. At Coweeta, where precipitation is distributed evenly over the year and the loamy soils are deep (up to 6 m) and capable of storing large amounts of moisture, the soil does not become fully recharged until early spring (April-May).

As a result, the presence or absence of a forest has little effect on the amounts of flow during this time of year (the soils being full of water anyway). However, at the onset of the growing season, increased flow due to reduced water use after clearcutting becomes evident and the contrast in streamflow from forested and cleared areas increases as the growing season advances. The effect continues well into the winter months (November-January), even though the trees have lost their leaves by then and evaporation is strongly reduced. This reflects the development of a much larger soil water deficit below the forest during the summer that takes an additional 2 months (February-March) to be refilled by the winter rains. Conversely, on catchments with shallower or sandier soils (having less water storage and a lower water retention capacity), soil water recharge and depletion occurs much more rapidly and increases in flow after forest clearance follow the pattern of forest water use much more closely (Hornbeck *et al.* 1970).

The effect of the timing of the cutting and the importance of controlling regrowth are demonstrated by a comparison of the results obtained for catchments 2 and 5 at Hubbard Brook (HB 2 and HB 5). On catchment HB 2, the forest was clearcut during the dormant season and regrowth eliminated by herbicide application the following spring. This produced a first-year increase in water yield of 347 mm. In contrast, on catchment HB 5, the removal of the trees took nearly a full year, while regrowth was not suppressed.

The resulting first-year increase in flow thus amounted to only 152 mm, or 44% of that observed for catchment HB 2. In addition, the gain in streamflow had largely disappeared after 3 years (Hornbeck *et al.* 1970, 1993). Such contrasting findings once more illustrate the effect of regenerating vegetation on soil water levels and stream-flow (cf. Adams *et al.* 1991). However, it should be noted that regeneration was particularly vigorous in the example from Hubbard Brook as it took place mainly via sprouting. As demonstrated by comparative work in West Virginia, elevated streamflow levels lasted much longer (15-20 years) when regeneration had to originate from seeds because of previous herbicide applications than when sprouting was allowed (6-7 years) (Hornbeck *et al.* 1993).

Similarly, when a regenerating hardwood forest at Coweeta was cut a second time after 23 years (when streamflow was still about 80mmyear^{-1} above that observed for mature mixed forest), the initial increase in water yield was nearly identical to that of the first cut (375 vs. 362mm). However, the subsequent decline in (extra) water yield was distinctly faster. The difference was attributable to a more rapid recovery of stand biomass during the second regeneration period in association with the greater sprouting potential of the even-aged forest, which contained numerous small stems prior to the second cut (Swank *et al.* 1988). As a result, the (projected) total duration of the second period of increased flows was estimated to be 18 years shorter than that associated with the first cutting (estimated at about 35 years). Such long durations reflect the time required by the roots to reoccupy the very deep soils at Coweeta compared with those of the north-eastern USA where effects are more likely to last 3-9 years (Swank *et al.* 1988; Hornbeck *et al.* 1993; cf. Trimble *et al.* 1963).

A rather different pattern of changes in forest water use and streamflow with time after clearing has been documented for native mountain ash *(Eucalyptus regnans)* forest in south-eastern Australia (Haydon *et al.* 1996; Vertessy *et al.* 1998). Following clearing and burning, there is an initial rise in streamflow lasting 4-6 years. This is followed by a rapid decrease in flows until the regrowth is about 27 years old, after which run-off totals slowly return to predisturbance levels. The latter may take as long as 150 years. Vertessy *et al.* (1998) provided a mechanistic explanation for this long-term pattern in terms of concurrent changes in overstorey and understorey leaf biomass and transpiration rates, as well as changes in rainfall interception and evaporation from the forest floor.

Results from paired catchment experiments in the humid tropics also show a proportionality in flow increase with percentage of forest removed, as observed under humid temperate conditions. Reported first-year increases after clearfelling range from 125 mm in Nigeria to 820 mm in Peninsular Malaysia (Bruijnzeel 1990) and show little relation to amounts of precipitation.

This led Bruijnzeel (1996) to suggest that perhaps the results were determined more by the degree of surface disturbance than by climatic or soil factors (cf. Malmer 1993; Van der Plas & Bruijnzeel 1993). However, in view of the large variability in total evapotranspiration among tropical forests, it may be rewarding to reanalyse the data in the light of contrasts in rainfall interception between regions as well.

Effects of converting natural forest to other land cover types on water yield

Whilst streamflow totals are observed to eventually return to preclearing levels where regrowth is allowed, the conversion of native forest to other types of vegetation cover may produce permanent changes. For example, permanent increases in annual water yield are associated with the conversion of deciduous or evergreen native forest to agricultural cropping. Reported increases range from 60-125 mm $year^{-1}$ under humid warm temperate conditions (Johnson & Kovner 1956) to 450mmyear–[1] in the equatorial tropics (Edwards 1979). The diminished water use of annual crops compared with that of a full-grown forest reflects the diminished capacity of low vegetation not only to intercept rainfall but also to extract water from deeper soil layers during periods of drought.

The former relates primarily to the lesser aerodynamic roughness of short annual crops (and possibly to their smaller leaf area and thus storage capacity as well), whereas the reduced water uptake of crops reflects their more limited rooting depth (Calder 1982). For the same reasons, conversion to pasture generally produces permanent increases in streamflow as well, although the magnitude of the increase depends on precipitation patterns and elevation (Holmes & Sinclair 1986). Interestingly, Hibbert (1969) noted that replacing deciduous hardwood forest in the south-eastern USA by vigorously growing *Festuca* grass did not lead to increased water yields, although increases of up to 125 mm $year^{-1}$ were observed after the productivity of the grass declined.

Such results can be explained in part by the fact that serious water shortages that could have reduced water uptake by shallow-rooted plants do not develop in the rainy climate at Coweeta, whereas in addition the contrast between forest and grass was lessened further by the deciduous character of the forest (cf. Swank *et al.* 1988). In contrast, the conversion of mixed deciduous hardwoods by eastern white pine *(Pinus strobus)* in the same area brought about a reduction of 250mmyear–[1] after 25 years.

The decline in flow was ascribed both to a steady increase in intercepted rainfall as the pines grew older and to higher transpiration by the evergreen pine trees during the dormant season (Swank *et al.* 1988). Similarly, the higher total water use *(ET)* of mature *Pinus radiata* plantations in south-eastern Australia compared with that of native eucalypt forest has been explained in terms of the distinctly higher rainfall interception by the pines (Dunin & Mackay 1982; Pilgrim *et al.* 1982). However, where pine plantations replaced non-deciduous native forests elsewhere in the world, streamflows have been reported to return to preconversion levels within 8 years, such as in Kenya (Blackie 1979) and New Zealand (Rowe & Pearce 1994; Fahey & Jackson 1997).

The results presented thus far pertain mostly to small headwater catchment areas involving a unilateral change in cover. Although these experiments provide a clear and consistent picture of increased water yield after replacing tall vegetation by a shorter one, and *vice versa,* such effects are more difficult to discern in large river basins having a variety of land-use types and temporal changes therein. In addition, there are the complications associated with strong spatial and temporal variability in rainfall, especially in tropical areas with largely convective rainfall, and the often large-scale withdrawals of water for municipal, agricultural and industrial purposes in populated areas. Qian (1983) was unable to detect any systematic changes in streamflow from catchments ranging in size from 7 to 727km^2 on the island of Hainan, southern China despite a 30% reduction in tall forest cover over three decades. Dyhr-Nielsen (1986) arrived at the same conclusion for the 14 500 km^2 Pasak River basin in northern Thailand, which lost 50% of its tall forest cover between 1955 and 1980.

On the other hand, Madduma Bandara and Kurupuarachchi (1988) observed an increase in averaged annual flow totals for the 1100 km^2 upper Mahaweli catchment in Sri Lanka over the period 1940-80, despite a weak negative trend in rainfall over the same period. Although both trends were not statistically significant at the 95% level, the associated increase in annual run-off ratios was highly significant.

The increased hydrological response was ascribed to the widespread conversion of tea plantations (not forest) to annual cropping and home gardens without appropriate soil conservation measures (Madduma Bandara and Kurupuarachchi 1988).

However, when analysing a longer time series (1940-97) for the 380 km^2 upper Nilwala catchment in Sri Lanka, which experienced a 35% reduction in forest cover during the observation period, a less consistent picture was obtained (Elkaduwa & Sakthivadivel 1999). Such contrasting findings illustrate the need for high-quality rainfall and streamflow data in historical hydrological data analyses, not only in the context of evaluating the effects of land-use transformations but also those associated with climatic change.

Effects of forest clearing on streamflow regimes

In areas with seasonal rainfall, the distribution of streamflow throughout the year is often of greater importance than the total annual amount *per se*. Reports of greatly diminished streamflows during the dry season after forest clearance abound in the literature, particularly in the tropics (see examples in Hamilton & King 1983; Bruijnzeel 1990). At first sight, this seems to contradict the evidence presented earlier, that forest removal leads to higher water yields, even more so because the bulk of the increase in flow after *experimental* clearing is observed during baseflow or dry-season conditions (Bosch & Hewlett 1982; Bruijnzeel 1990). However, the controlled conditions imposed during catchment experiments differ from those encountered in many real-world situations.

The continued exposure of bare soil after forest clearance to intense rainfall (Lal 1987), the compaction of topsoil by machinery (Malmer 1993; Van der Plas & Bruijnzeel 1993) or overgrazing (Gilmour *et al.* 1987), the gradual disappearance of soil faunal activity (Aina 1984) and increases in the area occupied by impervious surfaces such as roads and settlements (Ziegler & Giambelluca 1997) all contribute to gradually reduced rainfall infiltration opportunities in cleared areas. As a result, catchment response to rainfall becomes more pronounced and the increases in storm runoff during the rainy season may become so large as to seriously impair the recharging of soil water and groundwater reserves.

When this critical stage is reached, diminished dry-season flow is the result, despite the fact that the removal of the forest has led to reduced evaporation and thus should have induced higher baseflows. On the other hand, if the surface characteristics after forest clearing are maintained sufficiently to allow the continued infiltration of (most of) the rainfall, then the effect of reduced *ET* associated with forest removal will show up as increased dry-season flow. This could be achieved through the establishment of a well-planned and maintained road system plus the careful extraction of timber in the case of logging operations (cf. Bruijnzeel 1992; Dykstra 1994), and by applying appropriate soil conservation measures (Young 1989; Hudson 1995) when clearing for agricultural purposes.

However, even with minimum soil disturbance, there will be local increases in stormflow volumes and peak flows after forest removal because the associated reduction in *ET* causes the soil to be wetter and thus more responsive to rainfall. Relative increases in stormflow response associated with minimum disturbance operations are largest for small events (up to 300%), declining to less than 10% for large events (Gilmour 1977; Pearce *et al.* 1980b; Hewlett & Doss 1984), although the effect will be more pronounced if soil disturbance is severe (Swindel *et al.* 1983; Malmer 1993).

Also, whilst increases in stormflow response after (well-conducted) forestry operations tend to diminish or disappear altogether as the new vegetation cover becomes established (Swindel *et al.* 1983; Hsia 1987; Fritsch 1993; Fahey & Jackson 1997), they also may become structural. Examples include run-off contributions from roads or residential areas where there were none before (Ziegler & Giambelluca 1997) and permanently wetter soil conditions associated with reduced water use (e.g. grassland; Fritsch 1993). However, it is important to remember that caution is required when trying to extrapolate the undoubtedly adverse effects of indiscriminate forest clearing on local infiltration opportunities and storm run-off generation over large river basins (see Hewlett 1982 and Bruijnzeel 1990 for a fuller discussion).

Hydrological effects of (re)forestation

In response to the widely observed degradation of formerly forested land and the rising demands for industrial wood and fuelwood, the need for large-scale reforestation programmes has been expressed repeatedly (e.g. FAO 1986; Postel & Heise 1988). It is of interest therefore to examine to what extent such plantations are capable of restoring the original hydrological conditions, i.e. ameliorate peak flows and, above all, enhance low flows. Whilst there is little doubt that annual water yields from forested areas are reduced compared with those for non-forested areas, it must be granted that almost no catchment forestation experiments have been carried out on seriously degraded land.

As such, it could be argued that the clear reductions in total and dry-season flows observed after afforesting natural grasslands and scrublands or pasture in South Africa (Dye 1996; Scott & Smith 1997), New Zealand (Dons 1986; Fahey & Jackson 1997), south-eastern Australia (Holmes & Sinclair 1986) and Fiji (Waterloo *et al.* 1999) only serve to demonstrate the difference in water use between the two vegetation types. In other words, the potentially beneficial effects on streamflow afforded by improved infiltration and soil water retention capacities during forest development could not become manifest in these experiments. The key question is therefore whether the reductions in storm run-off generating overland flow incurred by such soil physical improvements can be sufficiently large to compensate the extra water use by the new forest, and so (theoretically) boost low flows (Bruijnzeel 1989).

There is no easy answer to this question for several reasons. First, the effect of an increase in topsoil infiltrability on the frequency of occurrence of HOF depends equally on prevailing rainfall intensities.

For instance, rainfall intensities in the Middle Hills of Nepal were generally so low that the 140mmh^{-1} increase in infiltration capacity 12 years after reforesting a degraded pasture site with *Pinus roxburghii* made no difference in the generation of HOF (Gilmour *et al.* 1987). Similarly, whilst topsoil infiltrabili-ties had roughly doubled over 12 years since reforesting *Imperata* grassland with teak in Sri Lanka, at 30mmh^{-1} the hydrological impact of this increase is probably limited (Mapa 1995). A much longer time span may be required therefore to restore infiltration capacities to the high values normally found in undisturbed forests.

Secondly, the reductions in catchment response to rainfall observed after forestation (Tennessee Valley Authority 1961; Fahey & Jackson 1997) may well reflect the drier soil conditions prevailing under actively growing forest rather than a reduction in peak-generating HOF (cf. Hsia 1987).

However, none of the studies documenting decreases or increases in stormflows after land-use change has attempted to quantify the associated changes in relative contributions by subsurface and overland flow types (Bruijnzeel 1990, 1996). Third, there is also the effect of soil depth, which determines both the maximum amount of water that can be stored in a catchment under optimum infiltration conditions and the possibilities for water uptake by the developing root network of the new trees (Trimble *et al.* 1963). And last but not least, there is the confounding effect of rainfall patterns (seasonal vs. well distributed) and general evaporative demand, which both exert a strong influence on tree water use.

Needless to say, the soil and climatic factors, plus the absence of detailed information on the prevailing stormflow mechanisms before and after the conversion, all render comparisons between different sites more complicated.

The only documented real-world case in which the kind of compensation mechanism supposed by Bruijnzeel (1989) seems to have occurred may be the White Hollow catchment in Tennessee, USA (Tennessee Valley Authority 1961).

Prior to improvement of its vegetation cover, two-thirds of this catchment consisted of mixed secondary forest in poor condition (due to fire, heavy logging and grazing), with another 26% under poor scrub. About 40% of the catchment was estimated to be subject to more or less severe erosion. Following extensive physical and vegetative restoration works, peak discharges decreased considerably within 2 years, especially in summer.

However, neither annual water yield nor low flows changed significantly over the next 22 years of forest recovery and reforestation. It was concluded that the extra water needed by the recovering and additionally planted trees was balanced by improved infiltration (Tennessee Valley Authority 1961). However, it is quite possible that the absence of major changes in total and low flows at White Hollow mainly reflects the lack of contrast between tall and short vegetation, as would have been the case when reforesting a truly deforested and degraded catchment.

Support for this contention comes from the observation of Trimble *et al.* (1987) that reductions in flow from several large river basins in the south-eastern USA, which had suffered considerable erosion before being partially reforested, were largest during dry years. In addition, the effect became more pronounced as the trees grew older.

A similar case was recently described for a once seriously degraded catchment in Slovenia (former Yugoslavia), where the spontaneous return of forest produced a steady reduction in annual water yield over a period of 30 years, with the strongest reductions again occurring during the dry summer months (Globevnik & Sovinc 1998).

Therefore, in both these real-world examples the water-use aspect overrides the infiltration aspect, despite the rather modest contrasts in water use between forest and grassland/cropland in the south-eastern USA.

Such findings offer little prospect for the possibility of significantly raising dry-season flows by forestation in the humid tropics. Observed maximum differences between annual water use of fast-growing pines or eucalypts and short vegetation (grass, crops) under well-watered (subtropical conditions attain values of 500-700 mm at the catchment scale and even higher values (> 1100 mm) on individual plots with particularly vigorous tree growth (Dye 1996; Waterloo *et al.* 1999).

The hydrological benefits incurred by the limited increases in topsoil infiltration capacities observed after forestation of degraded land in Nepal and Sri Lanka cited earlier are dwarfed by such high water requirements.

The conclusion that already diminished dry-season flows in degraded tropical areas will decrease even further upon reforestation seems inescapable.

In view of the extent of the low-flow problem, the testing of alternative ways of increasing water retention in tropical catchments without the excessive water use associated with exotic tree plantations should receive high priority (cf. Van Noordwijk *et al.* 1998).

Modelling the hydrological impacts of forest manipulation and land-use change

As shown in the preceding sections, different types of forest manipulations affect the water (and material) flows through catchments differently. Traditionally, foresters have relied on time-consuming paired catchment experiments to evaluate such effects. Whilst this approach enabled the construction of simple nomograms from which reductions in annual streamflow after afforestation could be read as a function of stand age and annual rainfall (Nänni 1970), or first-year increases in flow as a function of percentage basal area reduction and catchment aspect (Swank *et al.* 1988), the results were often so variable as to render their applicability for more detailed water resources planning rather limited (Bosch 1982). Afforestation with eucalypts produced similarly variable responses (curves 1 and 2) that also differed markedly from those for pine. The black-box nature of the paired catchment technique is unable to evaluate the relative importance of the various factors underlying such differences and this severely limits the possibilities for extrapolation of results to other areas or periods.

Process-based hydrological models represent an alternative way of predicting how catchments might respond to different forms of management. Because many practical forest management questions have a spatial dimension to them, and because landscapes usually comprise a complex mosaic of different land uses, such models should preferably be of a 'distributed' nature, i.e. capable of taking into account spatial variations in topography, soils, vegetation and climate (Vertessy *et ah,* 1993). During the last 10-15 years, considerable progress has been made in the modelling of forest hydrological and ecological processes over a range of spatial and temporal scales (e.g. Running & Coughlan 1988; Shuttleworth 1988; Hatton *et al.* 1992; Sivapalan *et al.* 1996; Vertessy *et al.* 1996; Watson *et al.* 1999).

Arguably, one of the most comprehensive process-based distributed models is the topography-driven TOPOG model (Vertessy *et al.* 1993). TOPOG integrates the water, carbon, solute and sediment balances at the small catchment scale (typically < 10 km^2) and is thus particularly useful for exploring complex feedback mechanisms between system properties.

Examples of within-catchment applications of TOPOG relevant to forestry include the prediction of steady-state soil moisture distributions and saturated zones in the landscape during wet and dry periods (O'Loughlin 1986; Moore *et al.* 1988), the spatial distribution of surface erosion, gully initiation and landslide hazards (Vertessy *et al.* 1990; Dietrich *et al.* 1992; Constantini *et al.* 1993), and the evaluation at the hillslope scale of the water balance and growth performance of different tree planting configurations (block planting vs. strip planting) under subhumid conditions (Silberstein *et al.* 1999).

Off-site applications of TOPOG include the successful simulation of changes in tree growth and water yield for a small catchment after clear-felling during 20 years of regeneration (Vertessy *et al.* 1996).

To address forestry-related questions of catchment water management at larger scales (e.g. 100-1000 km^2) as well, a simpler derivative of TOPOG (Macaque) has been developed recently. Macaque proved capable of effectively simulating the changes in water yield associated with the occurrence of a major wildfire (in 1939) and subsequent forest regeneration in a 163-km^2 catchment over an 82-year period (1911-92). It also enabled the prediction of the hydrological effect of the 1939 fires in a spatially explicit manner (Vertessy *et al.* 1998; Watson *et al.* 1999).

Models like TOPOG and Macaque constitute powerful tools whose predictions can help rational land-use decisions. However, whilst distributed models represent the only class of simulation models capable of capturing the complex feedbacks that occur upon disturbing hydrological systems, they are also data-demanding. Model outputs are especially sensitive to variations in LAI, soil hydraulic conductivity, the rainfall interception coefficient and canopy conductance, whereas at larger scales there is the problem of adequate spatial representation of rainfall inputs (Vertessy *et al.* 1998).

However, there is reason for optimism as various remote sensing technologies that are currently still in their infancy can be expected to become widely available within the next decade. This will greatly facilitate data acquisition and scaling-up of results.

OUTLOOK

As evidenced by the material collated in this chapter, considerable progress has been made since the mid 1960s in the conceptual understanding and mathematical description of such key forest hydrological processes as evaporation, from a wet canopy (rainfall interception) and from a dry canopy (transpiration) and including from sparse canopies.

Yet, the precise turbulent transfer mechanisms underlying the very high rates of wet canopy evaporation that have been observed under conditions of advected energy in maritime climates are not well understood. Neither do we know very much about the magnitude and hydro-logical significance of fog interception by the forests of montane cloud belts, particularly in the tropics. Furthermore, there are indications that low flows may be reduced considerably upon clearing such cloud forests (presumably due to the loss of the extra inputs of water afforded by fog interception), although experimental evidence based on process research is lacking.

Whilst the database on transpiration by temperate forests is expanding steadily, such information is still very limited for tropical forests, especially for fast-growing plantation species and montane (cloud) forests. Given the adverse effect of reforesting degraded tropical areas with fast-growing evergreen trees on low flows, the identification and evaluation of alternative ways of improving dry-season flows should also receive high priority. The quantification of the water budgets of agro-forestry systems assumes particular importance in this respect. Finally, very little information exists on the long-term changes in soil hydraulic properties associated with land-use change and how these affect storm run-off generation patterns.

The last decades have seen the waning of the empirical age of catchment treatment experimentation and ever more rapid developments in our ability to model complex natural systems in a spatially explicit way. The arrival of process-based distributed hydrological models and ongoing improvements in equipment, remote sensing technology and computational facilities guarantee that there are exciting times ahead for forest hydrologists.

4

Trees in the Urban Environment

INTRODUCTION

Trees in the urban environment are often referred to as the urban forest, comprising trees in civic woodlands, parks and the street. Earlier, urban trees were mainly regarded as aesthetic elements, whereas today they are recognized as having a positive impact on the environment as well as providing economic and social benefits. Monetary evaluations reflect the various benefits arising from the urban forest, covering such aspects as reduction of pollution and energy use, environmental amelioration, savings in public health care and increase in economic investment. Hence, the value of the urban forest is being increasingly recognized as a vital component in the maintenance of a sustainable urban environment in cities around the world. Meanwhile, the population living in urban areas has increased rapidly since the 1950s and the lack of space makes it tempting to use green areas for infrastructure and buildings.

Collins (1997) emphasizes that urban forestry, the planning, management and maintenance of the urban forest, is more closely aligned to traditional forestry than might be immediately apparent. As implicit in the term, the principle of sustained yield has been adapted to the urban environment, applying rural land-use forestry to the management of the urban forest. Hence, the overall objective in urban forestry is not that of timber production but, through a balanced structure of age and species, a sustained production of environmental, social and economic benefits. These social benefits also accrue if local communities are encouraged to contribute to their own environment by promoting projects and activities involving local residents. These kinds of projects often prove effective in promoting social interaction and lead to increased local involvement in other aspects as well.

The planning and management of a healthy urban forest requires that coordinated strategies are agreed between the professions more or less directly involved, such as planners, landscape architects, arboriculturists, foresters, engineers, legislators, developers and utility managers. Management of the urban forest resource is moving towards the achievement of a healthy, well-distributed urban forest, which is increasingly becoming an essential and integral part of the urban infrastructure. In this chapter, we outline the science that underpins such forests.

DEFINITIONS

Trees in the urban environment have been defined in several ways, although 'urban forestry and arboriculture' is probably the most used term in relation to trees in or near the urban environment. Many different research disciplines are involved in the fields of arboriculture and urban forestry. Harris (1992) defines arboriculture as being 'primarily concerned with the planting and care of trees and more peripherally concerned with shrubs and woody vines and groundcover plants'. However, many people consider urban forestry to consist primarily of two types of planting: urban forests and urban trees. Also, definitions of urban green areas and urban forestry vary significantly throughout the world. There seem to be different opinions as to what urban forestry covers, depending on whether professionals have a background within or outside forestry or have experience of working in the USA or other parts of the world such as Europe.

In many cases foresters have argued that urban forestry concerns 'forestry in urban areas'. Volk (1986) stated that:

Green areas such as tree lined streets, cemeteries, and parks, which are not predominated by trees and as such do not come under forestry influence should be excluded from consideration [of being considered urban forestry]. On the other hand, park forests which come under forestry supervision, should be included in our considerations. The fear of involvement of foresters in urban plantings has been described by Chambers (1987): 'Misguided resistance to the concept [of urban forestry] is still often mistakenly assumed to imply the take over of public open space and existing amenity trees for timber production.' Americans tends to look at urban forestry as the 'management of trees in urban areas on larger than an individual basis' (Harris 1992). In Europe this broad concept now seems to be accepted on a wider basis. Urban forest stands are now often considered as resources where an economic yield is not required, and traditional forestry practices are combined with both aesthetic and recreational considerations.

Costello (1993) suggested that urban forestry be defined as 'the management of trees in urban areas', including single trees. In this definition, 'management' is described as the planning, planting and care of trees; 'trees' as individuals, small groups, larger stands (e.g. green belts) and remnant forests; and 'urban areas' as those areas where people live and work. The location of urban forests can be anywhere, from urban settings to the countryside, as long as there are human structures on the site; these structures can be related to ecological functions, protection, merchandise or tourism and recreation.

Using this concept, we categorize trees in the urban environment as both urban forests and urban trees. Urban forests can be defined by their placement in or near urban areas and by their multifunctional aspects, giving shade, amenity values, etc. Therefore, we define urban forestry as the establishment, management, planning and design of trees and forest stands with amenity values, situated in or near urban areas (Nilsson & Randrup 1996).

Trees in the urban environment may be divided into three different types: trees in urban woodlands, park trees and street trees. These types of plantings differ distinctively in several ways. Most importantly, they have significantly different growing conditions, which means that they have different needs with regard to planning, management and maintenance. The methods used and the research problems related to urban green areas are common throughout the world due to the fact that urban 'greening' concerns not only natural spheres (such as trees, growing conditions, etc.) but also the environment in close proximity to human populations.

URBAN GROWING CONDITIONS

Urban growing conditions differ significantly from those in the rural landscape, and produce difficulties as a result of both above- and below-ground influences.

Stress factors

The harsh soil and air conditions that exist in urban planting are problems that do not play the same role in landscape planting. Growing conditions may also be difficult due to shading effects, recreational users, etc. (Harris 1992; Bradshaw *et al.* 1995). The modified urban mesoclimate affects the quantity of contaminants in urban areas, which is raised by a factor of around 25 (Flint 1985; Harris 1992). In general, the average lifespan of a newly planted street tree may be as low as 10-15 years (Moll 1989).

During the last 30-40 years, the vitality of street trees has fallen drastically (Bradshaw *et al.* 1995). Heavier traffic patterns have increased demands for road construction, which consequently has changed the growing conditions of many roadside trees. Also, pollution from traffic has a highly detrimental impact on street trees (Pedersen 1990). The fact that 50% of the trees planted in an urban environment die within the first year emphasizes this point (Gilbertson & Bradshaw 1985). Nowak *et al.* (1990) found that 34% of 480 trees died within 2 years of planting, while Miller and Miller (1991) found that the mortality rate was 25-50% for a number of species planted in Wisconsin, USA.

Temperature extremes can occur, especially where trees are widely spaced and where heat is reflected from hard surfaces (Bradshaw *et al.* 1995). Harris (1992) described that, occasionally, tree limbs up to 0.6 m and trunks up to 1.2 m in diameter break and fall during hot calm summer and autumn afternoons and subsequent evenings. Roots are more sensitive to temperature extremes than the tops of plants (Harris 1992).

Wind speed will vary according to the shape and height of buildings. Areas with tall buildings will usually be relatively cool in summer due to shading effects, and warmer in winter due to wind-protection effects. On the other hand, winds are more variable and more extreme at exposed corners of tall isolated buildings. Buildings deflect strong winds downwards and concentrate their force at the base and corners of buildings, forming 'wind tunnels'. Trees planted in these exposed gaps may suffer scorched leaves and shoots, which lead to a stunted canopy, especially on the windward side. Newly planted trees will transpire more rapidly in windy situations, which can lead to the death of a tree already severely stressed by drought (Harris 1992; Bradshaw *et al.* 1995). The wind stability of trees is determined by tree species, stand structure, spacing, thinning regimes, soil classes, breeding and tree age at the time of anchorage.

The presence of airborne pollutants in the atmosphere has been a characteristic feature of the urban environment since the beginning of the Industrial Revolution. Air pollution can occur in a variety of forms but the principal ones are dust, SO_2

and NO_x (Bradshaw *et al.* 1995). Leaves are the plant parts most likely to show symptoms of air pollution injury. On broadleaved plants, leaves may develop interveinal necrotic areas, marginal or tip necrosis, stippling of the upper surface, or silvering of the lower surface (Harris 1992).

However, trees in the urban environment also play a role in the quest for cleaner air in the cities. Scott *et al.* (1998) showed that daily uptake of NO_2 and particulate matter represented 1-2% of anthropogenic emissions for the county of Sacramento, California.

In areas with winter temperatures below 0°C, the use of de-icing salt is a well-known problem. De-icing salt is applied to the surrounding environment by surface run-off, wet spraying and airborne drifting.

The initial and most common symptom of de-icing salt damage on trees and shrubs is reduced growth. This is often difficult to recognize or may be confused with other stress factors.

Reduced growth is usually followed by early autumn colours and premature leaf fall. De-icing salt is usually accumulated on the windward side of trees. The damage is easily recognized because it faces the road and is normally regarded as the best indication of de-icing spray damage. The majority of trees and shrubs subjected to either soil salt or salt spray typically show necroses at the edges of the leaves or needles. Wounds, often related to pruning, are a common place for spray salt to infect the plants. The damage may cause lack of sprouting and eventually dieback. Conifers are very susceptible to de-icing salt spray damage because they are green all through the winter maintenance season. Trees and shrubs damaged by de-icing salt and showing dieback are difficult to cure. (Dobson and working zones because the soil is certainly 1991; Brod 1993; Gibbs & Palmer 1994; Pedersen going to be compacted during the construction of & Fostad 1996; Randrup & Pedersen 1996).

Characteristics and restriction of rooting in the built environment

Urban soils as a growing medium are poorly understood and often misunderstood. Therefore plantings are carried out with little appreciation or attention to the character and quality of the material that lies beneath the surface (Craul 1992). One major problem in relation to planting in the urban situation is soil compaction, which may occur in small as well as large urban sites.

Soil compaction can be divided into two types: (i) intentional soil compaction, which occurs when soil is deliberately compacted for site stabilization under roads, houses, etc. and (ii) unintentional soil compaction, which occurs when traffic uses areas intended for planting (Randrup 1997). In the urban situation, unintentional soil compaction is primarily found along roadsides and on construction sites.

When soil is compacted, its bulk density increases and its porosity decreases. These effects inhibit plant growth because the soil becomes impenetrable to root growth and, furthermore, restricts the water and oxygen available to the roots. For example, root growth of most plants is impeded once soil bulk density rises above 1.6. One consequence of compacted soil is waterlogging, which can kill roots around existing trees. Soil loosening has proved to be effective in alleviating compacted soil (Håkansson & Reeder 1994; Rolf 1994).

However, there is no doubt that the best treatment for compacted soil is to protect the soil from being compacted in the first place. Florgård (1987) suggested protecting trees growing on construction sites by dividing the site into zones in which different types of construction traffic are permitted. The principle of construction site zoning was adapted by Randrup and Dralle (1997) to protect the soil from being compacted. They suggested that the entire construction site be divided into a building zone, a working zone and a protection zone.

URBAN CHARACTERISTICS/ENVIRONMENT ANALYSED

The city is characterized by paving and buildings, which variously results in decreased wind speed, but an increase in windthrow (Harris 1992; Bradshaw *et al.* 1995), raised temperatures (Nowak & McPherson 1993; Miller 1997) and precipitation, lowered humidity and shading in street canyons (Bradshaw *et al.* 1995; Nowak 1995). The extent of the influences of these factors depends on the structure and amount of vegetation, as well as on the size of the city. Green areas in the city accessible to the public include areas at schools, public libraries and social institutions, as well as parks and churchyards. These are areas that are typically relatively small and geographically widespread, which is why they often suffer great recreational pressure, most often due to the overall proportion of green areas in the city.

Throughout Europe the proportion of urban green areas varies greatly, from over 60% of the area of Bratislava, the capital of Slovakia, to about 5% in Madrid, the capital of Spain (Stanners & Bourdeau 1995). In comparison, the figure for Mexico City is only 2.2% (Benavides Meza 1992); in relation to the number of inhabitants, this only provides 1.94 m^2 per inhabitant, which is far below the 9 m^2 recommended by the World Health Organization. A suggested measure of urban environmental quality is the location of green areas within a walking distance of 15 min or less from all housing areas. This criterion is met for all citizens in Brussels, Copenhagen, Glasgow, Gothenburg, Madrid, Milan and Paris and, in general, for more than 50% of the population in most European cities (Stanners & Bourdeau 1995).

The quality of urban green areas are increasingly recognized as being important to the overall quality of human life in the cities. Beyond this, the urban forests and trees are important as ecosystems in relation to the conservation of biological diversity (Kuchelmeister & Braatz 1993; Collins 1997). Though the urban population benefits from the urban green areas, the increase in population places great pressure on the existing green areas as a result of urban and infrastructural development. The importance of the urban green space, of which urban forestry is an integral part, increases as population increases. The growing urban population needs the environmental and social benefits associated with urban forests, as shown by Ulrich (1984) and Grahn (1989). In developing countries, urbanization has had a dramatic influence on creating environments practically without any amenities, as is the case in Mexico City, where the growth in population has not been matched by an increase in green space (Caballero Deloya 1993). It is an accepted reality that the growth of the cities cannot be stopped. Instead, the challenge is to control urban growth so that it results in economic growth and a satisfactory environment.

As more than two-thirds of the population of Europe live in urban areas, the quality of the urban environment, including green areas, is becoming increasingly recognized as one key to the economic reconstruction of European cities (Commission of the European Community 1990). Urban areas constitute the everyday environment of the greater part of the population and, in recent years, this topic has received considerable attention in the European Union, United Nations and the Organization for Economic Cooperation and Development, which will hopefully lead to an improvement in our knowledge of urban environments.

AMENITY VALUES/BENEFITS OF URBAN FORESTS AND TREES

Trees in the urban environment contribute significantly to the aesthetic appeal of cities, helping to maintain the psychological health of the inhabitants (Miller 1997). Besides the aesthetic and environmental aspects, urban forestry is also of importance in helping populations poor in resources to meet basic needs (Kuchelmeister & Braatz 1993). Urban plantings of fruit trees to provide firewood is one way of utilizing obvious benefits from the available natural resources, as done in Kampala, the capital of Uganda (Haque 1987). Research has shown that urban trees benefit communities economically (Dwyer 1992), socially (Schroeder & Cannon 1987; Michael & Hull 1994) and environmentally (Broderick & Miller 1989; Matthews 1991; Huang *et al.* 1992). The size, structure and condition of the urban forest directly affects the amount of benefits provided by the urban vegetation (Nowak & McPherson 1993). Nevertheless, the social and environmental benefits provided by the urban forest are often largely ignored in land-use planning (Dwyer *et al.* 1991; Tyrväinen 1997).

Economic impact

Though trees are not usually thought of as economic resources, the presence of trees has an impact on different economic factors, including the level of real-estate prices, economic investments and employment. Results of recent Finnish studies show that the benefits provided by urban forests are reflected in property prices, and that environmental variables, such as proximity to wooded recreation areas and water courses as well as an increasing proportion of total forested area in the housing district, had a positive influence on apartment prices (Tyrväinen 1997). The presence of trees may influence property values positively by as much as 20%, with an average increase of 5-10% (Ebenreck 1989; Kielbaso 1989).

Trees also provide different external environmental benefits. Costs for heating and cooling can be reduced by appropriate use of vegetation. Energy reductions for individual buildings have been shown to range from 5 to 15% for heating and 10-50% for cooling. Especially in areas with high summer temperatures, trees are important providers of shade. In areas with cool winters, it is of importance to use deciduous trees, as the loss of leaves in winter allows the sun to heat the house. Proper arrangements of vegetation around buildings can also reduce wind velocity and thereby reduce the heat loss from buildings (McPherson & Rowntree 1993).

Recreational use of green areas

Several studies have shown the importance of urban forests for participation in outdoor recreation activities (e.g. Gåsdal 1993; Sievänen 1993; Lindhagen 1996). In a Danish national survey it was found that around two-thirds of all forest visits take place in the forest situated nearest the housing area (Jensen & Koch 1997). Danish and Swedish studies have also showed that the use of green areas by people is associated with three highly esteemed values: (i) a high degree of natural elements, (ii) fresh air and (iii) the possibility of solitude (Grahn 1991; Holm 1998).

In general, people use green areas less than they would like. According to Swedish studies, distance and the fear of assault are the most prevalent reasons for people not visiting green areas. When the distance to the park exceeds 300 m, one person in four postpones a daily visit. As many as 56% refrain from regular walks in the park when the distance increases to 500m (Grahn 1991). American studies indicate that the removal of vegetation at strategic points can reduce the risk of assault, although this should not be the reason for removing all the vegetation (Michael & Hull 1994).

Psychological aspects

City life is stressful but research shows that urban green areas have a beneficial influence on the health and well-being of the urban population. Studies indicate that visits to green areas can counteract stress, renew vital energy and speed healing processes.

In Sweden, Grahn (1989) conducted extensive studies on the significance of parks to different groups of the population. For instance, he persuaded 40 schools, hospitals, sports associations, cultural associations and day-care centres to keep diaries of their outdoor activities for 1 year. For example, the diaries show that periods spent outside had an actual medicinal value for patients and residents of hospitals, old people's homes and homes for the sick. People became happier, slept better, needed less medication, were less restless and far more talkative.

Ulrich (1984) showed that hospitalized patients recovered faster when they had a view through a window, allowing them to see trees. Ulrich *et al.* (1991) showed a gory film on industrial accidents to 120 people. Half the people were then shown a nature film, whereas the other half were shown a film on the city, with sequences of buildings and traffic. The subjects' heart beat, muscular tension and blood pressure were monitored throughout. All subjects exhibited strong signs of stress during the first film on industrial accidents. The stress levels of the subjects that then watched the nature film returned to a normal level after 4-6 min, whereas the half that watched the film on buildings and traffic continued to exhibit high stress levels.

Kaplan and Kaplan (1989) have formulated a theory on the interaction between human attention and the surroundings. This theory distinguishes between spontaneous attention and conscious attention. Spontaneous attention demands no effort and occurs without premeditation. Conscious attention demands energy and leads to psychological exhaustion in the long term. Rapid movements, strong colours, sudden noises and strong odours are typical stimuli that demand conscious attention. These signals have a powerful effect on our attention, consciously and unconsciously, because they are perceived as potential dangers to which we should react. This means that urban living, with fast vehicles, flashing neon signs and strong colours, causes constant stress. Kaplan and Kaplan's research indicates that vegetation and nature reinforce our spontaneous attention, allow our sensory apparatus to relax and infuse us with fresh energy. Visits to green areas bring relaxation and sharpen our concentration, since we only need to use our spontaneous attention. At the same time, we get fresh air and sunlight, which have significance for our diurnal and annual rhythms.

Environmental education

The change and the continuity in nature provides not only a sense of time but also a sense of security and confidence, through the predictable change of seasons and the repetition of natural processes. The urban trees and forests play a role in educating young people and children in understanding the basic processes in nature and the complexities of the environment, either informally during play or as part of the school curriculum. Playing in nature or natural settings also helps children to develop their motoric senses (Holm 1998) and to regain and experience the human connection to nature through their imagination. Experiences with environmental education in the USA show that access to even a small area of the urban forest is of importance when learning about natural processes (Ebenreck 1989).

In England in 1985 a research project supported by the Department of Education and Science, the Countryside Commission and a consortium of local authorities resulted in the organization Learning through Landscapes (LTL). LTL was founded on the recognition of the impact that the physical surroundings has on children. LTL helps schools to design schoolyards that improve the quality of the environment and helps to create additional resources for the formal curriculum, such as the promotion of more effective teaching and learning in the outdoor classroom (Adams 1989).

The English Community Forests are examples of integrated programmes in which environmental education is integrated in social programmes by well-coordinated planning. The forests are charged with running and coordinating social programmes, involving information, consultation, participation, art, education, sport, recreation and cultural activities (Davies & Vaughan 1998).

Community involvement

Other benefits of urban forestry are those provided by involving people in planning, planting and caring for the trees and urban forests in their own locality. By promoting social interaction and strengthening local pride and identity, local public engagement benefits management greatly, encouraging people to act protectively towards their local forests and providing a potentially huge volunteer workforce (Collins 1996).

The possibilities for creating public awareness in any town are endless. In the USA there is a tradition of involving the public in all processes, from the policy-making to the care and maintenance of the urban forest. Through various types of tree programmes, public awareness has proved to be a valuable tool in the justification of tree activities because it develops a public interest group that helps to lobby for support. The projects that involve citizens have various aspects in common, such as planting, preserving, pruning, maintenance, public education, etc. (Dawe 1989; Sievert 1989). Examples of initiatives that enhance public awareness and engagement in a municipal tree programme are the Tree Boards, municipal non-profit groups with participants from a wide range of professions. The close cooperation between professionals and non-professionals provides direct communication of new ideas and research and helps to solve associated problems as experienced in a practical situation. Another way of involving the public is to encourage houseowners to adopt a tree, by taking part in the care and maintenance of a tree in their neighbourhood.

ENVIRONMENTAL ASPECTS

Trees influence the urban environment in various ways, whether individual trees or the entire urban forest. Urban trees can mitigate the environmental impacts of urban development by moderating climate, improving air quality, providing habitat for wildlife and reducing noise levels (Nowak *et al.* 1994). The environmental benefits associated with urban trees and woodlands are widely recognized. In large cities such as Chicago (Nowak & McPherson 1993) and Mexico City (Caballero Deloya 1993), the environmental aspects are integrated in the city greening programmes. At the UN Conference on the Environment and Development in Rio de Janeiro in 1992, all participating countries adopted Agenda 21, an action plan that obliges them to work towards sustainable development, an obligation that in turn devolves to the administrators of urban green areas (United Nations 1992).

Local-scale climate

The replacement of natural surfaces with buildings and roads, as typified by cities, has altered the thermal and moisture properties of the area, which modifies the local atmosphere and generates the 'urban climate', with poorer air quality and increased air temperatures (Nowak *et al.* 1994). By transpiring water and shading surfaces, trees lower local air temperatures (Nowak 1995).

In areas where the summer is hot, trees are important because of the shade they provide. Trees can even reduce energy use in buildings by lowering summertime temperatures, shading buildings during the summer and blocking winter winds and consequently reduce the emission of pollutants from power-generating facilities (McPher-son & Rowntree 1993; Nowak 1995).

Trees and shrubs can be used for manipulating air movement in order to control the impact of winds, by obstruction, guidance, deflection and filtration. The resulting effects depend on plant size, shape, foliage density and retention, as well as the placement of the plants. Combinations of trees and shrubs provide the most effective barriers, which may even be created by making use of already existing landforms. Windbreaks provide protection for considerable distances, up to 20 times the average windbreak height (Jensen 1955; Grey & Deneke 1978). A medium-porous windbreak (40-

60% reduction) reduces wind speed nearly as much as an impenetrable barrier. Meanwhile the shelter from this type of windbreak extends over a longer distance downwind, with much less turbulence present. However, the type of optimum windbreak depends on the situation. Hence, in some settings an impenetrable windbreak will provide the most appropriate protection, whereas in others the highly porous windbreak will be the optimal solution. Thus, the structure of windbreaks in terms of suitable provenances and clones of species, number of rows and density can be designed to provide the type of shelter needed (Forman 1997).

Air quality

Trees intercept particulate matter and absorb such gaseous pollutants as O_3, SO_2 and NO_2, thus removing them from the atmosphere. Trees also emit various volatile organic compounds, such as isoprene and monoterpenes, that can contribute to O_3 formation in cities. Studies conducted in Frankfurt am Main have shown that streets along which trees are planted contained 3000 polluting particles per litre of air, whereas streets that lacked trees had as many as 10 000-12 000 particles per litre of air (Bernatzky 1978). Protective plantations along heavily trafficked roads and around industrial areas are therefore an effective means of reducing air pollution. However, this should obviously not be taken as an excuse for neglecting to combat pollution at its source. In The Netherlands, some cities operate a tree-planting plan, the objective of which is to plant as many trees as needed in order to absorb the quantity of CO_2 emitted in providing the city with heating. To attain this goal, support is also given to reforestation programmes in eastern Europe and Africa, as well as to the extensive tree-planting carried out in the cities themselves.

Mexico City's Urban Forest Programme is another example of increasing awareness of the needs of urban greening as a means of altering the overall quality of life in the city. The fundamental goals of the programme are to mitigate the effects of the severe air pollution in the metropolitan area, to establish more green areas within the city and to give the city a more welcoming appearance (Caballero Deloya 1993).

Because trees can store carbon for long periods, they are an important carbon sink. Even though plants absorb CO_2 and produce O_2, it is important not to assign excessive significance to their role in the urban environment. Harris (1992) reminds us that plants really have only a minor effect on the CO_2 and O_2 content of urban air. Photosynthesis in the oceans accounts for 70-90% of the world's total O_2 production, for which reason it is absolutely vital that they be protected against pollution. However, even a minor reduction in the O_2 content of the air will cause a large percentage increase in its CO_2 content, which would reinforce the greenhouse effect, thus leading to a rise in the global temperature. Harris (1992) also stresses that urban vegetation has an especially beneficial effect on air pollution through its ability to reduce the quantity of airborne particles. Studies of 9000 trees in Chicago have shown that the trees reduce air pollution by 12 t of CO_2 and 10.8 t of O_3 per day (Nowak *et al.* 1994).

Biodiversity

Green areas play a vital role in urban biodiversity because these are the main habitats of urban plants and animals. The size and location of the urban green areas are of importance for their qualities as biotopes. Vacant urban wasteland in inner cities often possess a high diversity of species adapted to urban environmental conditions and pressures. For instance, older well-established installations attract birds and mammals whose natural habitat is the forest. The urban forest structures are also of great importance, providing wildlife corridors and stepping stones that connect the habitats in the urban green areas. Swedish examples emphasize that only if the urban infrastructure is integrated with the green infrastructure is it possible to achieve biotope protection within cities (Stanners & Bourdeau 1995).

Since a major part of Europe's population lives in urban areas and receives its daily perception of nature therein, nature in urban areas is important for environmental awareness and an understanding of nature.

Urban areas contain more of nature than is immediately apparent. Older gardens and parks, not to mention churchyards, often have noticeably rich biodiversity. Nature created by humans is often considered to be inferior to nature that evolved without human intervention.

In support of this, it is often asserted that, for example, the number of species is often greater in untouched nature. This is mainly related to the fact that many urban green areas do not boast particularly rich biodiversity. Most of them were established with large paved areas, gravelled areas, well-mown greens and isolated individual trees. However, Owen (1992) showed that in an urban private garden with variegated flower beds and a well-proportioned mixture of cultivated and uncultivated plants it was possible to attract a large proportion of the indigenous species of butterflies (34%), moth (30%) and hover flies (36%).

The presence of birds in the immediate environment is a vital element in the context of recreation. Their presence in urban areas depends on the character of the local vegetation. Variation in the structure of plantations also forms a basis for a rich assemblage of birds. As it takes many years for new plantations to mature, it is vital to preserve as much of the existing vegetation as possible when establishing new areas (Dwyer 1995).

Sustainable urban forests

Sustainable urban forests are defined by Clark *et al.* (1997) as 'the naturally occurring and planted trees in cities which are managed to provide the inhabitants with a continuing level of economic, social, environmental and ecological benefits today and into the future'. They will provide long-term net environmental, ecological, social and economic benefits (Clark *et al.* 1997; Miller 1997). To the components of a sustainable forest, McPherson (1998) includes features of adequate species and age diversity, a large percentage of healthy trees that are well adapted to local growing conditions, and a climate-appropriate treecover with native forests stands as one component of overall canopy cover.

THREATS TO GREEN AREAS

Besides the harsh growing conditions that plants experience in the urban environment, there are other, more immediate threats to urban trees and woodlands. These are the pressures of urbanization, which compete with the green areas in demand for land; hence the high recreational pressure on the areas left for urban green spaces.

Urbanization pressure

There is great pressure on urban space resources. Even where this is a question of public buildings, such as museums, where green area remains accessible to the public, it would in many cases detract from the overall recreational quality of the area. In Mexico City, the proportion of green areas within the city is falling by about 3.7% annually.

These are often replaced with buildings, especially in the poorest quarters of the city (Chacalo *et al.* 1994). Traffic installations and noise are other threats to green areas. Roads can isolate green areas from each other, which reduces their recreational value and their value as corridors for the propagation of flora and fauna. The annoyance caused by noise is more indirect. Dutch studies indicate that road noise annoys about 20% of the population, whereas about 11% is annoyed by air traffic (Stanners & Bourdeau 1995). These figures apply to indoor annoyance. Outdoors, people are exposed to even more noise, especially since part of the urban green areas consist of 'residual areas' along traffic constructions.

Social factors

Another important urban stress factor is vandalism. This is usually perceived to be a serious factor, although surveys shows that it is not: it is usually the result of careless play and affects only the most exposed trees (Bradshaw *et al.* 1995). Vandalism is predominantly a social problem. Successful community landscaping and gardening in densely populated inner-city neighbourhoods have shown that one deterrent to vandalism is the development of a spirit of proprietorship in residents (Flint 1985). Nowak *et al.* (1990) noted the highest tree mortality in areas of lower socioeconomic status. Percentage tree mortality was most strongly correlated with percentage unemployment.

Economic cuts

In addition, economic cuts are an obtrusive threat to green areas. Park administrations responsible for a large part of city green areas have been hit hard in recent years by cuts in appropriations and personnel. As an example it is typical of the trend in Denmark over the past 20 years that economic resources have dropped by 10-20% while green areas have increased by 20-40%. Similar trends have been observed in other countries, for instance Sweden, Germany and the UK. The sector responsible for the planning, establishment and operation of green areas in Denmark (including the administration of natural and recreational areas) has an annual turnover, public and private, of $US1.35 billion and employs the equivalent of 30000 full-time employees. The maintenance costs of urban green areas amount to approximately $US16 per inhabitant (Juul 1995). In this respect, if Denmark can be regarded as an average country in European terms, this gives a total European urban greening maintenance cost of approximately $US3.84 billion. In 1991, it was estimated that at least $US300-350 million was spent annually to enhance amenity tree resources in the UK (Ball *et al.* 1999).

PLANNING AND MANAGEMENT OF URBAN GREEN AREAS

The vigorous growth of urban areas has not only increased the need for intensified urban planting but also highlighted major problems related to species selection, establishment techniques, care and maintenance, and planning. Proper species selection, tree care and maintenance will ultimately result in a greater understanding of urban tree management. Consequently, this will ensure that planted trees remain healthier and live longer, thus reducing labour and replacement costs, while still providing an overall ameliorating effect. Money saved is therefore equivalent to money earned, since it becomes available for other purposes.

In Denmark, the major part of the public green area is administered centrally by a municipal park administration. The park administration is typically located in a local council's technical department and has its own operating organization that is responsible for the practical care of green areas. However, throughout Europe there is a trend towards an ever-more privatized operation of green areas, demonstrated by increasing use of private contractors, first and foremost when establishing new installations but also in the maintenance of green areas. Nevertheless, it is characteristic of issues concerning urban forests or green areas that there is a high level of public involvement. Also, self-administration is gradually gaining a foothold, for example in day-care centres, where the management and parents' committees are increasingly able to decide for themselves how their green areas should be operated.

In addition, there is a growing tendency towards reducing costs related to tree establishment and care. Urban trees and uneconomic forest stands are particularly exposed to such cuts. Therefore, better planning and management systems for urban green areas are often currently lacking (Konijnendijk 1999). Small individual economic cuts may not be very significant in themselves, but considered over an extended period the decrease in budgets can have detrimental consequences not apparent in the isolated individual case. One approach for solving this problem could be the introduction of overall green infrastructure planning.

Green infrastructure planning

The EU Green Book ascertains that there are many threats to green areas, for example from vehicles and advertising (Commission of the European Community 1990). It also stresses the need for an element of nature in the urban environment. Even if urban nature perhaps cannot compare to 'natural' nature, it is still of great importance. The nature that exists in the landscape is the source we should use for disseminating wild plants and animals into urban areas. This is why green corridors leading from the countryside into urban areas are vital, as is the transitional zone between urban and rural areas. In many places, the green structure is not cohesive and thus cannot provide the necessary transport routes. Just a minor interruption of a green corridor can prevent it from functioning. Although binding the green network together in urban areas demands a great effort, it is absolutely essential if we are to succeed in developing urban biotopes and creating the conditions needed for a richer flora and fauna. The EU Green Book recommends that public green space should be increased as much as possible. Hence, green infrastructure planning includes a holistic assessment of the green infrastructure, current conditions and plans for development that could be achieved, for instance, by making it possible for local councils to give a green plan formal status as a part of council planning.

Examples

Germany is one of the countries at the forefront of green infrastructure planning. The German nature and environmental protection legislation also regulates parks and urban green areas. Their green plans are included on several different levels in landscape planning (which is linked to general plans) and in green structure planning (which is linked to local plans). Although these plans are not legally binding they still play a significant role. Examples from three German cities illustrate the divergent ways in which these plans originate and how they are used (Nilsson *et al.* 1998).

In Hannover, the overall green structure is included in two planning phases. The park administration has the option of conducting a landscape analysis before work is started, in all forms of area utilization. In this way, planning takes landscape potential into account from the very beginning. Plans for the green structure are combined with the plans for building development in the next phase. Both phases are laid before the politicians, who thus gain the opportunity of seeing how consideration is given in the final proposal to the original, overall intentions. In cases where it is impossible to avoid damaging nature, the authorities can demand compensation. Advantage of this is often taken by the city head gardener to demand improvements elsewhere, for instance a builder can be obliged to undertake the improvement of a neighbouring park. In this way, nature - the green area - becomes a commodity that can be traded, for better or worse.

Stuttgart approaches superior green planning another way. This city has a long tradition of securing the expansion and improvement of its green structure through exhibitions held every 10 years, most recently in 1993. Stuttgart also offers a classical example of the fact that it is not only the lack of green areas that can present a problem; the problem can also be related to access to these areas and their lack of mutual cohesion. The major problem in Stuttgart was the cohesion of the old royal gardens in the centre of the city. For this reason 10 bridges, which linked the parks together across various arterial roads, were built in conjunction with the Bundesgartenschau of 1977. This was a phase in the long-term 'Green U' plan, which was completed in connection with the 1993 exhibition. The Green U now makes it possible to pass through green areas, from the central royal gardens to the forests at the edge of the city.

In Munich, a plan was adopted in 1992 for 14 green strips, totalling 584 ha, which are to link the city's green areas to the surrounding landscape. The green strips are to be established over a 25-year period and will cost a total of $US430 million. The reason for this major effort is the fact that the development of the city's green areas has not increased in proportion to building development. At the same time, increased awareness of the significance of green areas to ecology and recreational activities has meant that greater attention is being paid to the importance of the cohesion of green areas. A large part of the green areas are on the edge of the city and are owned by it. Only the innermost 10-m belt of this resembles a park and consists of small tree plantations, a green and perhaps a stream. It also contains a network of footpaths and cycle paths. The remainder of these areas is rented to farmers, who operate them with only limited use of pesticides.

In Denmark, a successful example of green infrastructure planning is the 'Finger Plan' for the area outside Copenhagen. The name relates to the fact that the overall structure is shaped like a hand, with the five 'fingers' being planned for urban development. The Finger Plan, which was born as long ago as 1947, had the goal of stopping the layered growth of the city and ensuring that urban growth would thereafter be concentrated in narrow urbanized areas ('fingers') along traffic corridors. The wedges between the fingers were to be used for agricultural and recreational purposes. This idea was very clear and was beneficial to the green areas. Subsequent developments have largely adhered to the guidelines of the plan.

In England the planning of the new towns was founded, even as early as 1900, on the concept of using trees and woodland as a setting for urban development. The aims of the new towns were to relieve the urbanization pressure on large cities such as London, Birmingham and Glasgow, and to create self-contained and balanced communities for living in, for employment and for recreation. The new towns were designed and developed by development corporations. The success of the new towns is to be found in the fact that they were produced as integrated structures with good communications, high levels of amenities and higher than average physical environment, based to a large degree on social commitment and the belief that good physical environment was good for people as well as for business (Simson 1998).

Conflicts in management

In the policy-making, planning and development of urban forestry, some general trends and challenges can be recognized. These comprise a growing complexity, an increasing role of public participation and conflict management, and the transition towards closer-to-nature forests. In a study of urban forest planning and policy-making in 16 European cities, the main conflicts were discovered to be conflicts in relation to nature conservation, forestry vs. urban development, conflicts between different types of recreation and recreation vs. conservation management (Konij-nendijk 1998).

CONCLUSIONS

Urban green areas are of great importance to the people living in cities. Nevertheless, urban green areas are also increasingly exposed to threats related to the development and progress of three main factors: the densification of cities, the construction of infrastructure and decreasing resources. Even though individual actions can seem insignificant by themselves, they can lead to detrimental consequences if an overall view of the green structure and its different functions is lacking. Only by emphasizing the environmental, social and cultural importance of urban green areas is it possible to create a base for the needed priorities, in order to protect and develop the urban green structure.

The importance of an overall green structure lies in its various functions: environmental, social and cultural. The ecological functions are conditioned by the whole system of plants, animals, soil, water, climate and human impact. Hence, the possibility of developing and utilizing the green structure in the long term depends on creating a complete picture of this system in order to utilize and consider the needs of the cities. The green structures of the cities are of great importance when it comes to quality of life. The social functions have been emphasized in studies from different cities, showing that the majority of people spend most of their spare time within the city or in nearby areas. The cultural and aesthetic characteristics related to urban green areas and structures are also of great importance for the quality of life in cities. The urban green areas, the gardens, parks and cemeteries, all add to and reflect the cultural history and identity of the city.

In general, an increasing interest in urban environmental problems can be traced. Over the coming decades this will probably cause a considerable increase in the development of parks and green areas, most of which will occur in the larger cities of Asia, Africa and Latin America. Similar expansion of the green infrastructure was carried out in North America and Europe during the years after the Second World War and up to the 1970s. It was done with a strong belief in high technology, heavy machines and the liberal application of chemical aids. Over the coming years, the main challenge will be to ensure that the development of green infrastructure in the world's urban areas is carried out within the framework of sustainable development, without the use of technology destructive to humans and nature and with as few chemical aids as possible. Humans are a vital resource in this context, not only because manual work is an alternative to many of the methods harmful to the environment but also because knowledge can in many instances replace the use of artificial methods.

5

The Importance of Social Values

SUSTAINABLE FOREST MANAGEMENT INVOLVES POLITICAL AND SOCIAL PROCESSES

The past decade may come to be known by foresters as the period when they, and just about everybody else, sought to define or to prescribe sustainable forest management (SFM). Many of these efforts have painted very detailed pictures of what a well-managed forest should look like. Others have established general principles. Whatever their form, the key ingredients are sustaining multiple values through forest management, and the rights of multiple actors.

The earliest initiatives to define SFM were unilateral, undertaken by industry associations or by environmental non-governmental organizations (NGOs), and consequently were mistrusted by other stakeholders. Most of the currently accepted SFM initiatives result from multistake-holder processes, and consequently reflect a range of these stakeholders' values. They generally comprise sets of principles, criteria and indicators that have to be interpreted in detail at the local level, offering further scope for incorporating local values. They include global/intergovernmental processes (notably the UN Forest Principles 1992), regional processes (e.g. the Ministerial Conference on the Protection of Forests in Europe 1993) and national standards (e.g. the UK Forest Standards 1998). Others are led by civil society (e.g. the Forest Stewardship Council's

Principles and Criteria). The International Institute for Environment and Development (IIED 1996) analysed 17 such initiatives and found that all had the following in common:

- sustaining yields of all socially valued goods and services from forests;
- ensuring positive impacts of forest use on different social groups;
- maintaining the state of the forest to enable continued production for future generations. These initiatives to define SFM all state or imply two premises.
    1. The purpose of forestry is to provide the highly varied needs of society; this requires that demands are signalled effectively in policy and markets, and necessitates means for making trade-offs.
    2. The basic principles of SFM need to be interpreted at the most local level at which specific goods and services are needed, e.g. the community level for recreation and firewood, the national level for major watersheds, and the global level for climate regulation. 'Sustain-ability' can be likened to liberty or justice, a goal we all understand and aspire to, but which has to be negotiated and defined locally to understand and achieve it in practice (Holmberg *et al.* 1991).

This all points to an emphasis on determining local values, on participation among interest groups, on using local decision-making processes, and on ensuring that forest management systems, markets and policies reflect social values.

Only recently, however, have foresters been expected to focus on social issues. There is little prior experience of foresters taking on roles of social development, although there are historical examples: the famous *taungya* system developed in Burma in the 1850s was a response to local people's needs for farmland. Yet foresters are being held increasingly accountable for social conditions (in various new regulations, voluntary codes and certification). There are many unresolved arguments. To what extent can forestry be an instrument of social development? For which communities should foresters be held accountable for social conditions, those close to the forest or also those further away? Clearly, forest managers have at least to understand which groups are most dependent upon the forest and who could contribute most to the success or failure of forest management.

FORESTS PROVIDE MULTIPLE SOCIAL VALUES

The social values of forests differ widely, depending on the culture and social group in question and the roles which forests play in their livelihoods and quality of life. These values are not static, but change over time. Key change factors appear to be the following.

Shortages of, and opportunities to develop, the five main forms of capital (natural, physical, financial, human/individual and social/community capital). Where natural capital such as forest is abundant, it tends to be valued as a resource for conversion to generate other forms of less-abundant capital, and vice versa.

- In a similar vein, the absolute and relative scarcity of particular forest resources, such as timber or biodiversity.
- The availability and price of substitutes for forest goods and services.
- Scientific discovery, education and technology changes.
- Access rights, and resources such as labour that alter capacities to exploit forests.
- An individual's allegiance to specific groups and their shared values.
- Factors that change individual allegiances: campaigning and the political influence of certain groups, tastes and

associated communications and media. The prevalence of individual consumerism has changed values away from those of the community.

- Changes in political culture.
- Changes in national development conditions.
- Changes in individual income.

Whilst the table begins with basic livelihood values such as food, and finishes with recreational and aesthetic values, it would be a mistake to assume that there is a universal, rigid hierarchy of needs. For example, for some groups, spiritual values are fundamental, while for others these are much less significant. It is therefore important to identify the relevant values from the point of view of the group in question. Indeed, certain groups define themselves (in part) by the values they hold in common. This is a source of many recent clashes between forest 'stakeholders'. These clashes can be exacerbated when some groups promote groundswells of broader opinion in favour of the values they hold most strongly, as we have witnessed with many environmental campaigning groups or forest peoples' groups. In other words, group values can be influenced by those of others. The outcome is, in large part, a function of power relations, something the forest manager may be able to do little about but must be aware of.

It is also crucial to be aware of the broader trends that affect social values. Policy, institutional and market conditions frequently make the realization of some values difficult. Furthermore, the role of forests in providing such values can be substituted by other sources (e.g. imported foods, non-forest employment and entertainment). The possibilities of substitution tend to be much greater for richer communities than for poorer, forest-based groups. Hence the need for an emphasis on working with the poor.

In developing countries, subsistence domestic products such as fuelwood, poles, fencing and fodder are a priority for forestry, the other priority area usually being food security from forest management or conversion: 'Over 1 billion people (about 20% of the world's population) depend either wholly or to a significant extent on forests, woodland or farm trees for their subsistence needs and/or livelihood' (WCFSD 1997). As Filer and Sekhran (1998) point out, many people who are perceived as rather passive 'indigenous forest dwellers' think of themselves more as forest gardeners and forest developers, with food a number one concern. Forest managers ignore these pressing social needs at their peril.

Some demands for forest values are now far stronger than they were even a few years ago. For example, 'biodiversity' is a word that was coined only in the late 1980s, and the idea of carbon sequestration as a prime value is only beginning to be accepted. Yet now there are all sorts of international environmental agreements, especially the Biodiversity Convention and Climate Change Convention, with significant financial transfer mechanisms emerging to match the political obligations to produce biodiversity and carbon storage values. At present, those who are pressing for such 'global' forest values tend to be the politically more powerful countries and groups such as international environmental NGOs; much remains to be done to ensure that the production of these values also benefits local groups, rather than squeezing out their (more parochial) concerns.

It is quite a challenge for the forest manager to make decisions about the relative weights of the values held by different groups, from local to global, and how to integrate them or how to make choices between them where integration proves impossible. Three trends are helping here. Firstly, there is the trend for certain markets to recognize some social/environmental values of forest management that were previously unrewarded, for example the market for certified forest products and the emerging market for carbon storage. Secondly, there is development of more inclusive systems of forest policy and management decision-making, such as Round Tables, forest fora, and stakeholder liaison groups, where consultation with different groups about their values is on the increase (even if there is as yet insignificant participation in decision-making and management). Thirdly, there is the work by economists to categorize values and to develop methodologies to assess them on a single (financial) scale. While these methodologies remain contentious (it is not so much the financial magnitude that counts as who bears the cost and who gains the benefits) and indeed have so far made little difference to major policy decisions, especially those regarding private forests, the economic categorization of multiple values is useful to information science if not yet to decision science.

Broadly speaking, it includes the following.

- Direct-use values: where the value is derived directly from the forest, either in a consumptive manner (timber, nuts, fodder, game, fish, etc.) or a non-consumptive manner (tourism, recreation, etc.).
- Indirect-use values: where the value derives from environmental services such as watershed and social protection, carbon sequestration or biodiversity protection, rather than from the forest directly.
- Passive-use values: where value is accorded by the mere fact that the forest exists (existence value), or for the future possibilities that the forest represents (option value) or for the ability to pass the forest on to future generations (bequest values) (Gregersen *et al.* 1997).

THE CHALLENGE OF ACHIEVING SECURITY OF FOREST VALUES

Despite the vast range of values that people seek in forests, few values have been evident in policies, markets and institutions until recently. This is largely because of the prevalence of governments and corporations in power structures and their relatively narrow requirements from forests (notably timber and foreign exchange).

Over time, the procedures of forest authorities that serve these interests have often become increasingly anomalous in the face of needs for multiple values. Their procedures have tended to become objectives in themselves, officers' rewards being based on observing hierarchical norms of behaviour and not on innovation or results, with an emphasis on narrow technical issues leading to a legitimation of increasing isolation from other forest interest groups and their values (Hobley 1996). The continued allocation and management of forests for timber alone, bolstered by such 'fortress forestry' authorities, hinders stakeholders from using forests to produce other goods and services.

There are usually several overlapping customary and legal interests attached to a piece of forest territory. Rarely is more than one set of interests, usually timber or mining, taken into consideration in forest policy, planning and land allocation. This is often exacerbated by local stakeholder rights having been removed through legislation. Moreover, because many governments tend to be weak, powerful (private sector) operators can appropriate these same rights. The net result is inequity in bearing the costs of forest use, and in enjoying the benefits. Means for dialogue, negotiation and partnerships between stakeholders that might improve the situation are weak; thus either the *status quo* is perpetuated or clashes over forest values escalate.

Consequently, many groups are experiencing insecurities in supplies of forest goods and services (Bass 1997). These insecurities will worsen as population grows, or more particularly as the consumption of richer groups increases, whilst forest resources continue to diminish. By the middle of this century, if present trends continue, there will be twice as many people relying on a much smaller area of forest. It is imperative that demands for wood production in particular are consistent with supplying the other forest values that people need, especially those that currently have no market or can never operate within a market, such as local livelihood needs.

In agriculture, the concept of 'food security' at household, national and global levels helped to galvanize action against food shortages and famine.

The concept of 'security of forest goods and services' may help in making more precise decisions about forests, i.e. what goods and services forests should produce and who should share the costs and benefits. The value of the recent initiatives towards SFM principles, criteria and indicators is that they force different groups to be clear about what they seek, in terms of goods and services and the state of forest values.

The challenge, then, must be to achieve security of those forest goods and services that are socially valued at specific levels. There are significant policy and fiscal challenges regarding security of the (indirect-use) values that are required at national level, notably the production of watershed, biodiversity and other public benefits from private lands or management companies. In addition, divisions between countries of the North and South have hindered attempts to secure global forest values in the face of the assertions of many countries that forests are sovereign territory.

It is suggested that the local level, especially the community and household in forest-dependent areas, should be accorded priority, for forests are key for livelihood security and poverty reduction; furthermore, local forest producers are often best placed to generate the values that are required at national and global levels (although they will require incentives).

Forestry that improves social values and reduces poverty will be of a type that empowers poorer groups as forest stewards, improving their security of access to forest goods and services necessary for livelihoods. It will also mitigate or restrain the power of those in whose hands forests are currently over-concentrated and who are wasting or asset-stripping them (Mayers 1997).

PEOPLE'S MEANS TO ACHIEVE SECURITY OF FOREST VALUES

People have always planted and managed trees *where* they want, for the goods and services they want, *if* they have the means at their disposal, i.e. the technology and resources, and recognized rights, responsibilities, rewards and relationships with other groups.

Traditional knowledge

There is much discussion about the need to reconcile traditional indigenous knowledge with 'scientific' forestry in order to improve local action to secure forest values. It is ironic that, at a time when we are seeking means to sustain multiple values, many traditional management systems that do precisely this are on the decline. For example, Lacandones forest farmers in Mexico cultivate 75 species in a single hectare, and a farmer will need to clear no more than 10 ha of rain forest in his entire farming career (Clay 1988). In Sweden, until the nineteenth century, rotational shifting cultivation sustained grain, root crops and livestock as well as timber (Hamilton 1997), and the government saw it as a legitimate form of forest management. As Ghillean Prance has said, traditional forest peoples 'who depend upon so many of the species in the forest will hardly want to destroy more than the absolute minimum necessary for their agriculture. The settler from outside the region, on the other hand, is perplexed by such diversity and tends to destroy rather than use forest [diversity]' (quoted in Bass 1997)

Traditional forest management systems comprise both knowledge and rules, some of which may be transferable to new SFM approaches. The challenge is partly a democratic one: to admit local groups into policy and management decisions and to ensure that their rights can be exercised. But it is also a challenge to the prevailing systems of knowledge, which by and large are scientific and commercial, to admit such knowledge into the pantheon of accepted practices that guides our forest management.

Rights

Different groups have particular rights associated with obtaining forest values. Some rights directly concern the forest and its use:

- territorial rights;
- ownership of trees and other resources, such as minerals, grazing and wildlife;
- rights of access, use and control (for specific purposes and times);
- intellectual property rights.

Several problems are commonly associated with rights. One is that different rights overlap on one territory. Furthermore, many rights may not be established in legal documents, especially customary rights.

Other relevant stakeholder rights concern communities and their cohesion:

- rights to protection of cultural heritage, landscapes and folklore;
- collective rights, e.g. a community's rights to represent itself through its own institutions;
- rights to religious freedom;
- rights to self-determination and to development;
- rights to privacy.

National laws tend to cover specific social issues linked to forests, notably rights to public consultation (planning laws), rights of access (public rights of way) and forest worker rights, etc.

Internationally, there is a growing body of relevant legally binding agreements, to which countries may be party, and which eventually find their way into national legislation. These include:

- UN Covenant on Economic, Social and Cultural Rights (1966);
- UN Covenant on Civil and Political Rights (1966);
- UN Declaration on the Human Right to Development (1986);
- International Labour Organization Convention 169 concerning indigenous and tribal peoples in independent countries (1989);
- UN Convention on Biological Diversity (1992). Many new laws are based on recent legal principles deriving from international consensus on sustainable development (such as the 'intergener-ational equity', 'polluter pays' and 'precautionary' principles). Laws on land, environment and forestry are being reviewed in many countries, especially regarding the links or conflicts between formal and customary rights.

Some groups are forceful in exerting their rights and/or have skills and resources to do so. Others are less well equipped. Irrespective of the stakeholders' powers and resources, forest managers are likely to experience problems if they ignore or violate these rights, and indeed claims. An informed approach is better. This would include anticipating future legal requirements by making provision for best practice in dealing with local groups, and continuous improvement of practice.

REASONS FOR NURTURING SOCIAL VALUES IN COMMERCIAL FOREST MANAGEMENT

Apart from the policy, legal and ethical reasons noted above, there are good commercial reasons to consider social values (Higman *et al.* 1999). Forest managers are increasingly subject to pressures from other interest groups, frequently concerning social values.

- Demands from forest peoples' groups may include greater respect for local populations' rights, carrying out or desisting from specific management practices, and support for their own environmental/social projects.
- Demands from local groups to contribute to social and economic development may include support for local enterprise, employment opportunities, excision of specific areas from management, and use of company inrrastructure.
- Demands from trades unions and their initiatives may include greater respect for workers' rights to organize and negotiate, fair wages and benefits, health and safety at work, and the right to skills development throughout the organization.
- Demands to recognize other forest actors' rights to monitor, control and negotiate may include the development of agreements, and procedures to manage conflicts and make compensation.

Unless an active, organized approach is taken to respond to such pressures, forest managers may find themselves facing:

- slow-downs, strikes, blockades, boycotts, legal battles;
- damage to forest stock;
- arson, sabotage or vandalism to equipment and infrastructure;
- reappropriation of forest lands for cultivation, or migration;
- development of 'cultures of resistance' among forest-dependent people and their supporters (such as some consumers).

Considerable management skill and time may need to be

invested in dealing with disputes, legal challenges and compensation claims, stalled negotiations, 'bad press' and political backlashes and general hostility towards forest managers and companies.

In contrast, participatory approaches that develop people's potential contributions can benefit forest managers, by:

- improving the reputation of forest managers and companies;
- uncovering and sharing useful local information;
- broadening the base of ideas, skills and inputs applied to forestry;
- efficient apportioning of responsibility, e.g. local groups may be better suited to managing recreation and harvesting of non-timber forest products;
- better understanding of broader social, and thereby market, trends;
- improving transparency, accountability and therefore trust between all parties;
- longer-run cost savings and risk reduction.

By taking an active approach to people as well as to trees, forest managers greatly increase the potential social benefits from forest management and their chances of support from others. Such experience should also increase their capacity to anticipate future developments regarding social values, for example in legislation or the market, and thus to gain 'first-mover' advantage from the situation.

If some social values are indicators of market trends (and they frequently are), then it behoves forestry organizations to keep close track of them. Many companies have made good business ventures by diversifying into recreation provision in particular. And it is increasingly clear that there is considerable financial value attached to brand names of certain leading companies which are known to produce social and environmental benefits alongside fibre. For example, the Greenpeace name has been estimated to be worth hundreds of millions of dollars (Anon. 1998).

CODES OF PRACTICE AND CERTIFICATION STANDARDS ON SOCIAL ISSUES

As noted earlier, all initiatives to define SFM principles and criteria cover social values. Some of these are becoming enshrined in legislation, while others face forest enterprises through market relations.

Current systems of forest certification specify various social requirements at the level of the forest management unit. Even so, social issues remain perhaps the most contentious of certification standards, and there are differences between standards, particularly regarding the required degree of involvement of different interest groups in forestry and treatment of peoples' rights. There are also differences in interpretation of the standards by certifiers/assessors. Whilst some confine themselves to assessing the local social outcomes of forest management, others assess the roles of local stakeholders in the management of the forest and indeed the enterprise, and call for changes that appear to reflect their own biases. Whilst it is increasingly clear that forestry should not be a principal means of social engineering, and less still should forest certification, it is generally agreed that social standards for forestry will become more stringent in future. Note that some require precise performance thresholds to be met, while others require only that the issue shall be measured. Still others consider that the social issue is a policy concern and require it to be covered in policies only.

CONCLUSIONS

There is a strong political and legislative tendency towards 'subsidiarity', i.e. making decisions at, and for, the most local level appropriate to the goods and services in question, and being held accountable for this. The trend implies an important role for the forest manager in understanding local groups and their values and reconciling them with national and global values.

Flurries of activity in recent years have resulted in a kind of 'policy inflation' facing local forest managers. Indeed, many managers might now feel, with some legitimacy, that they can hardly get started in forest management without consulting with various groups, conducting multiple assessments and being held up to scrutiny by public and market bodies alike. Whilst it is clear that this 'policy inflation' needs rationalization, and here the principles and criteria initiatives are a promising means to find common denominators and allow for local interpretation, the 'capacity paralysis' that is so out of balance with the new policies also needs addressing. At a practical level, many forest managers have just not made any effort at all in relations with their neighbours. Others have invested heavily in major public relations but without substantially changing management to manage social risk and opportunity in the first place. There is much disagreement on the limits to social responsibility of forest managers.

Some practical approaches now need to be installed and monitored, so that they can reduce the 'policy inflation' by indicating what is working and desirable.

6

Non-timber Forest Products and Rural Poverty: An Economic Analysis

WHY NON-TIMBER FOREST PRODUCTS AND RURAL POVERTY?

The term 'non-timber forest products' (NTFPs) refers to the wide range of species, both flora and fauna, that are produced by (or exist in) forests and woodlands and which are available to humans for uses other than commercial timber. In the past decade, there has been an enormous upsurge in research on NTFPs, reflected in, and promoted by, works such as Nepstad and Schwartzman (1992), Panayotou and Ashton (1992) and Godoy and Bawa (1993).

This upsurge was caused by a number of factors, including a shift in forestry research away from the traditional concentration on commercial or single-use forests, the rise of social forestry, and an increasing interest in indigenous forests and woodlands. However, the most important reason for the rise in work on NTFPs has been the prominence they are given in discussions surrounding the global protection of biodiversity in partnership with local forest-based communities.

Indeed, the greater commercial use of NTFPs has been widely promoted by researchers and international agencies as a means of simultaneously promoting the economic development of poor rural areas and of conserving critical tropical and temperate forests and woodlands. Exploring this argument forms the subject matter of this chapter.

If we are to understand the potential role that NTFPs might play in the socioeconomic development of rural areas, we need first to examine the role that these resources currently play in rural livelihoods, and the economic underpinnings of NTFP use in rural households. Here there is a disjunction between international and local perspectives. For the international community, NTFPs have two potential roles.

The first is what one can term the 'development imperative', namely that NTFPs are seen as a set of resources that are potentially exploitable to promote the socioeconomic development of poor, resource-dependent communities. NTFPs are often thought of as 'hidden' resources, whose production technology and ecology are well understood by local users and producers but whose economic potential has yet to be fully realized. More broadly, forests generally are regarded as having a wide range of potential products, particularly medicinal, whose utility can be expressed presently only as option values. Assuming that these products can be commercialized and that the benefits of commercialization can be captured by local communities, NTFPs it is believed might form the basis of significant income-raising trades for a reasonably substantial class of the rural poor.

The second reason for the focus on NTFPs can be termed the 'environmental imperative'. Since NTFP uses are generally non-destructive to the resource stock (unlike timber), utilization of NTFPs adds value to the forest without undermining the resource stock. If rural agents face the portfolio choice of either clearing land for agricultural purposes or leaving land as forest, then a higher return to land under forest use will lead to more forest being preserved. This property of nondestructive use value is what has led some inter national agencies to suggest that the development of NTFPs can be used as part of a strategy for forest and woodland conservation. So, given their potential role in promoting economic development and environmental conservation, the recent international interest in NTFPs hardly needs explaining.

However, from the perspective of rural households, there is nothing special or unique about NTFPs. In fact, rural households use NTFPs for prosaic reasons. That is to say, NTFPs are goods and services that households utilize according to the economic nature of the NTFP in question.[2] Indeed this is true of all forest products, whether timber or non-timber. As an example, an economic classification of the type of forest products generally used in Zimbabwe is given in Table 15.1, based on research in the south-east of the country. As this table suggests, some forest products are used as consumption goods, some forest products are inputs into other economic production activities, some forest products can be sold and some forest products are transformed to produce durable goods. Note that although the particular items categorized in this table reflect utilizations based on species endemic to miombo woodlands, similar lists could be drawn up for forest products derived from tropical forests, including of course the Amazonian rain forest.

Thus NTFPs are simply goods and services with particular physical, technical and economic characteristics that may or may not make households desire to use them. In deciding whether and how to use NTFPs, rural households will assess the economic characteristics of these NTFPs against other uses of their time, labour or income, and against other competing products. For example, take the decision of the household to collect and consume wild fruits. The decision to do this will depend, amongst other things, on the physical qualities of the wild fruit (taste, nutrients, etc.), the accessibility of the wild fruit in terms of the time taken to collect it, the availability of alternative wild or exotic fruits, the cost to the household of collecting the fruit in terms of other tasks forgone, and the cost to the household of consuming the wild fruit rather than selling it if a market is available. Similarly, the use of firewood by rural households will depend on the quality of firewood species available, their collection costs, and the quality, availability and cost of alternative technologies such as kerosene stoves, paraffin lamps, solar-powered batteries and so on. In short, rural households will use NTFPs if it is economically rational for them to do so.

Furthermore, the use and value of NTFPs is just one, possibly quite small, part of a whole set of economic activities within the household. Rural households in developing countries have the distinct characteristic of being at the same time both a consumption and a production unit, that is to say they have the characteristics simultaneously of both firms and households (the classic economic model of rural households is analysed in Singh *et al.* 1986). In consequence, rural household economic activities are multifarious, usually comprising agricultural production for own consumption and for sale; livestock rearing for own use, own consumption and sale; a variety of non-farm enterprises; migration and economic connections to formal labour markets; goods trading; involvement in networks of reciprocal exchange; investment in education, agricultural equipment and other productive capital; and the collection and use of freely provided environmental goods, some of which come from forests and woodlands. From the perspective of rural households, then, NTFPs form just one component of a set of livelihood activities.

So, if we are going to understand the role and value of NTFPs to rural households, we need to ask some questions. What are the general economic characteristics of these households? How do NTFP activities fit into the broader set of economic decisions or portfolio allocations that are being made by these households? Understanding this will allow us to relate the economic characteristics of rural households to the economic characteristics of NTFPs, and hence understand why households use these resources. This understanding of the economic underpinnings of NTFP use is employed to examine the potential of NTFPs to drive rural socioeconomic development. As I shall argue, there are many serious economic constraints to the use of NTFPs for this purpose, with the result that I believe that the recent enthusiasm of the international community for NTFPs in development projects is considerably misplaced.

ECONOMIC CHARACTERISTICS OF RURAL HOUSEHOLDS

It may seem pointless to attempt to generalize about the characteristics of rural households, given the many different production activities rural households undertake and the many different agroclimatic zones in which such households live. For example, in sub-Saharan Africa alone the term 'rural household' encompasses settled agriculturalists, settled agropastoralists, nomadic pastoralists and extractivist forest-dwellers.

These households can be found in ecological zones as varied as the arid Sahel, the Central African rain forests, and the semiarid plains and woodlands of southern Africa.

However, despite the huge variety of production types and climatic zones in which households are located, there are many ways in which rural households share quite similar economic characteristics. (For a comprehensive overview of the economic analysis of rural households, see Dasgupta 1993.)

The first, and perhaps most important, is that rural households are generally either poor or have very low standards of living. Exact figures on rural household incomes and rural poverty are hard to find, not least thanks to a lack of rural household survey data, the incommensurate nature of many of the rural household surveys that are carried out, and genuine problems in comparing the welfare of rural households across countries and across time. However, what evidence there is proves fairly conclusive.

For example, the United Nations Development Programme (UNDP) has estimated that 72% of rural households in the developing countries as a whole have standards of living below the poverty line (UNDP 1992, p. 161). In Africa, the same organization estimated average incomes to be $US475 per capita in 1992; this is low enough, and yet we know that rural incomes are quite a bit lower than these country-wide means. Zimbabwe itself has reasonably good data on rural standards of living. The latest reliable statistics come from the national Income, Consumption and Expenditure Survey (ICES) of 1995/96, which shows mean rural per-capita consumption levels of $US217 per annum and median levels of only $US146 per annum (CSO 1998, p. 33).

That is to say, half of the individuals living in Zimbabwe's rural areas exist on per-capita consumption levels of less than $US146 per annum. Not surprisingly, rural poverty rates are high. The same survey calculated that 86.4% of rural dwellers could be classified as suffering from poverty, while an astonishing 62.8% of rural dwellers suffered extreme poverty (CSO 1998, p. 33). (Extreme poverty is defined as an inability to reach the food poverty line, defined as the minimum food intake an individual needs to satisfy basic calorific requirements.) Note that by African standards, Zimbabwe is by no means a poor economy, suggesting that in many other countries on the continent the situation is still worse.

Alongside this poverty and these low standards of living is the second feature of rural households, namely their economic remoteness. By this is meant the fact that many rural households are a considerable economic distance from the formal markets in which serious income-raising trades can be made (Dasgupta 1993, pp. 234-45). This is often a result of physical distance: rural households are simply a long way away from urban markets. However, it can also be the result of poor infrastructure provision, essentially a lack of roads (Barwell 1996). For example, in Zimbabwe a government study found that rural households were on average 20 km away from a tarred road and 3 km away from a dirt road.

The results of this are that the unit transactions costs of trading in formal markets are high: rural households must traverse substantial physical distances if they are to connect to formal markets. Simply getting produce to the market is expensive, and this is what is meant by the term 'economic remoteness'. The fact that many rural households face such high transactions costs severely restricts their economic opportunities and their exploitation of gains to trade (Platteau 1996; Risopoulos *et al.* 1999). (Conversely, rural households close to formal markets, especially urban areas, are often better off than most others.) Indeed, these high mobility/transactions costs lead to pervasive formal product market failures (de Janvry *et al.* 1991; Dasgupta 1993, p. 234), which impose significant welfare costs on rural households and constrain their responses to economic incentives. (Concomitantly, rural households are also distant from basic amenities such as banks, health services and grid electricity and this limits use of these facilities and services by rural households; Barwell 1996.)

The third feature of rural households is their high exposure to risk.[3] Almost all rural households are highly dependent on natural resources, whether for crop production, livestock fodder and browse, or the use of environmental resources. These in turn are strongly influenced by climatic conditions, particularly rainfall, which are highly variable. As well as this natural risk, due to their comparative remoteness rural households also face considerable idiosyncratic risks, such as exposure to health shocks (both human and animal) and crop pests that can have devastating consequences. However, the main problem is that in the face of this natural variability, rural households' exposure to risk is high because they do not have access to formal insurance or credit markets. Indeed, given the structure of rural economies, there are good economic reasons why formal markets in risk fail to exist.

These reasons are well known in the economics literature and include the high covariance of rural households' agricultural and livestock outputs, a lack of collateral to underpin credit markets, and the high costs of information acquisition and contract monitoring in remote rural areas. The consequence of these factors is that formal trading in risk is rendered unprofitable. The combination of missing formal product markets and missing markets in risk explains the fourth feature of rural households, namely the fact that their economic production is only partially monetized and the fact that local goods trading is often vibrant. The low share of cash transactions in rural households' total budgets is explained by the lack of formal product markets: rather than trade goods and incur the high transactions costs of trading, it is more economical for the household to consume the goods it has produced itself.

Thus, for example, in Zimbabwe the 1995/96 ICES suggested that amongst poor rural households, fully 42.5% of food consumption was derived from the household's own production. These sorts of figures are typical of other African rural households. However, if a household does wish to trade in goods or factor services, the absence of formal markets means that it has no other choice than to trade in local markets. It is common therefore to find active local product markets and markets in labour. In almost all settled agricultural or agropastoral areas, there is localized trading in crops, livestock and in labour for agricultural tasks such as ploughing, weeding, harvesting and threshing. Likewise, local markets also tend to exist for other goods and services, in particular NTFP goods and the goods made from NTFPs. Thus, Cavendish (1999a) found that of the wide variety of NTFPs and NTFP-based goods used by households in his survey, many were traded locally and therefore had recognizable local prices. However, the fact that trading is restricted to the rural life space means that these goods and services face low demand levels, so prices also tend to be low.

A fifth feature of rural households is that they tend to have lower levels of human capital than their urban counterparts. There are two reasons for this. Development patterns in general in poorer countries have been urban-centred, so that public and private education has been much more available to urban households than to rural (Chambers 1983). However, there is also the impact of urban households' higher income levels, which allows them to invest much more heavily in their families' education than poorer, cash-constrained rural households.

The lack of human capital again constrains the economic welfare of rural households. In general, higher educational levels raise labour productivity in all activities (Psacharopoulos 1994). Even in agriculture, it has been shown that higher education levels lead to greater output (Jamison & Lau 1982). Perhaps more important though is that a low education level disbars rural individuals from competing for more highly paid formal sector jobs. Low-education individuals are only qualified to compete for relatively unskilled jobs, which pay low wages due to the excess of supply over demand in this segment of the labour market. Thus, low human capital levels often act to 'lock in' the lower economic status of rural households (Eswaran & Kotwal 1986). In consequence, rural households tend to share a sixth feature, namely low levels of physical or productive capital. Both because of the low incomes of these households and also due to the failure of capital markets for rural agents, rural households find capital accumulation extremely hard.[5] So the main factor of production for rural households is relatively unskilled labour: it is this that they must allocate to the highest return activities in their economic reach.

VALUE OF NTFPS TO RURAL HOUSEHOLDS AND THE CAUSES OF NTFP USE

Evidence on rural households' use of NTFPs

There is much descriptive evidence that NTFPs are used

widely by rural households. Two themes run through the case study literature on rural households' NTFP use: first, that the level of NTFP use by rural households could be substantial; and second that these NTFP utilizations are seldom quantified or valued in conventional household surveys, so that little is known about their economic contribution. Looking at Africa first, the breadth of the goods and services that environmental resources potentially offer rural households is vividly apparent from the overarching literature review of Sale (1981). In this work, Sale presents a list of the various different utilizations of wild plants and animals, most of which are derived from forests or woodlands, in order to summarize the work of many other researchers. It is clear from this table that wild resources provide rural households with a wide range of sources of economic value. Naturally the exact resources that households use, and the extent of their use, will differ across regions, if only due to differences in species distribution across Africa's various ecological zones.

The existence of widespread NTFP utilization by African rural households has been confirmed by a number of other studies. For example, the literature on the contribution of woodlands and woodland products has been exhaustively reviewed in Townson (1994). This study quotes many references as to the extent of rural households' use of forest foods, firewood use and sales, basketry and handicrafts, furniture and carpentry and other extractive products, all based on NTFPs. In similar fashion, Falconer (1990) has detailed the importance of a wide range of usually unnoticed forest products to the livelihoods of rural households in West Africa. Arnold *et al.* (1994) review data from surveys in six countries in eastern and southern Africa suggesting that forest products have an important role to play in the growth and functioning of rural households' small-scale enterprises.

More evidence on the importance of wild foods and wild products to African rural households is given in Eltringham

(1984) and Scoones *et al.* (1992), the latter referring to the 'hidden harvest' because much of the resource utilizations that they review are not usually uncovered by conventional research programmes. In Zimbabwe, Campbell *et al.* (1991, 1997) have used various methods to estimate the contribution of a wide range of woodland products to rural households, suggesting these might generate around $US50 per household per annum, equivalent to roughly one-quarter of household cash incomes. More recently, Brigham *et al.* (1996) have reported a small number of traders in Zimbabwe and South Africa earning substantial cash incomes from wood and wood-based products, and Shackleton *et al.* (1998) found a small number of traders in South Africa earning high incomes from edible wild herbs. However, in none of these case studies has an accurate analysis been carried out of the role and value of NTFPs in the context of the broader household economy.

African households are not unique in using NTFPs so extensively. In a classic work, Jodha (1986) calculated that amongst poor Indian families the proportion of household income derived from common property resources, of which NTFPs would be a large subset, was between 9 and 26%. Working in one forest area of India, Hegde *et al.* (1996) estimated that the cash income from NTFPs potentially comprised a stunning 48-60% of household incomes. Falconer and Arnold (1991), in their review of rural households generally, argue that local forest products are central to household livelihoods, and draw out the particular importance of NTFPs to rural women and children. There is a substantial case study literature on households and NTFP use from Latin America, summarized in Godoy *et al.* (1993) and Lampietti and Dixon (1995).

These suggest that rain forests are rich in products used by rural households; that these NTFP use values are seldom captured in conventional measures of household consumption or well-being; and that poorer households depend on these resources more heavily than richer households. The latter work reviews 16 studies of the economics of NTFP extraction in the Amazonian rain forest and suggests that the value of these minor forest products is approximately $US70 per hectare annually.

However, the literature on rural households' NTFP use has not focused on the value of NTFPs in the context of the household's overall level of economic well-being, so rigorous quantifications of NTFP values *vis-à-vis* other sources of economic value are rare.

The only source of detailed economic data on rural households and NTFP use comes from a panel household survey conducted in 1993/94 and 1996/97 by the author in Shindi Ward, Zimbabwe.

These data are examined at some length, as it is the only study that systematically links NTFP use to the broader household economy; indeed, the whole purpose of this particular data survey was to examine the use, value and management of environmental resources generally in the context of a rigorous and quantitative household survey[7] It must be remembered of course that the results of this study represent only one set of households in a particular agroclimatic zone at particular points in time; none the less it is the best dataset available to analyse the issues covered in this chapter.

Thus, Tables 15.3 and 15.4 contain summarized data from this study, presenting the aggregate value of NTFP use and other sources of household income across all households and by income quintiles, and the budget shares of NTFP use and other income sources expressed as shares of household total income. (Total income refers not just to cash income but to cash income plus the household's use of its own production plus net gifts and transfers to the household plus the use of freely provided environmental resources collected by the household itself. It is therefore a very broad conception of income, and much closer to a conceptually accurate measure of household welfare than cash income alone.)

It is clear from these data that the households in question depend reasonably heavily on a broad set of environmental goods. On average, these goods comprise 35% of total household income, a share almost equivalent to that of subsistence consumption (37%) and substantially greater than non-environmental cash income (26%). Further, the majority of these environmental goods are NTFPs.

The consumption and sale of NTFP goods alone comprises 21.5% of household total income on average. As we saw earlier, there is a very wide range of NTFPs being used by the households; thus this significant total share is made up for some households by a large number of small utilizations, the type of activities usually overlooked in conventional economic studies of rural households. None the less, there are certain NTFP uses that stand out for these households, namely the value of firewood use, the value of livestock browse and graze offered by woodlands, and the cash income arising from the sale of NTFP goods (e.g. thatching grass, carpentry products).

Another striking feature of these figures is the fact that in total value terms the use of NTFPs generally rises as overall household incomes rise. Take firewood for example. There is a systematic relationship between the total value of firewood used and the income quintile of the households.

Indeed, top quintile households use roughly 2.5 times as much firewood per household as those in the bottom quintile. In similar fashion, top quintile households use roughly twice as much NTFPs for housing inputs as those in the bottom quintile, and 5.5 times as much woodland browse and graze for their livestock.

The value per household of cash income from NTFP sales appears to peak in the 4th quintile; none the less, top-quintile households still source over 2.5 times as much cash income from NTFPs as bottom-quintile households. So in absolute terms, NTFP resource demands appear to increase as households within the rural life space become more wealthy.

Conversely, dependence on NTFPs, and indeed environmental goods more broadly, appears to decline with income. That is to say, the income budget shares of NTFPs and total environmental goods basically decrease as the income quintile of households rises. The overall NTFP shares in Table 15.4 display this property less clearly than the overall environmental income shares. Thus, for the bottom four quintiles, the share of total income derived from NTFPs hovers between 22 and 24%. However, for the top quintile this falls fairly decisively to 16.5%. The decline in the share of total environmental income is more pronounced: from 40% for the bottom quintile it consistently decreases to reach 29% for the top quintile. Note that some of the individual NTFP subgroups also display this property of declining dependence as incomes rise. Income budget shares for the consumption of own-collected NTFP foods, own-collected firewood and other own-collected NTFPs all decline systematically with income. (Income budget shares for the use of NTFPs as housing inputs and fertilizers also basically decline as income rises but the relationship is not smooth.) What this means, of course, is that while it is true that richer households consume quantitatively greater amounts of NTFPs, it is poorer households that depend more heavily on NTFPs for their livelihoods.

Economic underpinnings of rural households' extensive use of NTFPs

We have seen that rural households, particularly poorer rural households, indeed use NTFPs extensively. What explains this pattern of use? We do not believe it is because rural households are innately more environmentally minded or naturally more orientated towards using environmental goods. Rather, it is because the economic characteristics of NTFPs match the economic characteristics and constraints of rural households that we listed earlier: NTFPs 'fit in' naturally to the current economic system of poor constrained rural households.

First, there is the fact that the great bulk of forests and woodlands in developing countries are held under communal tenure, with NTFPs (a largely non-destructive resource use) generally available under conditions of effective open access. This implies that households do not have to purchase NTFP goods in order to consume them; rather they can be collected and consumed.

As we noted earlier, rural households' economic transactions are only partially monetized, thanks to the large number of missing product markets caused by the high unit transactions costs of trading. The economic remoteness of many rural households therefore results in them being cash constrained. When they do acquire cash, there are often economic priorities that can only be purchased using cash, such as basic foods (cooking oils, salt, sugar, etc.), clothing, school fees and the like. What freely provided NTFPs offer, then, is an alternative source of goods and services that economizes on the household's use of its scarce cash resources. Rather than purchase fuel, the household can collect firewood; rather than purchase agricultural implements, it can collect the wood and make them itself; rather than purchase fruits, it can collect them from the wild. Take for example the household data in Table 15.4. For the bottom quintile, only 27% of their total income is actually monetized; although this figure rises, even for the top quintile less than half of their total income is monetized. It is no coincidence that as the share of cash income in total income rises, the share of environmental resources and NTFPs in total income falls. Thus one reason for the widespread use of NTFPs is as a response by poor rural households to their cash-constrained nature, caused ultimately by the pervasive failure of formal markets and the absence of trading opportunities.

Second, and leading on from this point, NTFPs can overwhelmingly be collected using unskilled labour, and this matches the factor endowments of rural households as described earlier. For some NTFPs, collection involves simply the application of labour, such as picking up dead wood or plucking foods. This is one of the reasons why children and older people are often heavy users of NTFPs: not only do these groups tend to have less control over cash resources, but they can also simply help themselves to resources using their own labour. For the majority of NTFPs, collection does require the use of some equipment, such as an axe for cutting wood, a machete for grasses and leaves, snares for hunting wild animals and so on. In general though this equipment is inexpensive and is fairly durable, and use of equipment does not need a high level of education or skills. Even where local rules exist about the harvesting or collection of NTFPs (e.g. about how to take bark from medicinal trees), these are simple to learn and do not stop individuals collecting the resource should they choose to do so.

Third, not just NTFP collection but NTFP processing also is a set of activities that requires the application of either unskilled labour alone or unskilled labour augmented by low-level capital equipment. As an example, a common set of NTFP-based products is baskets and mats made from leaves, creepers or rushes. Weaving these baskets and mats is labour-intensive but it is not highly skilled, most case studies reporting that these products are said by local respondents to be the type of things that anyone can make. Likewise the only capital equipment required is a weaving needle, which is a very cheap item to buy. Similarly, wood is often used to make a variety of household implements and agricultural tools, or is carved to make products aimed at the tourist market. Once again, interviews with resource makers stress that the skills used to make these objects can be acquired in a very short time and the capital equipment required is minimal.

Finally, where NTFP foods are processed to make commercial products, such as fruit wines, palm wines, dried meats, dried fish and dried insects, again the skills and capital equipment required are low: it is essentially a matter of allocating sufficient household labour to complete the task. As discussed earlier, due to the difficulties that rural households face in capital accumulation, because formal credit markets generally fail in rural areas and because education levels are low, rural households are usually endowed with unskilled labour but poorly endowed with capital. So another reason for the extensive use of NTFPs by rural households is that the factor inputs required to collect and process NTFPs (unskilled labour, little capital equipment) match closely the factor endowments of the classic rural household. (These required factor inputs, combined with open access to the NTFP resource, means that NTFP activities have very low entry barriers. In such circumstances we would therefore expect the returns to NTFP activities to be correspondingly low.)

Fourth, households also use NTFPs in response to the general riskiness of rural economic activities. The use of NTFPs, particularly what have been classified as 'minor forest products', during times of household stress is an observation common to much of the NTFP case study literature. NTFPs display a certain degree of non-covariance with respect to agricultural output. When crops fail due to drought or disease, or when shocks hit the household such as unemployment, death or disease, some NTFPs will still be available for the household to either consume or use to generate cash income to purchase its essential needs.

Thus it is economically rational for risk-averse rural households to hold a portfolio of production opportunities that exploits this non-covariance. In this sense, commonly held forests and woodlands can be regarded as providing a set of back-stop resources that insure households against the failure of other, higher return production activities. Thus, even if the returns per hectare of woodland were systematically below that of agricultural land, rural villages would still retain common lands for this purpose.

Finally, the argument comes full circle. One of the reasons that rural households use NTFPs so extensively is precisely because they are open-access resources. There are a number of reasons for the survival of communally held resources, for example the insurance element noted above; however, a major reason for the survival of such resources is the very low income levels of rural households. Resource privatization is an expensive business: households taking charge of privatized resources usually need to spend time and money on creating exclusion (e.g. by building fences), on enforcement (e.g. employing guards to monitor incursions) and on punishing infractions (by going through the courts).

Particularly where a resource has previously been held in common, privatization is often strongly contested and consequently these various costs can be expected to be high. Where households are generally poor, the private costs of resource privatization are likely to be far higher than the potential private gains from control of the resource. Thus the low incomes of rural areas underpin the existence of commonly held resources, which in turn underpins the extensive use of NTFPs by those very same low-income households (on the relationship between efficient property rights regimes and transactions costs, see Coase 1960; Bromley 1989; de Meza & Gould 1992).

CAN RURAL DEVELOPMENT BE BASED AROUND NTFPS?

We have presented evidence that rural households' use of NTFPs is widespread and significant in terms of their overall livelihoods. We have also suggested that the cause of this extensive NTFP use by poor rural households is the match between the economic characteristics of NTFPs and the economic endowments and constraints of those same rural households. Can we therefore conclude from this that the commercialization of NTFPs is economically feasible and likely to bring substantial economic benefits to rural poor? Further, if commercialization were feasible, what would it be likely to do to the resource base that produces these NTFPs? In other words, what light does the analysis above shed on the possibility of using NTFPs to meet the twin goals of economic development and environmental conservation? I argue that there are substantial difficulties here, arising from the same economic characteristics of rural households and the causes of their NTFP use that were listed earlier. I look at a number of issues in turn and draw on the case study literature to illustrate where they have led to problems for various NTFPs.

The problem of preferences

We saw earlier that one of the reasons for rural households' NTFP use was their low incomes and the still-partial monetization of many of their economic transactions. However, it is a truism that as individuals and households become more affluent, their demands for goods and services change. In particular, people choose to consume more highly preferred goods or goods of a higher quality. (There is abundant evidence for these demand shifts in the higher-income developed countries.) However, evidence from academic studies and from history suggests that NTFPs do not have high product quality or are not in general highly preferred goods. One way of showing this is to look at income elasticities of demand for NTFPs, as these elasticities reveal what the demand response of households will be to any increase in their incomes.

Unfortunately, demand elasticities for NTFPs are not easy to come by, due to the lack of attention paid to such goods by formal economic studies. Thus we have culled evidence from two sources. The first is the author's own study of households and environmental resources in Shindi, Zimbabwe and the second is from a recent literature review reported in Köhlin (1998).

In only one case, wild fish demands, is the recorded elasticity greater than 1 (i.e. a luxury good), although it is believed this has much to do with the supply conditions of wild fish in the study site. Otherwise most elasticities are closer to zero than to 1. For example, wild fruits collectively and mice have income elasticities of 0.3-0.4; woodland-derived wild vegetables have an elasticity of 0-0.2; firewood has an elasticity of 0.4; and NTFP-derived goods have income elasticities of 0.4-0.5. While these elasticities are positive, so that increases in income within the range of incomes spanned by the sample will increase overall NTFP demands, the budget shares of these goods will decline, to be replaced in importance by other more preferred goods. Table 15.5 gives one example of this, by comparing the income elasticities of woodland-derived and field-derived wild vegetables. The fact that the latter are much higher than the former reflects the higher preference households have for these foods, and also means that as their incomes rise rural households will switch to field-derived wild vegetables and away from their woodland-derived counterparts.

Further, the positive income elasticities in this table for NTFPs reflect the rather low income levels of Shindi households. Evidence from the regressions suggests that at higher income levels these elasticities would turn negative, so that at higher incomes these NTFPs would actually be inferior goods.

While this table draws on the wider literature on NTFPs, most of the quoted elasticities refer to firewood, as this has been the main quantitative focus of the literature. Three studies of firewood demands conclude that income elasticities turn negative as incomes rise (Amacher *et al.* 1993 for Nepal; Bagahawatte 1997 for Sri Lanka; Shyamsundar & Kramer 1996 for Madagascar). Further, the other elasticities cited are all either low and positive, or negative. This implies that as households get richer, the absolute quantities of NTFPs that they wish to consume will decrease until at some point NTFP demands will fall to zero. This evidence from formally estimated income elasticities is also backed up by classic observations of consumption shifts that occur as rural households become richer. For example, one immediate shift is from natural construction materials (earth bricks, poles, thatching grass) towards higher-quality purchased substitutes (breeze blocks, zinc roofing). Likewise, richer households choose to consume more purchased foods and beverages and less wild foods and locally produced alcohols. As the income elasticities suggested, richer households also prefer to switch away from firewood towards other sources of energy and lighting.

There are good economic reasons why NTFPs are regarded as inferior goods by richer households. Their production is variable, the quality of the goods cannot be controlled and other substitutes have been bred or produced with higher product quality in mind. Thus more affluent households shift to better substitutes when they can afford to do so. However, the key point is that the inferiority of NTFP goods creates a real problem for NTFP commercialization projects. Dependence on, and use of, NTFPs are linked to poverty and to market failure rather than to household choice: the current prevalence of NTFP use by rural households is a result of their low incomes rather than the attraction of NTFP products themselves. A dramatic illustration of this is given by Hegde *et al.* (1996), who argue that the very high rates of NTFP utilization of their sample households are caused by the fact that these households earn barely more than the Indian minimum wage, and present empirical evidence that as households get richer so their NTFP use declines. So where NTFPs are inferior, attempts to commercialize them will founder on a lack of long-term product demand.

High transactions costs of trading

In our discussion of the stylized features of rural areas, we stressed the role that economic remoteness played in underpinning low rural incomes and in causing the failure of formal product markets. This is also a major cause of the low monetization of rural households' activities, since trading in formal markets outside the rural area is so often uneconomic.

These transactions costs will affect NTFP commercialization projects just as much as they would affect any other project aimed at commercializing rural produce. The high unit costs of transportation imply that NTFPs which have a low unit value relative to their weight will have low if not negative margins in the marketplace.

This may be the case for a number of NTFPs. On account of the open-access nature of the resource rules surrounding forests and woodlands in developing countries and the fact that many are inferior goods, NTFP prices tend to be fairly low. Some NTFPs will have high weight-to-price ratios, especially those made of wood. For example, it is noticeable that despite the reasonable prices being attained for carvings on the major roads of Zimbabwe, production activity is contained within a reasonably narrow area, close enough to the road to make transporting the wood inputs an economic proposition. High trading costs have also been implicated in the lack of NTFP commercialization in Latin America (Richards 1993). Of course, the converse of this point is the effect that road building has on reducing trading costs and thereby stimulating the marketization of rural produce generally. The impact of the Belem-Brasilia and the Transama-zon highways on economic conditions in the Amazon basin has been widely noted. However, assuming that NTFP projects take the physical infrastructure as given, the impact of transactions costs on the profitability of NTFP commercialization will remain a serious constraint for remoter rural areas for a number of NTFPs.

Storage problems

Another feature of rural areas we noted was the generally low levels of physical capital. This is true both at the household level and at the community level. Rural areas not only lack household-based productive capital but also the area-wide capital stock, such as power supplies and communications, on which the productivity of household-based enterprises depends. One key problem that this raises is a lack of appropriate storage facilities, such as an absence of refrigeration and refrigerated transport. Indeed, storage of goods is often a major difficulty for rural households. Even for longer-lasting foods such as grains, losses are regularly incurred thanks to mould, rotting and crop pests despite the careful construction of granaries and the use of locally available goods to line and protect these granaries.

Problems with storage could be a major constraint to the commercialization of NTFPs where these goods are perishable. A substantial fraction of the NTFPs examined under the 'Hidden Harvest' programmes are exactly these types of goods: fruits, fruit-based beverages, wild meats and even wild fish. All these would require reasonably capital-intensive storage if commercialization projects were to succeed. Appropriate storage provides two major economic functions, the absence of which would cause problems to emerge. The first function is that of product preservation. Given that the commercialization of NTFPs requires transportation of products to new markets, an absence of adequate storage would result in high losses of products due to spoilage (rotting, bruising in transit, excess fermentation of liquids, etc.). The other function that storage can play is that of interseasonal supply smoothing. Without it, products can only be supplied to the market during the season of their production, resulting in glutted markets, lower product prices and unsmoothed income streams. Thus seasonality and perishability lower the economic returns of NTFPs to rural communities, thereby making these activities less attractive.

Production risk

As discussed earlier, rural households face considerable levels of risk, and one reason for the preservation of woodlands for NTFPs is as a risk-spreading insurance mechanism against severe shocks to the other economic activities of the household. However, in the medium to long term risk-averse rural households will wish not just to spread risk but to reduce it.

If NTFP activities themselves still involve considerable production risks, then such activities will be less attractive to rural households than other, more certain income flows. This will be a consideration where the supply of NTFPs is dependent on climatic conditions, such as some of the foods mentioned earlier, or where NTFPs are prone to disease.

Open access and the costs of privatization

A further concern derives from the fact that many forests and woodlands in developing countries are held under communal tenure, with usufruct rights to NTFPs very often being effectively open access. If NTFPs were to be commercialized, then one immediate concern would relate to the degree of exploitation of the resource. Raising the value of an NTFP will naturally increase supply pressures on the resource. Where NTFP use is nondestructive to the resource stock, this is not necessarily a problem. However, where NTFP use can diminish the resource stock, then the commercialization of the resource can have serious implications for objectives of environmental conservation. Indeed, there are a number of cases where increases in resource pressure consequent on increased demand for NTFP goods has had serious environmental consequences.

One such case is the impact of basket-making on an indigenous tree in Botswana. The main source of leaves for baskets is *Hyphaene petersiana*, which stands up very well to intense harvesting pressure. However, the main source of dye for these baskets is the bark of *Berchemia discolor*, and harvesting the bark can harm the tree if done too frequently. The increase in demand for Botswana baskets has increased substantially the demand for dye inputs, and this in turn has led to the death of many *B. discolor* in basket-making areas (Cunningham & Terry 1995). Similarly, the high demand for *Warbergia salutaris* as a source of medicines in Zimbabwe has led to the almost complete extinction of this species within the country (Mukamuri & Kozanai 1999). There are numerous cases of this dynamic in the Amazonian rain forests, where palm heart production has resulted in the near elimination of *Euterpe edulis* and *Euterpe oleracea*; the cutting of palms for fruits in Peru has rapidly depleted the numbers of *Mauritia flexuosa, Mauritellia peruviana* and *Jessenia bataua*; and the felling of trees for rosewood oil production had led to the virtual extinction of *Aniba rosaeodora* and *Aniba ducke* in economically accessible parts of Brazil (Richards 1993). Commercialization of a destructive NTFP use when held under open access can thus have severe environmental consequences for the species in question (though not necessarily for the forest as a whole).

A longer-term concern relates to the question of who gains from NTFP commercialization. We noted earlier that the existence of communal tenure over woodlands is related to the high costs of exclusion, monitoring and enforcement relative to the benefits to be gained from private woodland control. In other words, the tenurial arrangements over woodlands are related to the ratio of costs and benefits faced by rural households and communities. If as a result of NTFP projects the per-hectare returns to woodland rise, then this ratio changes and economic incentives will arise to change tenurial arrangements. In particular, privatization may emerge as a cost-effective option. However, this is only likely to be cost-effective for households that are already more affluent than others, since only these will be able to bear the private costs of resource control.

Two groups stand out here. The first is local élites. There is evidence that as open-access resources rise in value, these resources become co-opted by local élites. The classic study of this phenomenon is Ensminger's (1990) analysis of resource privatization in rural Kenya. In response to the lowering of trading costs via cheaper transportation costs, communal grazing lands were privatized with the consent of rural elders who themselves benefited from this process. However, this process of élite partitioning of commons resources in response to changing economic conditions has also been found in India (Jodha 1986) and Brazil (Hecht 1985). The second group is outsiders. Town-dwellers or traders/middlemen with superior technology and access to capital may gain control of either the NTFP resources or the NTFP goods' trade and thereby arrogate to themselves the economic returns to these goods. In either case, commercialization-induced changes in local tenure could not only stymie the expected socioeconomic gains from NTFP products to the generality of rural households, but also by triggering the privatization of woodlands and other common resources may leave the rural poor worse off by removing from them a vital consumption back-stop and a source of insurance goods.

Incentives for domestication and technical substitution

We have discussed the many reasons above why NTFPs are currently often low-value goods, such as missing markets, the prevalence of local trading, low local demand and the open-access nature of NTFP resources. One implication of these low values is that neither rural households nor outside agencies currently have an incentive to invest in any sort of resource management or product improvement, since the costs of such actions would far outweigh the benefits. However, this would change if NTFPs were to become higher-value goods.

There are two processes to mention here: domestication and the development of technical substitutes.[9] It is globally true that when natural resources become valuable, there is pressure to intensify production and to domesticate the resource. Take as an example a wild fruit. While prices for the fruit remain low, it is unprofitable for households to do anything other than collect the fruit from the wild. However, as fruit prices rise, at some threshold value it becomes economic for the household (or some other agency) to incur the time and resource costs of establishing the resource under their own control, through planting and tending the relevant species.

Furthermore, domestication also allows resource managers to improve product quality through the development of a constant, uniform or standardized product, thereby maintaining or even increasing product prices. This dynamic is the general story of the development of agricultural products and there is no reason why NTFPs should be any different. Indeed, there are ample examples of cases where rising NTFP values have led to precisely this response. Perhaps the most famous is that of Brazilian rubber *(Hevea brasiliensis)* collection from natural forests. As rubber prices rose in the early part of the century, so it became economic to establish rubber plantations in South-East Asia; more recently, rubber plantations have been established in Brazil as well and these now supply 60% of Brazil's market (Browder 1992).

Another classic NTFP affected in this way is brazil nuts. In response to rising nut prices, several thousand hectares of *Berthol-letia excelsa* plantations have now been established within Brazil itself. So neither rubber nor brazil nuts provide a solid foundation for NTFP commercialization in the Amazon in the long run. Indeed, it is difficult to point to a wild resource which, once valuable, has remained undomesticated (an extensive list of other Amazonian NTFPs that have been domesticated is given by Homma 1992). Beyond a certain point, then, the commercialization of NTFPs will almost certainly lead to the product being removed from the forest and being placed on the farm instead.

Additionally, if NTFPs become high-value goods, there is an economic incentive to invest in the search for cheaper synthetic substitutes, if this is technically feasible. Once such substitutes are developed, the market for NTFPs often collapses - the 'bust' following the 'boom'. Richards (1993) discusses many such examples of substitute-induced market collapses in commercialized Amazonian NTFPs. At various times these have included dyewood *(Caesalpinia echi-nata)*, vegetable ivory *(Phytelephus macrocarpa)*, balata *(Manilkara bidentada)*, leche caspi

(Couma macrocarpa), barbasco *(Lonchocarpus* spp.), babaçu oil *(Orbignya phalerata)*, cumaru nuts *(Dipteryx odorata)*, sorva latex *(Couma utilis* and *C. rigida)* and of course rubber. Such technical substitutions are problems for the entire goal of NTFP-based economic development, since they raise the spectre of entire markets disappearing just as rural households have come to depend on the NTFP resource for a high proportion of their livelihoods.

CONCLUSIONS

We should not therefore underestimate the problems associated with the use of NTFPs for the economic development of rural areas. Although rural households currently use NTFPs quite extensively, this is a consequence of the low incomes, capital scarcity, missing markets, riskiness in production and tenure conditions that characterize rural areas. It is these that make it economically rational for households currently to use NTFPs, as these are low value, depend on unskilled labour for their collection and processing, and offset to a degree the riskiness of other production activities.

However, this is no guarantee of success when it comes to the commercialization of NTFPs:

(i) there is little evidence that NTFP dependence in the long run is desired at all by rural households;

(ii) there are economic problems associated with the costs of both trading and storing NTFPs;

(iii) NTFPs still have levels of production risk that may make them unattractive;

(iv) the commercialization of NTFPs is likely to lead to the elimination of some species;

(v) NTFP development may also undermine the communal tenure system, thereby removing the wider benefits of NTFP use from poorer households; and

(vi) NTFP projects aimed at raising product prices will have to face the twin pressures of domestication and technical substitution that have affected almost all other wild products. In the face of these problems, NTFP extraction-based rural economies are likely to be highly unstable, thereby undermining the goal of improved rural household welfare.

So what type of NTFPs might meet the twin desires of increased rural incomes and greater protection for forests? Based on this review, such products would need to have a number of characteristics:

1 a market amongst high-income consumers in order to surmount the low-income elasticities of rural households for these products;

2 prices high enough to overcome the transactions costs of collection and trading but which are not high enough to trigger investment in technical substitutes where these could feasibly be developed;

3 be a reasonably durable product, so that storage is not a binding constraint;

4 have a fairly low production-risk profile;

5 harvesting that is non-destructive to the resource stock;

6 returns per hectare that make it economically rational to conserve forests and woodlands but which are not high enough to trigger resource privatization;

7 a species ecology that rules out domestication of the resource.

Whether such products exist is a moot point. One goal for the next phase of forestry and NTFP research might be to identify and publicize such products. Only then are the initial aspirations for NTFP use to both protect the forest and alleviate rural poverty likely to be fulfilled.

7

Ecophysiology of Forests

INTRODUCTION

The global significance of forests has grown with our awareness that they contain a disproportionate amount of the earth's biodiversity and its terrestrial carbon stores. In addition, forests are recognized as major buffers to climate change because they can absorb energy efficiently and dissipate a large fraction of heat in the evaporation of water. Recently, trees have also been recognized as a major source of compounds that interact with ozone and create haze (Lerdau & Keller 1997). To understand the ramifications of these kinds of ecological interactions requires an appreciation of the underlying processes. If such understanding can be extended to large areas, the implications of climatic change and other alterations in the environment can be assessed more realistically.

Over the last half-century, the study of ecophysiology has slowly emerged from the laboratories of physiologists into the field where ecologists labour. Improvements in technology allowed this extension by the introduction of instruments suitable for making *in situ* measurements on individual trees. Portable gas-exchange cuvettes for measuring CO_2 consumption and O_2 outflow, branch bags, open-top chambers that allow experimental control of atmosphere for large trees, weighing lysimeters and heat pulse meters are a few examples of these technological improvements.

This emergence of ecophysiology has required that the forest be viewed as whole assemblages rather than the sum of individual components. Moreover, this expanded view of forests has led to collaboration with other types of scientists, such as micrometeorologists, who developed instruments and mathematical models to estimate energy and gas exchange from extensive areas. Starting in the 1960s, ecologists also contributed by constructing quantitative models to describe the movement of radioisotopes through food chains. During the International Biological Program in the 1970s, these food-chain models were extended to describe the capture, storage and release of carbon, water and minerals cycling through forest ecosystems (Reichle 1970, 1981).

In this chapter, we confine our discussion to living vegetation, which generally represents less than 50% of the total organic content in an ecosystem. Even with this restriction we illustrate that it is possible to predict the probability of disturbances that could result in tree death and lead to alterations in the pools of resources available to regenerating forests. The presentation is organized around a selected set of ecological concerns for which ecophysiological research has provided critical insights. These concerns include how alterations in climate, atmospheric chemistry and management practices affect the growth, composition and susceptibility of forests to insects and pathogens.

RESPONSES OF FORESTS TO VARIATION IN CLIMATE

The absolute limits on tree distribution are generally associated with climatic limitations. There has therefore been an effort to define these limits, as well as the optimum conditions of temperature and moisture for broadly representative types of forests. In this section we review the contributions of ecophysiology in defining functional limitations of temperature and moisture conditions (Mason & Langenheim 1957).

Determination of temperature optimum and limits

Ecophysiological studies have established the lower temperature limits for tropical, subtropical, temperate and boreal forests. Many subtropical species are able to concentrate solute and thus lower the freezing point in cells below that tolerated by tropical trees. Some temperate trees extend the freezing threshold down to -45°C via the mechanism of supercooling, whereas boreal species are able to transfer water out of the nucleus into cell walls and thereby withstand exposure to liquid nitrogen at -196°C. These adaptations to low temperatures serve to define the potential geographical limits of various types of forests.

Defining the optimum temperature for growth or photosynthesis has traditionally been made in the laboratory on seedlings or from excised branches or buds of mature trees. By measuring the production rates of metabolic heat and CO_2 efflux of excised buds at varying temperatures, Anekonda *et al.* (1993, 1994) described relationships with growth and geographical origins of *Sequoia sempervirens*.

However, the temperature optimum for photosynthesis often exhibits seasonal adjustment (Neilson *et al.* 1972; Strain *et al.* 1976; Slatyer & Morrow 1977). Intuitively, we would think that optimal growth for a species would occur at temperatures typical of those that occur in the species' native range. In fact, this is not true. Studies by Hawkins and Sweet (1989) demonstrated that optimum temperatures for a broad array of tree species native to New Zealand averaged nearly 8°C above typical midsummer temperatures, whereas faster-growing species introduced from North America were closely adapted to the present New Zealand climate.

Further refinements in growth-room experiments identified the importance of root temperature (Babalola *et al.* 1968; Bowen 1970; Donovan & McLeod 1985). Root temperature affects the rate that water may be taken up through root membranes, which helps explain the distribution patterns of closely related genera across broad climatic zones (Waring & Winner 1996).

Physiological definition of soil drought

Inadequate precipitation can lead to a soil water deficit. Ralph Slatyer (1967) set forth the basic principles of how plants respond to soil drought but until Per Scholander and colleagues at Scripps Institution of Oceanography constructed a portable pressure chamber, ecophysiologists were unable to measure water potential gradients in tall trees (Scholander *et al.* 1965). With the pressure chamber, relationships between relative water content, solute potential and incipient plas-molysis could be assessed and seasonal comparisons made to evaluate the physiological impact of drought. In drought-prone areas, seedlings often experience near-lethal water potentials because their roots do not extend as deeply as those of mature trees. The pressure chamber provided the first direct measure of water availability to deeply rooted trees when measurements were taken at night under conditions when transpiration approaches zero. The fraction of water extracted from different depths within the soil profile has more recently been determined through analysis of the isotopic composition ($8^{18}O$ and $8^{2}H$) of xylem sap.

Sapwood as a water reservoir in trees

Trees contain a large volume of sapwood, which is significant because this tissue serves during the day and through periods of drought as a temporary reservoir of water that extends the opportunities for trees to photosynthesize (Waring & Running 1978; Holbrook & Sinclair 1992; Borchert 1994; Tognetti & Borghetti 1994; Goldstein *et al.* 1998). The extraction of large amounts of water from stems and branches involves some cavitation in the water-conducting elements of the xylem. Rapid recharge of the sapwood reservoir occurs through uptake of water by roots and through foliage and twigs (Katz *et al.* 1989; Goldstein *et al.* 1998). The amount of water released from sapwood for a specific increase in the water potential gradient defines the 'capacitance', an essential term in modelling the water balance of trees (Edwards *et al.* 1986) and forests (Waring & Running 1978). As more water is extracted from the sapwood, the water transport pathway between the soil and evaporating surfaces of the foliage becomes less efficient, with implications for both transpiration and photosynthesis.

Transpiration by forests

Transpiration was the first physiological process directly measured for an entire forest by employing an energy budget analysis (Monteith & Unsworth 1990). A forest, unlike vegetation of shorter more uniform stature, represents an aerodynamically rough surface, a property that creates turbulence in the flow of air, even under calm conditions. As a consequence of this aerodynamic roughness, forests can absorb large amounts of solar radiation without experiencing temperatures that would be lethal to shorter vegetation, even when transpiration is restricted.

Stomatal response is closely linked to the pho-tosynthetic process. Consequently, accurate transpiration models separate the photosynthetically active component of solar radiation (400-700nm) from the total and take into account hydraulic constraints and variation in ambient concentrations of CO_2 (Williams *et al.* 1997). Most models that predict the mean canopy conductance of whole forests are still empirical, developed from responses recorded under a range of environmental conditions using gas-exchange cuvettes or inferred from flux measurements determined when the forest canopy is dry.

From the extensive literature published on leaf and canopy stomatal conductance, some important generalizations have emerged. First, the maximum canopy conductance for a wide variety of forests averages two to four times the maximum value measured on individual leaves. The leaf area of woodlands and forests is expressed in terms of leaf area index

(m^2 of projected leaf surface per m^2 of ground) and ranges from less than $1 m^2 m^{-2}$ to $12 m^2 m^{-2}$. The maximum canopy conductance for forests is lower than the maximum that would be expected from the maximum canopy conductance of individual leaves because the illumination of individual leaves decreases as they shade each other when the total canopy leaf area increases. This reduces the stomatal conductance of individual leaves below that which would occur in full sunlight. As a result of self-shading, the maximum canopy conductance approaches a constant at leaf area indices greater than $3.0 m^2 m^{-2}$ (Kelliher *et al.* 1995). These two generalities greatly simplify the estimation of maximum stomatal conductance and reduce the need for accurate assessment of leaf area indices above $3.0 m^2 m^{-2}$ for purposes of estimating transpiration.

Although the *maximum* canopy conductance may not differ significantly among forests, this does not mean that reliable estimates of *actual* canopy stomatal conductance can be extrapolated from measurements made on seedlings or saplings to tall trees. As noted above, trees have deeper root systems and a larger volume of sapwood than seedlings or saplings, yet even with these benefits mature trees offer an increasingly long and tortuous path for water movement from roots to leaves (Mencuccini & Grace 1996).

As a result, comparative studies between young and older trees often show that when water is readily available in the soil, older trees may be more sensitive to atmospheric vapour pressure deficits (Ryan & Yoder 1997). The differences are not simply in response to height and the hydrostatic gradient of $0.01 MPa m^{-1}$ (Goldstein *et al.* 1998). The spacing between individual trees also plays a role. As trees increase in size, branches elongate as a function of the space between trees. Longer branches offer a less efficient pathway for water transport than the main stem, and can reduce transpiration and photosynthesis per unit of leaf area by hastening stomatal closure during the day (Walcroft *et al.* 1996; Hubbard *et al.* 1999).

RESPONSES OF FORESTS TO VARIATION IN NUTRIENT AVAILABILITY

One of the more challenging problems for eco-physiologists is to assess the supply of nutrients available to sustain forest growth. As noted in Chapter 7 (this volume), little insight is gained by simply analysing the elemental content in the soil because many nutrients are present in unavailable forms, and trees differ in their abilities to extract essential nutrients from throughout the soil profile. In addition, a range of nutrients can be acquired from the air via aerosol deposition on foliage (Tagliavini *et al.* 1998) and additional nitrogen can be acquired through root associations with symbiotic nitrogen-fixing bacteria. Physiologists and chemists, starting with Liebig in 1840, have established those elements essential for growth, defined specific deficiency symptoms and related concentrations in foliage to minimum requirements. In this section, we emphasize two additional components of nutrition that have significant impact on the growth of forests: balance and internal recycling. In a later section, we discuss how nutrient imbalances increase the susceptibility of forests to insects and pathogens.

Optimum nutrition

Torsten Ingestad (1979) developed a hydroponic system where the balance and total amount of nutrients could be varied daily to maintain relative growth rates constant over short periods. In a series of experiments he defined 'optimum nutritional balance' as that state when the ratios of nutrients in solution and leaf tissue maintain similar values. Under controlled laboratory conditions, the optimum nutrient balance, relative to the concentration of nitrogen, is similar for a wide range of tree species.

Further refinement in understanding and assessment of nutritional status is gained by defining 'metabolically active forms' in plant tissue (Attiwill & Adams 1993). For phosphorus, the inorganic form best reflects its availability (Chapin & Kedrowski 1983; Polglase *et al.* 1992).

For nitrogen, most reserves are in the form of proteins. Above a certain concentration, excess nitrogen accumulates as free amino acids. This may be symptomatic of a generally unfavourable physiological status (Näsholm & Ericsson 1990; Ericsson *et al.* 1993) or it may be evidence that the rate of photosynthesis does not depend exclusively on substrate concentration.

Sune Linder, a compatriot of Ingestad, extended these optimum nutrient addition experiments into the field, providing convincing evidence that the growth of boreal forests of pine and spruce are more limited by slow release of nutrients through decomposition of organic matter than by climatic restrictions on photosynthesis and growth (Axelsson & Axelsson 1986; Linder & Flower-Ellis 1992).

Internal recycling of nutrients

It has been long recognized that evergreen forests can accumulate large amounts of foliage in excess of that required for efficient interception of solar radiation (Waring & Franklin 1979; Wang *et al.* 1991). It is also known that a linear correlation exists between the total nitrogen content in foliage and wood production (Ågren 1983; Hunter *et al.* 1987; Waring 1989). By comparing the nutrient content in leaf litterfall with that in new and older foliage, it has been estimated that initially well-fertilized plantations can maintain favourable growth rates over decades by recycling stored nutrient capital acquired during development of a dense canopy (Millard & Proe 1992; Miller *et al.* 1992, 1996; Miller 1995).

Ecophysiologists have contributed to our understanding of nutrient uptake and internal recyling by defining seasonal patterns more precisely and by identifying the dynamic exchange from one internal pool to another. Insights gained from such analyses include recognition that:

- fast growth of evergreens results in a greater proportion of shoot nitrogen reserves going into new growth at the expense of older foliage (Müller 1949; Hawkins *et al.* 1998);
- when low growth rates prevail, elements in short supply are preferentially translocated to new growth (Müller 1949; Hawkins *et al.* 1998);
- deciduous trees may obtain more than 50% of their nitrogen from internal sources (Weinbaum & van Kessel 1998);
- during periods of rapid leaf expansion, uptake of nutrients from the soil plays a minor role in meeting demands for deciduous as well as evergreen trees (Mead & Preston 1994; Weinbaum & van Kessel 1998);
- understorey vegetation may contribute disproportionately to the acquisition and recycling of nutrients within forest ecosystems (Raison *et al.* 1993; Buchmann *et al.* 1996).

These insights have important implications in the management of vegetation and in the assessment of forest ecosystem response to atmospheric deposition of nitrogen and sulphur-rich compounds (Aber *et al.* 1989; Steudler *et al.* 1989; Johnson 1992). For example, significant changes in the ratio of calcium to aluminium and the concentrations of essential trace elements in annual growth rings of trees bear witness to the impact of air pollution (Baes & McLaughlin 1984; Bondietti *et al.* 1989).

8

Carbon Balance Analyses

With increased concerns about how forests may respond to changes in atmospheric chemistry and climate, there has been a major effort to gain a better understanding of the processes controlling tree growth. This effort has been accentuated by observations that historical measures of production no longer apply, possibly as a result of changes in genetic composition of trees, application of fertilizers, control of competing vegetation and alterations in atmospheric chemistry (CO_2, ozone, acid rain, etc.). Developing a more integrated picture of how processes such as photosynthesis, respiration and allocation combine to affect the structure and function of the autotrophic component of forest ecosystems is critical to predicting forest growth under changing global conditions. Although net primary production represents all carbon products produced annually from photosynthesis after subtracting losses from respiration, the components of respiration and growth vary significantly depending on the environment, composition of tissue, and allocation of resources above and below ground.

Canopy photosynthesis

Photosynthesis is among the best understood of all physiological processes. Historically, most research on photosynthesis has been done under laboratory conditions on individual trees. A series of basic equations have been developed for individual leaves that describe the capture of light energy, the diffusion of CO_2 and the enzymatic transformations involved in the photosynthetic process (Farquhar *et al.* 1980; Farquhar & Sharkey 1982). To apply these basic equations to whole canopies involves an analysis of how photosynthetic capacity and environment vary spatially. Sophisticated models have been constructed to predict the quantity of direct and diffuse radiation absorbed within a forest canopy (Norman & Jarvis 1975; Leuning *et al.* 1995; Le Roux *et al.* 1999).

Although such models are useful for predicting the maximum rates of photosynthesis, they are not able to predict rates under varying environments. To extend estimates of photosynthesis to whole canopies two important simplifications are generally made: (i) the canopy is considered to represent a single large leaf with varying ability to absorb radiation; and (ii) the relation between photosynthesis and light absorption is extended in time to achieve a more linear response than occurs instantaneously (Wang *et al.* 1991). Further simplifications are possible by combining the effects of subfreezing temperatures, drought, vapour pressure deficits and nutritional limitations on the conversion of absorbed radiation into photosynthetic products into a general equation as suggested by Landsberg (1986).

Gross photosynthesis:

:a^(I)=e/(H_2O)/(*D*)/(*T*)

where a is the light conversion efficiency established by nutrition, $ is the photosynthetically active radiation absorbed by the canopy, and modifying factors /(*i*), which range from 1 to 0, describe fractional reductions in relation to soil water deficits (H_2O), unfavourable temperature (*T*) and vapour pressure deficits of the air (*D*). At weekly or monthly time steps, models based on these simplifying assumptions show good agreement with integrated estimates of gross photosynthesis obtained using eddy-flux covariance techniques (Dang *et al.* 1998).

Autotrophic respiration

A large fraction of gross photosynthesis is expended through autotrophic respiration in the construction and maintenance of plant tissue. Physiologists generally separate respiration into three major components: photorespiration *(R)*, construction respiration (R_c) and maintenance respiration (R_m).

Photorespiration

In light, photorespiration occurs in the process of generating the substrate for the enzyme ribulose bisphosphate carboxylase-oxygenase (Rubisco), essential for the primary fixation of CO_2. Under conditions where the CO_2 concentration within the leaf is depleted relative to the concentration of O_2, the enzyme releases CO_2 rather than fixing it into carbohydrates. In general, higher temperatures stimulate photorespiration to the extent that simple estimates of gross photosynthesis may be overestimated by as much as 10%. Conversely, rising CO_2 concentrations in the atmosphere tend to moderate the effects of rising temperature on photorespiration and shift the optimum temperature for photosynthesis upward. At temperatures above 40°C, gross photosynthesis decreases abruptly because of changes in chloroplast and enzyme activity (Berry & Downton 1982).

Construction respiration

The synthesis of plant tissue requires the metabolism of more resources than found in the final product. Rates of construction respiration for various tissues differ, depending on their composition. From an analysis of biochemical pathways Penning de Vries (1975) estimated that the production of 1 g of lipid would require 3.02g of glucose, whereas 1 g of lignin, protein or sugar polymer might require 1.90, 2.35 and 1.18 g of glucose respectively. More recently, empirical relations have been derived to estimate the total cost of construction based on a correlation with the heat of combustion, ash, and organic nitrogen content of tissue and its biochemical composition

(McDermitt & Loomis 1981; Vertregt & Penning de Vries 1987; Williams *et al.* 1987; Griffin 1994). In general, 1.25-1.35 g of carbon are required to produce tissue containing 1 g of carbon. Although the amount of tissue produced may be a function of temperature, the construction cost per gram is fixed. This fact makes it possible to assess construction respiration at annual time steps from forest inventory data using allometric relations between measured increases in stem diameter and the production of foliage, branches, stemwood and large-diameter roots (Ryan 1991).

Maintenance respiration

Maintenance respiration (R_m), the basal rate of metabolism, includes the energy expended on ion uptake and transfer within plants. Repair of injured tissue may greatly increase respiration above the basal rate. Because trees accumulate a large amount of conducting and storage tissue as they age, the observed decrease in relative growth rates associated with age has often been assumed to reflect increasing maintenance costs (Whittaker 1975; Waring & Schlesinger 1985). However, most of the tissue in trees is wood and, of this, only the sapwood contains any living cells (5-30%). It is unlikely that the metabolism of this extra sapwood is enough to limit growth. Enzymatic activity associated with protein turnover can be predicted as a function of nitrogen content, the fraction of living cells in foliage, branches, stems and roots, and temperature of the tissue (Stockfer & Linder 1998). Maintenance respiration generally increases exponentially with temperature within the range of biological activity, as described by the formula

$$R_m(T) = R_0 Q_{10}$$

where R_0 is the basal respiration rate at $T = 0°C$ (or other reference temperature) and Q_{10} is the respiration quotient, which represents the change in the rate of respiration for a 10°C change in temperature (T). The Q_{10} is usually about 2.0-2.3. Under field conditions, where daily temperature variation is large, the non-linearity in the response of maintenance respiration can be important because the respiration rate will depend on the pattern of temperature variation even in sites with the same mean temperature. This has been modelled by fitting a sine function to minimum-maximum temperature differences and integrating the response not only daily but annually (Hagihara & Hozumi 1991; Ryan 1991). From analyses made in pine forests growing at mean annual temperatures from 5 to >20°C, Ryan *et al.* (1995) concluded that the annual above-ground woody tissue maintenance respiration represents 5-15% of gross photosynthesis and that other factors must therefore be responsible for commonly observed reductions of more than 50% in above-ground production as forests age.

Net primary production

Annual net primary production (NPP) is conceptually easy to define as the residual carbon products remaining after autotrophic respiration $(R + R_c + R_m)$ has been subtracted from gross photosynthesis. In practice, it is difficult to obtain accurate estimates of seasonal changes in foliage and fine-root mass, variation in metabolic reserves, and precise measurements of tissue temperatures throughout a forest, thus making estimates of NPP difficult. None the less, carbon balance estimates that take into account construction and maintenance respiration along with estimates of annual growth come fairly close to independent estimates of gross primary production (GPP), modelled or derived from microme-teorological measurements.

If one assumes that half the carbon allocated below ground goes into the production of roots while the rest is expended in construction and maintenance respiration, an estimate of total NPP can be made from datasets. When this was done for 12 temperate forests, the ratio NPP: GPP approached a constant, 0.47 + 0.04 (Waring *et al.* 1998). Similar analyses in boreal forests indicate that NPP : GPP = 0.3 (Ryan *et al.* 1997). This lower ratio in the boreal forest zone is attributed to delayed recovery in photosynthetic capacity of evergreen canopies in spring when solar radiation peaks (Jarvis *et al.* 1997; Ryan *et al.* 1997). Similar constant relationships between the ratio of autotrophic respiration and gross photosynthesis have been reported in growth-room experiments where pine and eucalypt seedlings have been raised under a range of temperatures from 15 to 25°C (Gifford 1994). It is important to emphasize that the fraction of carbon allocated to wood production can vary by more than threefold as a result of differences in the way that carbon resources are allocated to growth.

Allocation of carbon resources

Although the overall NPP : GPP ratio derived from carbon balance analyses may approach a constant, the proportion of carbon allocated to roots increases with climatic limitations on gross photosynthesis (Runyon *et al.* 1994). The availability of nutrients alone can alter above- and below-ground allocation as much as climatic limitations, as demonstrated by deriving carbon budgets for plantations of *Pinus radiata* provided with different levels of available nitrogen.

For ecologists, the seasonal dynamics of carbon uptake and allocation are critical for they define the growing season, the time of flowering and seed production and, often, the susceptibility of forests to damage from frost, herbivores and pathogens. To meet this challenge, ecophysiolo-gists have applied insights developed from growth-room studies where photoperiod, nutrition, temperature and available water have been controlled (Partanen *et al.* 1998). A number of empirical models have been developed to predict budbreak, foliage and stem elongation, and bud set in temperate and boreal forests from accumulated daily temperature values (heat sums) above a threshold after photoperiodic and chilling requirements have been met (Cleary & Waring 1969; Hari & Hakkinen 1991; Dougherty *et al.* 1994; Whitehead *et al.* 1994).

In tropical and subtropical forests, the onset of a wet season (or the end of a dry season) may initiate conditions that can be predicted to favour the initiation or cessation of growth (Borchert 1973, 1994; Reich 1995).

Although the theoretical basis for developing allocation models is still weak (Farrar 1996), some progress has been made. Various schemes have been proposed to model carbon allocation, as summarized by Cannell and Dewar (1994). These schemes are based on different assumptions about the controls on resource allocation as defined by: (i) sink strengths (Ford & Kiester 1990; Luxmoore 1991; Thornley 1991); (ii) resource deficiency (Ewel & Gholz 1991); (iii) functional balance (Davidson 1969); (iv) distance from essential resources (Weinstein *et al.* 1991); and (v) growth optimization (Ågren & Ingestad 1987; Johnson & Thornley 1987). Although the various schemes on allocation are interrelated, none deals with underlying processes, and some are in direct conflict with one another.

Models that relate root uptake of nitrogen and shoot uptake of carbon have been improved by incorporating more details. Initially, growth was assumed to be a simple function of the amount of carbon and nitrogen available, with the product of carbohydrate and nitrogen resources in foliage and roots determining the relative allocation. Then models began to include resistance to transport and demands for resources by intermediate structures between roots and shoots. More recently, models consider sugar and amino acid transport separately through phloem and sapwood (Cannell & Dewar 1994).

Root-to-shoot gradients in water potential also influence rates at which resources are transported through the two vascular systems. The majority of these models assume that growth at any instant is determined by the availability of substrate (C, N, etc.); however, availability is difficult to define. When plants are dormant, hormonal controls limit growth regardless of the concentration of carbohyrates and other resources in tissues. When shoot extension is rapid, root growth may be inhibited, even when starch concentrations are high (Ford & Deans 1977).

Hormonal control is again involved in root development (evidence in McWilliam 1972 discussed by Dewar *et al.* 1994) and there is also evidence that current photosynthate rather than starch reserves is required to produce new roots (Marshall & Waring 1985) or to support the process of symbiotic nitrogen fixation (McNabb & Cromack 1983). With the present state of understanding, it is reasonable to focus on developing accurate phenological models to define seasonal timing in growth activity as a function of daylength, temperature, drought and chilling requirements. Such phenological models would predict the fluctuating strength of competing sinks, while substrate availability would determine how much growth is possible.

With knowledge of phenology and environmental conditions, the pools of available carbon and nitrogen can be allocated into biomass, storage reserves and losses through respiration. Wein-stein *et al.* (1991) generated seasonal estimates of carbon allocation for red spruce *(Picea rubens)* by assuming priorities based on proximity to the resources (scheme iv in the list above). In this model, leaf growth has first priority for carbon after maintenance requirements of all living tissue are met. Storage of carbon in leaves is followed by growth and storage in branches, stem, coarse roots and, last, fine roots. Carbon in excess of that needed to meet the maximum growth rate of an organ was passed down the priority chain.

The priority ranking for allocation of water and nutrients would, according to this proximity logic, be opposite, with fine roots ranked first and new foliage ranked last. Similar proximity logic was discussed by Thornley (1976). Because critical resources come from opposite directions, no given organ is likely to grow at its full potential unless phenology limits all growth elsewhere. Predictions of photosynthate allocation seasonally in *Picea rubens* based on phenology and proximity logic showed reasonable growth patterns and matched measured storage reserves within 10% and total carbon content within 2% at the end of the year.

Most seasonal models of carbon allocation require specific knowledge of tree phenology, definition of the limits to growth of various organs, and specification of the size of storage reserves in all major organs. In reality, storage reserves should encompass not only starch but also amino acids, as well as a host of other compounds that protect against injury from temperature extremes and attacks from insects and diseases. Seasonally, trees are most susceptible to attack from insects and pathogens when storage reserves are low, a condition that occurs during rapid leaf expansion or when growth is prematurely halted during extended drought.

SUSCEPTIBILITY OF FORESTS TO HERBIVORES AND PATHOGENS

As emphasized in earlier sections, knowledge of the biochemical composition of tissue provides more insight into nutrient availability and the regulation of photosynthesis than a simple analysis of the total elemental content. In this section, we continue this emphasis in a review of the major types of biochemical defences that trees have evolved in response to herbivores and pathogens (see also Chapter 6, this volume). Although plant defence systems are highly variable, some general measures of stress have been developed to assess the susceptibility of forests to attack from herbivores and pathogens.

Biochemical and structural defences

Although each species has a unique suite of protective defences, some general symptoms of stress have emerged from comparative studies. Defensive chemicals present in plants are broadly classified into compounds that contain nitrogen and those that do not contain nitrogen. Compounds that contain nitrogen include cyanogenic gluco-sides, alkaloids and non-protein amino acids; compounds without nitrogen include tannins, terpenes, phytoalexins, steroids and phenolic acids. Each kind of compound may serve to protect the plant in a variety of ways.

Some trees produce fungistatic and bacteriosta-tic compounds that prevent colonization by pathogens. Other compounds act as physical barriers, such as waxes on the leaf surface or resins or lignin in cell walls. Increasing fibre and lowering water content decrease digestibility of plant tissue and reduce herbivore growth rates and survival (Scriber & Slansky 1981). Tannins precipitate protein, inhibiting most enzyme reactions and making protein present in plant tissue nutritionally unavailable to most animals and microbes (Zucker 1983). Phytoalexins are lipid-soluble compounds activated following an attack by pathogens and exhibit antibiotic properties (Harborne 1982). The alkaloids found in many angiosperms are particularly toxic to a variety of mammals (Swain 1977).

Changes in host biochemistry may also affect the colonization of organisms helpful to the host tree. These include protective ant colonies, macroorganisms that graze on bacteria, and symbiotic associations of nitrogen-fixing bacteria and mycorrhizal root fungi. These beneficial organisms may directly infect or prey on attacking organisms, release antibiotics or provide essential nutrients. Many of the compounds released as exudates, which include a variety of polysaccha-rides, organic acids and amino acids, are essential to beneficial associates, but when these organisms are absent they can also be assimilated by herbivores and pathogens.

In general, defensive compounds that lack nitrogen reach high concentrations in cells, often 10-15% by weight, whereas nitrogen-containing defensive compounds are usually at concentrations below 1%. Plants expend less total energy in the synthesis of small amounts of nitrogen-containing defensive compounds than when producing large amounts of carbon-rich compounds, although variations in the turnover rates of defensive compounds and differences in the relative growth rates must be considered in the assessment of synthesis and maintenance costs (Bryant *et al.* 1991). Nitrogen-containing compounds are most frequently found in deciduous fast-growing vegetation, whereas defensive compounds without nitrogen are more characteristic of slow-growing plants, particularly evergreens with long leaf lifespans (Bryant *et al.* 1986; Coley 1988). Plants that depend on defensive compounds rich in nitrogen are at a competitive disadvantage where nitrogen is in short supply. On the other hand, plants producing carbon-rich defensive compounds are at a disadvantage when growing in shade with an abundant supply of nitrogen. Those plants adapted to more fertile soils may be expected to build a variety of defensive compounds from nitrogen.

Thus, alkaloids predominate in the foliage of trees in many lowland tropical forests where nitrogen is relatively abundant (McKey *et al.* 1978). Plants growing in areas where nitrogen is scarce generally produce tannins and related carbon-based defensive compounds. Thus, in some tropical forests growing on sterile sands, primates must survive mainly by eating fruits (Gartlan *et al.* 1980). A similar pattern in distribution of vegetation with nitrogen-based or carbon-based defensive compounds to that observed in tropical forests has been reported in boreal and temperate forests (Rhoades & Cates 1976; Bryant *et al.* 1991).

To meet the challenge of insects and pathogens, many plants are able to produce toxic compounds quickly and construct barriers that consist of dead or resin/gum-filled tissue almost immediately after attack (Schultz & Baldwin 1982; Raffa & Berryman 1983). In response to localized insect activity, foliage throughout an entire tree may become less palatable (Haukioja & Niemelä 1979; Karban & Myers 1989). Morphological responses, such as stiffer thorns on *Acacia* trees, may also be induced by grazing (Seif el Din & Obeid 1971). Bark sloughing is a response to attack by woolly aphid (*Adeleges piceae)* and the aphid only reaches epidemic populations when balsam fir *(Abies balsamea)*, which lacks the ability to shed bark, replaces native forest species (Kloft 1957). The extent to which local environmental conditions can alter a plant's biochemical and structural properties, and affect their selection by insects and pathogens, has been demonstrated under precisely controlled laboratory conditions (Waring *et al.* 1985; Larsson *et al.* 1986; Coleman & Jones 1988a,b; Coleman *et al.* 1988). Field experiments have also demonstrated that plant susceptibility can be altered by varying the availability of light and nutrients (Bryant *et al.* 1985; Coley *et al.* 1985). Because many defensive compounds have high rates of turnover, it is essential that their assessment be made at critical times when the plants are being attacked (Lorio 1986; Reichardt *et al.* 1991).

The linking of ecology and physiology has explained unexpected responses to management practices designed to favour the abundance of certain game species. In the Lake States of the USA, protection of large areas of aspen *(Populus tremuloides)* forests beyond a certain age would be detrimental to the winter survival of ruffed grouse, which depends on a favourable biochemical composition of aspen buds that is found only with younger stands (Jakubas *et al.* 1989).

Similarly, in the Alaskan coastal forest of western hemlock *(Tsuga heterophylla)*, cutting old-growth forests increased the biomass of a prime browse species of blueberry *(Vaccinium ovalifolium)* by nearly fourfold but the population of Sitka black-tailed deer *(Odocoileus hemionus sitkensis)* decreased.

Field experiments, combined with feeding trials, demonstrated that blueberry plants become less palatable to deer when grown under high light conditions. An increase in tannins and non-tannin phenolics reduced the digestibility of protein nitrogen in plant tissue below that required to sustain female deer with one or more fawns through the winter months (McArthur *et al.* 1993). Structural properties, such as specific leaf weight, also change in parallel with leaf biochemistry.

Biochemical and allocation ratios

Ecophysiologists have searched for simple indices of stress that might aid managers in quantifying the risk of attack to forests from native insects and pathogens. Various ratios were considered, following success in reinterpreting nutrient status in terms of elemental ratios. Ratios that contrast the relative concentrations of defensive compounds to those compounds that promote the growth of insects and pathogens have obvious merit. For example, the incidence of infection by pure cultures of the root pathogen *Armillaria ostoyae* shows marked sensitivity to the ratio of phenolics/sugars and lignin/sugars in the root cortex of Douglas fir (Entry *et al.* 1991).

Structural ratios also have value in the assessment of risk, as noted in the correlation between specific leaf weight and digestible nitrogen. The two most widely used indices are based on allocation differences:

(i) light-use efficiency, i.e. annual above-ground growth per unit of absorbed radiation (Monteith 1972); and

(ii) growth efficiency, i.e. wood growth per unit of foliage (Waring 1983).

Light-use efficiency has the advantage that satellite technology can be used to predict solar radiation, the fraction absorbed by the canopy and above-ground growth (Goward *et al.* 1987; Dye & Goward 1993; Prince & Goward 1995; Lefsky *et al.* 1999; Means *et al.* 1999). Growth efficiency has the advantage that it can be applied to assess the risk of insect or disease attack to individual trees (Oren *et al.* 1985; Christiansen *et al.* 1987). For some species, leaf area is correlated with sapwood basal area (Waring *et al.* 1982).

ECOPHYSIOLOGICAL MODELS OF FOREST GROWTH

There are two classes of forest growth models that are well developed:

(i) those that focus on the whole ecosystem and

(ii) those that concentrate on the life-cycle dynamics of trees in the forest.

Both classes are process models: ecosystem models compute growth from the seasonal dynamics of canopy carbon balances and allocation rules based on limiting resources; and life-cycle models emphasize disturbance, recruitment and mortality processes that affect the establishment, growth and death of individual trees. In this section we refer to only the first, ecosystem models. Examples of widely applied ecosystem models are reviewed and contrasted with life-cycle models by Ågren *et al.* (1991), Ryan *et al.* (1996), Landsberg and Gower (1997) and Waring and Running (1998).

These models are driven within environmental inputs: rainfall, solar radiation, temperature and atmospheric vapour pressure deficit (*D*). Some models require daily weather summaries while others operate with weekly or monthly averages (see Aber & Federer 1992; Landsberg & Waring 1997). The canopy and forest floor intercept radiation, precipitation and aerosols. Some water recharges the soil and enters streams, while the rest is converted to water vapour and evaporated or transpired into the atmosphere. The upper limit on photosynthesis is set by the amount of visible light intercepted by the canopy and the maximum quantum efficiency or maximum photosynthetic capacity, the latter two being a function of nutrition. Reductions in stomatal conductance reduce the rates of water vapour loss via transpiration and CO_2 uptake via photosynthesis. Stomatal conductance is affected by all the climatic variables and by the availability of soil water. The products of photosynthesis are partitioned into growth and plant respiratory losses of CO_2 back to the atmosphere. Carbon is partitioned into foliage, stems and roots differentially, depending on the extent that different resources limit photosynthesis and growth.

Eventually plant components are shed and converted into detritus that is incorporated into soil organic matter, leached or converted into CO_2 via het-erotrophic respiration (not shown in the schematic diagram). This type of process-linked model demands reasonable agreement in estimates of carbon, water and nutrient cycling. By extending the analyses to decades one can quickly identify unreasonable assumptions because they lead to unrealistic leaf areas, wood production and litter accumulation. The models generally predict the total light absorbed by the canopy as well as leaf area index so that calculations of light-use efficiency and growth efficiency are easily acquired. In addition, the content of nitrogen (if not other elements) can be predicted by the models.

Some models keep track of diameter distributions of trees as well as stocking (Korol *et al.* 1991; Landsberg & Waring 1997), and all make separate estimates of above-and below-ground production. One of the main advantages of process-linked models is that they can serve to diagnose the extent to which forest growth is now limited or may become limited in the future by climate. They can also be used to compare the influence of climate with that of site variables that may be manipulated, such as the floristic composition of the forest (changes in allocation) and the fertility of the soil (changes in allocation and photosynthetic capacity).

SUMMARY

By combining the traditional empiricism of ecology with the process orientation of physiology, ecophysiology has helped expand the reliability and generality of models designed to forecast the status of individual stands, forests and regional assemblages of vegetation.

This merger of fields has contributed to a better understanding of the processes controlling forest growth and the susceptibility of forests to biotic disturbances. As a result, forest managers have acquired diagnostic tools that allow them to judge better the implications of various options today and in the future.

9

How to Save Tropical Rainforests

Today tropical rainforests are disappearing from the face of the globe. Despite growing international concern, rainforests continue to be destroyed at a pace exceeding 80,000 acres (32,000 hectares) per day. World rainforest cover now stands at around 2.5 million square miles (6 million square kilometers), an area about the size of the contiguous 48 United States or Australia and representing around 5 percent of the world's land surface. Much of this remaining area has been impacted by human activities and no longer retains its full original biodiversity.

Deforestation of tropical rainforests has a global impact through species extinction, the loss of important ecosystem services and renewable resources, and the reduction of carbon sinks. However, this destruction can be slowed, stopped, and in some cases even reversed. Most people agree that the problem must be remedied, but the means are not as simple as fortifying fences around the remaining rainforests or banning the timber trade. Economic, political, and social pressures will not allow rainforests to persist if they are completely closed off from use and development.

So, what should be done? The solution must be based on what is feasible, not overly idealistic, and depends on developing a new conservation policy built on the principle of sustainable use and development of rainforests. Beyond the responsible development of rainforests, efforts to rehabilitate and restore degraded forest lands along with the establishment of protected areas are key to securing rainforests for the long-term benefits they can provide mankind.

PAST EFFORTS

Historic approaches to rainforest conservation have failed, as demonstrated by the accelerated rate of deforestation. In many regions, closing off forests as untouchable parks and reserves has neither improved the quality of living or economic opportunities for rural poor nor deterred forest clearing by illegal loggers and developers. Corruption has only worsened the situation.

The problem with this traditional park approach to preserving wildlands in developing countries is that it fails to generate sufficient economic incentives for respecting and maintaining the forest. Rainforests will only continue to survive as functional ecosystems if they can be shown to provide tangible economic benefits. Local people and the government itself must see financial returns to justify the costs of maintaining parks and forgoing revenue from economic activities within the boundaries of the protected area.

LIMITED RESOURCES

Countries with significant rainforest cover are generally among the world's poorest. As such, people's day-to-day survival is dependent upon natural-resource use. Most local people living in and around forests never have an option to become a doctor, sports star, factory worker, or secretary; they must live off the land that surrounds them, making use of whatever resources they can find. Their poverty costs themselves, their country, and the world through the loss of biodiversity and ecosystem services like erosion prevention, flood control, water treatment, and fisheries protection.

Governments in these countries are in the unenviable position of having to balance the well-being of rural poor with the interests of industry, demands from foreign governments, and requirements from the international aid community. In this climate, it can be easier to simply neglect the continued destruction and degradation of environmental assets than to come up with a long-term plan to ensure that economic development is ecologically sustainable. Success in conserving wildlands in these countries will require reconciling the inevitable conflicts between short-term needs of local people and the long-term nature of the benefits that conservation can generate on a sustainable, ongoing basis.

Forces behind rainforest loss

Rainforests are being cut mostly for economic reasons, though there are political and social motivations as well. A significant portion of deforestation is caused by poor farmers simply trying to eke out a living on marginal lands. Beyond conversion for subsistence agriculture, activities like logging, clearing for cattle pasture and commercial agriculture are sizeable contributors to deforestation on a global scale. Agricultural fires typically used for land-clearing are increasingly spreading outside cultivated areas and into degraded rainforest regions.

ADDRESSING DEFORESTATION

Addressing deforestation will need to take the very different needs and interests of these groups into account.

Poor farmers:

Poor farmers are simply trying to put food on the table for their families. A better approach to addressing the needs of the rural poor may be improving and intensifying currently existing agricultural projects and promoting alternative cultivation techniques—notably permaculture. Permaculture adds a mix of crops to the farmer's palette that both enables him to diversify his income stream and enhance degraded soils by restoring nutrients. An added benefit of such techniques is that they maintain forest systems, soils, and biological diversity at a far higher level than do conventional agricultural approaches. As long as such fields are adjacent to secondary and old-growth forest, many species will continue to thrive.

One promising area of research looks at ancient societies that lived in the Amazon rainforest before the arrival of Europeans in the 15th century. Apparently these populations were able to enrich the rainforest soil, which is usually quite poor, using charcoal and animal bones. By improving soil quality, large areas of the Amazon that have been deforested could be used to support agriculture. This could help reduce pressure on rainforest areas for agricultural land. Further, the "terra preta" soil could be used to help fight global warming since it absorbs carbon dioxide, an important greenhouse gas.

A second important part of aiding poor farmers is helping them gain formal title to their land. Right now, in places where it is difficult to gain ownership rights to land and where land is relatively open and abundant, there is little incentive to maintain or improve holdings. Once local people have a stake in the land they are farming, they will have an interest in using it efficiently instead of moving on to a new area of forest once soils are prematurely exhausted.

The creation of credit facilities for poor farmers to both save their earnings and borrow in times of need is also important to improving their quality of life. Micro-credit facilities can provide significant economic benefits to the local economy while bringing dignity to and promoting entrepreneurship among local people.

Finally, improved access to markets is important in enabling farmers to get their agricultural products. Improved access can be a doubled-edged sword if it means increased road-building, which often spurs further deforestation. Any infrastructure improvements should be carefully planned to minimize the future impact on remaining ecosystems.

INDUSTRIAL/COMMERCIAL DEVELOPERS:

Thus far it has proved difficult to apply the same permaculture agricultural techniques mentioned above to industrial operations. As currently practiced, large-scale agriculture is typically quite destructive of native ecosystems and does not maintain biodiversity at levels commensurate with adjacent forest areas. Incremental steps like the use of natural pest control and fertilizers can help reduce pollution caused by agricultural operations, while leaving strips of forest as corridors linking sections of forest helps moderate biodiversity losses.

Sustainable logging, while possible, has met resistance from the timber industry for its lack of efficiency relative to traditional harvesting methods, and it remains controversial among conservationists as to the impact on the environment. Illegal logging and counterfeit labeling are major obstacles facing sustainable forest management for timber, but in time the development of higher yielding timber plantations will help alleviate pressures on natural forests.

Restoring and rehabilitating ecosystems

There is no use bemoaning past deforestation of large areas. Today the concern is how to best utilize lands already cleared so they support productive activities, now and for future generations. Without improving the well-being of people living in and around forests, we cannot expect rainforests to persist as fully functional systems and continue to cater to our needs.

In addressing environmental problems in rainforest countries, it is important that decision makers not only be concerned with the transformation of existing natural ecosystems, but also the more rational utilization of already cleared and degraded areas. To lessen future forest loss, we must increase and sustain the productivity of farms, pastures, plantations, and scrub land in addition to restoring species and ecosystems to degraded habitats. By reducing wasteful land-use practices, consolidating gains on existing cleared lands, and improving already developed lands, we can diminish the need to clear additional forest.

Research and experience has shown that the restoration of entire ecosystems is most possible in regions where parts or at least remnants of the original forest still remain and there are few human population pressures. Small clearings surrounded by forest recover quickly, and large sections may recover in time, especially if some assistance in the reforestation process is provided. After several years, a once-barren field can again support vegetation in the form of pioneer species and secondary growth. Although the secondary forest will be low in diversity and poorly developed, the forest cover will be adequate for some species to return (assuming they still exist). In addition, the newly forested patch can be used for the sustainable harvest of forest products and low-intensity logging and agriculture.

Funding rainforest conservation efforts

Conservation efforts and sustainable development programs are not going to be cost-free. Even countries that already get considerable aid from foreign donors have trouble effectively making such initiatives work in the long term. Since handouts, which in and of themselves have the tendency to breed dependency, are not going to last forever, funding these initiatives may require more creative sources of income to be truly successful. Here are some other funding strategies for consideration:

- **Ecotourism**—Ecotourism can fund efforts both through park entrance fees and employing locals as guides and in the handicraft and service sectors (hotels, restaurants, drivers, boat drivers, porters, cooks).
- **Bio-prospecting fees**—Rainforest countries can earn revenue by allowing scientists to develop products from

the island's native plant and animal species. The pioneer in this area was Costa Rica, which entered into an agreement with the American pharmaceutical company, Merck, to look for plants with potential pharmaceutical applications. Under the agreement, a portion of the proceeds from compounds that do prove commercially valuable will go to the Costa Rican government, which has guaranteed that some of the royalties will be set aside for conservation projects. Similarly, in 2001 Givaudan, a Swiss fragrance and flavor company, sent a team to look for new exotic smells and flavors in Madagascar. Following their survey, Givaudan researchers "reconstituted" 40 aromas that could be used in commercial products. The company has agreed to share a portion of the profits from these products with local communities through conservation and development initiatives.

- **Carbon credits**—For setting aside forest for the purpose of atmospheric carbon mitigation, developing countries can receive payments from industrialized countries looking to offset their carbon emissions. Carbon-offset programs are popular in many circles, since they can "provide a mechanism for motivating wealthy countries to pay for a benefit of forest conservation that transcends national borders." In effect, such programs promote "the transfer of funds from industrialized countries to tropical countries as a commercial transaction rather than an act of charity" (Costa, P.M. "Tropical forestry practices for carbon sequestration: a review and case study from Southeast Asia," Ambio Vol. 25 No. 4, June 1996)).
- **Corporate sponsorship**—Corporations have been a bit slow in "adopting" parks, but they have the money and a marketing-driven interest in taking a closer look at such schemes. See below for more details on a potential plan.

- **The Linden-Lovejoy-Phillips plan**—One interesting idea proposed by Eugene Linden, Thomas Lovejoy, and J. Daniel Phillips for tropical rainforests consists of dividing natural areas into blocks and then soliciting funding commitments from international environmental groups, development institutions, corporations, and other credible donors. There would be a bidding process, after which an entity would take responsibility for maintaining forest cover and forest health in each block of the entire forest system. This plan could be a road for corporations to become involved in conservation as a public-relations/marketing tool. A given percentage of the proceeds could be put into a trust fund with the payout ear-marked for ongoing conservation and sustainable development programs.

FURTHER STEPS ONCE FUNDING IS IN PLACE

- **Expand protected areas**—As many areas should be protected as soon as possible. If protected areas can be developed in such a manner to generate income for local communities, an increasing number of parks should theoretically create more economic benefits for a greater share of the population.
- **Increase surveillance of and patrols in protected areas**—This can be done at a reduced cost if local communities benefit from the success of the park. If locals have a vested interest (i.e. are compensated via entrance fees, hired as guides, make handicrafts to sell to tourists, and learn to value their ecosystem for the services it can provide), they will want to watch the park so that the source of their income is not diminished. Community surveillance is the most effective way to patrol a protected area, though it will probably be necessary to have park staff conduct patrols as well. Guides should be trained as well to keep watch for

activities that are damaging to the ecosystem and report suspicious activities at park headquarters.

- **Build research facilities for training local scientists and guides**—The average rainforest country needs to build its intellectual capital to grow its economy and make the best use of the country's resources. There need to be further studies on endemic species (many just have a name and a location and new species are being discovered every year) for both pure-research reasons and potential commercial applications. Improved crop yields and reduced erosion could also be possible with future research.
- **Establish programs that promote sustainable use**—Programs that promote sustainable use are key to elevating the standard of living for people living around protected areas. Not all members of a community will see the direct benefits from employment in the service or production sector, and many people will still rely on traditional use of the natural resources around them. These resources must be used in a more effective manner to maximize productivity and minimize the impact on the environment.
- **Compensate displaced people**—As more protected areas are set aside, it is inevitable that some people may be asked to move. It is important that these people are compensated for abandoning their existing livelihood and homes. While direct cash payouts is an option, a better strategy is providing these displaced people with long-term income possibilities through training in better agricultural techniques or alternative crops.
- Involve indigenous people, where they still exist, in park management. Indigenous people know more about the forest than anyone and have an interest in safeguarding it as a productive ecosystem that provides

them food, shelter, and clean water. Research has found that in some cases, "indigenous reserves" may actually protect rainforest better than national parks in the Amazon.

- **Promote ecotourism**—Ecotourism is perhaps the best hope for developing the economy of some rainforest countries. Planners should seek to minimize the environmental impact and maximize the benefits for local communities.
- **Ensure economic success does not result in increased deforestation**—As rural populations begin to reap benefits from conservation-related activities, it is important that they not reinvest this income in activities that result in further deforestation. Traditionally, in many villages, the more money someone made, the more money was put back into land clearing. Rural banks and savings institutions are virtually unknown in many parts of the developing world. Such facilities, which would enable both saving and lending, could rapidly change the lives of millions through increased entrepreneurship and the ability to put away money for the future.
- **Encourage entrepreneurship**—Encouraging entrepreneurship through such a micro-credit strategy could pay significant dividends for a country's economy as a whole. Studies in developing countries have found that entrepreneurial skills among the poor are actually quite high when people are given access to capital. Default rates are typically quite low as well (do the poor have a greater respect for money?). Stimulating entrepreneurship through small, low-cost loans is possibly a better approach than handouts, which may do little more than breed dependency and reduce human dignity.

Bibliography

Aukland, L.: (1997). *The Effect of Selective Logging on Amphibian Diversity of Budongo Forest*, Uganda. B. A.:, Oxford University.

Bahati, J.: (1995). *Impact of Arboricidal Treatments on the Natural Regeneration of Species Composition in Budongo Forest*, Uganda. M. Sc., Makerere University.

Bethell, E.: (1998). *Vigilance in Foraging Chimpanzees*. University College, London University.

Johnson, K.: (1993). *Local Uses of Budongo's Forest Products*. M. Sc., Oxford University.

Johnson, K.: (1996). *Hunting in the Budongo Forest*, Uganda. SWARA.

Miller, P. L.: (1993). *Some dragonflies of the Budongo Forest*, Western Uganda. Opusc.

Owiunji, I.: (1996). *The Long Term Effects of Forest Management on the Bird Community of Budongo Forest Reserve*, Uganda. M. Sc., Makerere University.

Reynolds, V.: (1965). *Budongo: A Forest and its Chimpanzees*, London, Methuen.

Reynolds, V. & Reynolds, F.: (1965). *Chimpanzees of the Budongo Forest*, New York, Rinehart and Winston.

Shiel, D.: (1997). *The Ecology of Long-term Change in a Ugandan Rainforest*. D. Phil., Oxford University.

Spini, L.: (1998). *The Frequency and Significance of Social Grooming in the Sonso Community of Chimpanzees at the Budongo Forest*, Uganda. M. Sc., Oxford University.

Index

□□□